WARFARE
under the
ANGLO-NORMAN
KINGS
1066–1135

WARFARE
under the
ANGLO-NORMAN
KINGS
1066–1135

Stephen Morillo

THE BOYDELL PRESS

First published 1994
The Boydell Press, Woodbridge

ISBN 0 85115 555 3

The Boydell Press is an imprint of Boydell & Brewer Ltd
PO Box 9, Woodbridge, Suffolk IP12 3DF, UK
and of Boydell & Brewer Inc.
PO Box 41026, Rochester, NY 14604–4126, USA

British Library Cataloguing-in-Publication Data
Morillo, Stephen
    Warfare Under the Anglo-Norman Kings,
    1066–1135
    I. Title
    940.1
    ISBN 0–85115–555–3

Library of Congress Cataloging-in-Publication Data
Morillo, Stephen.
    Warfare under the Anglo-Norman kings, 1066–1135 / Stephen Morillo.
        p.   cm.
    Includes bibliographical references and index.
    ISBN 0–85115–555–3 (acid-free paper)
    1. Great Britain – History, Military – 1066–1485. 2. Great Britain –
History – Norman period, 1066–1154. 3. Military art and science –
England – History. 4. Normans – England – Kings and rulers.
5. Knights and knighthood – England. 6. Normans – England – History.
I. Title.
DA60.M67 1994
942.02–dc20   94–18931

The paper used in this publication meets the minimum requirements
of American National Standard for Information Sciences –
Permanence of Paper for Printed Library Materials, ANSI Z39.48–1984

Printed in Great Britain by
St Edmundsbury Press Ltd, Bury St Edmunds, Suffolk

Contents

Maps and Drawings

Preface

This book has a long history, and I have accumulated many debts in the process of writing and revising it. J.F.A. Mason guided my research at Oxford, and I will always be grateful for the advice and wisdom he offered. The D.Phil. dissertation that resulted was read by John Prestwich and Frank Barlow, who offered many useful suggestions and corrected many errors. The generosity of the Rhodes Trust made my three years at Jesus College both possible and enjoyable.

The revisions that turned dissertation into book were assisted at many stages in many ways. Charles Davis and the late Jim Alexander read early versions of the manuscript and offered valuable advice and support. Warren Hollister (whose books got me interested in this topic back in high school), Eleanor Searle and Richard Abels read later versions; all gave criticisms and advice that have made me think harder about Anglo-Norman warfare and society and that have saved me from many mistakes and oversimplifications. I am grateful to them as colleagues and as friends. I have also profited from discussions with friends at the Haskins Society Conference, the International Medieval Conference in Kalamazoo, and the Battle Conference. I thank all of those friends, and especially Bernie Bachrach and John Gillingham, for helping me hone my ideas.

My association with Wabash College has also nurtured this book in various ways. The generosity of the Byron K. Trippet Fund and the Wabash Faculty Development Fund made much additional research and writing possible, and sent me to many conferences. My colleague and friend Peter Frederick was, as always, full of good advice. And I thank the many students who have reciprocated my interest in medieval warfare – nothing makes one understand a topic more than trying to teach it. Several students in particular deserve special mention. Rob Vega has read and commented perceptively on the entire manuscript; Joe Longtin assisted with research tasks during a summer internship; and Chris Rowland, Jason Hand, and the other students at the Wabash student newspaper lent their hardware, software and expertise to help me produce the maps and drawings.

As for deeper roots, the germ of this study first emerged as a paper for one of Steven Epstein's tutorials at Harvard College. I thank him for encouraging me to go farther with it. My wife Kim Milone now knows more about Anglo-Norman warfare than she ever thought she would, because she not only provided moral support but also read the manuscript several times, asking incisive questions, proofreading thoroughly, and skillfully editing many rough spots out of my historian's prose. Finally, I won't blame my parents, Marvin and Carolyn, for my long-standing interest in military history, but I will credit them with encouraging and supporting my interests of all sorts, and for infecting me with an appreciation for the academic life. This book is for them.

Crawfordsville, IN
June 1994

Abbreviations

ASC
: *The Anglo Saxon Chronicle.* A revised translation by D. Whitelock, with D.C. Douglas and S.I. Tucker. London, 1961.

Battle
: *Anglo-Norman Studies (Proceedings of the Battle Conference).*

BT
: *The Bayeux Tapestry. A Comprehensive Survey.* Ed. Sir F. Stenton. 2nd edn. London, 1965.

CDF
: *Calendar of Documents Preserved in France, Illustrative of the History of Great Britain and Ireland.* Vol. 1, AD 918–1206. Ed. J.H. Round. London, 1899.

Carmen
: *The Carmen de Hastingae Proelio of Bishop Guy of Amiens.* Ed. C. Morton and H. Muntz. Oxford, 1972.

Chaplais
: *Diplomatic Documents Preserved in the PRO.* Vol. 1, 1101–1272. Ed. P. Chaplais. London, 1964.

Eadmer
: Eadmer. *Historia Novorum in Anglia.* Ed. M. Rule. RS, 1884.

EHD
: *English Historical Documents.* Vol. 2, 1042–1189. Ed. D.C. Douglas and G.W. Greenaway. London, 1953.

EHR
: *English Historical Review.*

EcHR
: *Economic History Review.*

Florence
: Florence of Worcester. *Chronicon ex Chronicis.* 2v. Ed. B. Thorpe. London, 1848–9.

HH
: Henry of Huntingdon. *Historia Anglorum.* Ed. T. Arnold. RS, 1879.

John of Hexham
: John of Hexham, in *Symeonis Monachi Opera Omnia,* 2:284–333. Ed. T. Arnold. RS, 1885.

LHP
: *Leges Henrici Primi.* Ed and trans. L.J. Downer. Oxford, 1972.

Malmesbury, GRA
: William of Malmesbury. *Gesta Regum Anglorum.* 2v. Ed. W. Stubbs. RS, 1887–9.

Malmesbury, HN
: William of Malmesbury. *Historia Novella.* Ed. K.R. Potter. London, 1955.

OV	Orderic Vitalis. *Ecclesiastical History*. 6v. Ed. and trans. M. Chibnall. Oxford, 1969–72.
P&P	*Past and Present*.
PR	*Pipe Rolls*. Pipe Roll Society, London, 1884.
PR 31 H1	*The Pipe Roll of 31 Henry I. Michaelmas 1130*. Facsimile from the 1833 edition, ed. J. Hunter. 1929.
RRAN	*Regesta Regum Anglo-Normannorum, 1066–1154*. Vol. 1, ed. H.W.C. Davis. Oxford, 1913. Vol. 2, ed. C. Johnson and H.A. Cronne. Oxford, 1956. Vol. 3, ed. H.A. Cronne and R.H.C. Davis. Oxford, 1968.
RS	Rolls Series.
Symeon, HR	Symeon of Durham. *Historia Regum*. Ed. T. Arnold. RS, 1885.
TRHS	*Transactions of the Royal Historical Society*.
Vegetius	Flavius Vegetius Renatus. *Epitoma Rei Militaris*. Ed. C. Lang. Stuttgart, 1967.
WJ	Guillaume de Jumièges. *Gesta Normannorum Ducum*. Ed. J. Marx. Rouen, 1914.
WP	William of Poitiers. *Histoire de Guillaume le Conquerant*. Ed. R. Foreville. Paris, 1952.

Chapter One

INTRODUCTION

By the evening of October 14, 1066, William the Bastard, Duke of Normandy, would earn a new nickname. On that day, he led an army of horsemen, footsoldiers and archers drawn not only from his duchy but from all over northern France against Harold Godwinson, the reigning king of Anglo-Saxon England, and his army of footsoldiers wielding fearsome battle axes. They fought on a hill near Hastings, in a battle that lasted all day. The outcome was long in doubt. William's army nearly broke in panic early in the day, and only William – by baring his head and riding up and down the lines to show he was still alive – stemmed the rout. The Anglo-Saxon army would not break until the final attack of the day, as darkness closed in. Harold fell then, surrounded by his best warriors; his death made William's victory decisive. By the end of December, after a brief campaign along the south coast and a destructive approach to London, the Duke of Normandy would be crowned king of England. He would be known as William the Conqueror.[1]

As king, William became heir to a rich, well-governed realm, now joined to his own patrimony of Normandy, itself a prosperous and united province. Several years of campaigning and government by military occupation would in fact be necessary to ensure his safety in his new kingdom, and in the process England was to receive a new Norman class of leaders. But from remarkably early in his reign, many of the resources of the kingdom were available to him, including its military resources. Anglo-Saxons, William's enemies in October 1066, were fighting with him at Exeter in the spring of 1068.[2] Both military systems and both armies, Anglo-Saxon and Norman, contributed to the new Anglo-Norman military system and army. Both were transformed by the union.

The Anglo-Norman realm, born in battle and weaned on war, was to fight constantly throughout its existence. But the Battle of Hastings,

---

[1] The Battle of Hastings is discussed in more detail with full references below, pp. 163–68.
[2] OV, 2:212; William was fighting less cooperative Anglo-Saxons, showing that not all of the kingdom's military resources were at his disposal yet.

though it gave birth to the realm, was a poor indicator of the shape of its wars to come. Battles in medieval warfare were rare events. Ravaging and plundering the land, building and besieging castles, and indeed actively avoiding battles were the normal, everyday activities of war, activities punctuated only in unusual and almost accidental circumstances by set piece engagements. There were good reasons for the battle-shy nature of medieval war, as this study will show. But though medieval leaders avoided battles, they waged war all the time.

In fighting constantly, the Anglo-Norman realm was like every other medieval European state. Warfare was the central activity of government and the ruling class across the continent. Understanding how this activity was conducted is therefore central to understanding medieval Europe.

This is a study of how the kings of the Anglo-Norman realm, William and his sons William Rufus and Henry, waged war between 1066 and 1135. It is designed to present as complete a picture as possible of this topic, linking the military system to armies in the field, and putting both in a set of wider contexts. The intent is to take a 'slice of time' during which the patterns and practices of Anglo-Norman warfare were relatively stable, and examine those patterns and practices thematically rather than chronologically. Thus, I have not provided a narrative account of the various wars fought by the Anglo-Norman kings,[3] but an analytic account of all royal warfare during the period 1066–1135. This intent has guided the organization of the book.

Chapter Two places the Anglo-Norman military system and warfare in their contexts.[4] First, the military system was a branch of the government, as it were; understanding the relationships this entailed is vital in understanding the structure of the military system, as well as the whole development of royal governmental machinery. Second, in an age of personal government, it is also necessary to examine the relationships and attitudes of the ruling class, whose function was, at heart, military. Thus not all royal government (or military enterprise) can be analysed neatly as 'governmental machinery'.[5] Third, warfare was a tool of policy.

---

[3] A chronological table of the major wars and campaigns may be found at the end of this chapter. A clear narrative of the history of this period, including the wars the kings waged, is available in F. Barlow, *The Feudal Kingdom of England*, 4th edn (London, 1987).

[4] I will also consider to some extent what effect warfare had reciprocally on these same factors, though Ch. 2 is not a chapter on the effects of war on society. For discussion of the direct effects of warfare on the population and countryside, see Ch. 4.

[5] 'Government machinery' is in fact anachronistic terminology, though useful nonetheless.

Thus, it is important to know what policy, or what 'strategic principles', guided the use of warfare by the Anglo-Norman kings, and what other tools they had available in preference to warfare. Fourth, it is necessary to see the problems imposed by the strategic situation of the Anglo-Norman realm. Where were the major threats likely to arise? What problems would meeting them entail? The answers to these questions influenced warfare greatly.

Chapter Three examines the Anglo-Norman military system, showing its administrative structure and how it performed its tasks. To create and maintain armed forces, a military system performs two types of tasks. First, it must obtain manpower, i.e. secure the services of leaders, soldiers, sailors and the various other specialists it may need. Second, it must organize that manpower into administrative units for the purpose of disciplining, housing, supplying, and training it – in short, it must transform men into an army. A military system is also faced with the problem of demobilizing troops who are no longer needed.

Chapters Four and Five then examine the nature of Anglo-Norman warfare and the particulars of how it was waged. The two vital elements of Anglo-Norman warfare were castles and armies in the field. The first step in understanding the basic nature of Anglo-Norman warfare – the patterns of campaign action; why certain actions were regularly taken – is an examination of the respective roles of castles and field forces. The particular actions taken by field forces – movement, maintenance, tactical action – in the execution of their tasks then fit into this framework; the details of these actions show how field forces performed their role. Chapter Four examines the roles of castles and field forces, the normal patterns of campaigning, and the usual actions of forces on campaign. Chapter Five focuses on tactical action: the techniques royal forces used in assaulting and defending fortresses and on the field of battle.

Finally, Chapter Six reviews the main conclusions about Anglo-Norman warfare that this study highlights. One of these is the crucial role of leadership to the effectiveness of Anglo-Norman armies, so I include here an assessment of the Anglo-Norman kings as military leaders.

The contexts of Anglo-Norman warfare and my desire to present a thematic study of a stable system have largely determined the limits of this study. Baronial warfare, either of the local feud variety or border warfare, particularly on the Welsh marches, carried on with baronial resources and leadership, is excluded, for it differed from royal warfare in organization and purpose, though the line separating baronial from royal warfare is admittedly not always perfectly clear. On the other hand, I have placed the broadest possible geographical limits on the study, for it would be impossible to understand the campaigns in Britain without reference to concurrent events on the continent, and vice-versa.

Finally, context has influenced the chronological limits and divisions of the study. The conquest is the obvious starting point. Although some Anglo-Saxon military institutions survived to be used by the Normans, they survived in altered form, beside new institutions, under new leadership. Most important, they formed part of a system called upon to defend England and Normandy, not just the former. Cross-Channel obligations were fundamental to the Anglo-Norman military system until 1135. William Rufus was not duke of Normandy, but he had a significant faction of the Norman barony supporting him and operated regularly in the duchy against Duke Robert; when the latter left for the Holy Land in 1096, William became de facto ruler of the duchy. Henry I also had his supporters in Normandy before he finally won the duchy by force in 1106. Therefore I have taken the period 1066–1135 as a whole, and have made it the focus of this study; I have tried to present the details of every aspect of the military system and warfare during these years.

In Stephen's reign (1135–1154), the disputed succession altered the strategic context of warfare dramatically. The machinery of government and the military system was split by desertion and civil war; Normandy was ignored by the king, probably mistakenly, in the face of his English troubles, and by 1144 he had lost it permanently. And perhaps most importantly, the character of the leadership exercised over the Anglo-Norman military system changed. Initially the strategic context of warfare was unchanged, and the basic patterns of military organization and warfare remained substantially unchanged throughout the reign. But conditions of division and weak leadership, in contrast with the unity and strong leadership of 1066–1135, produced warfare that was different in character from that of the earlier period, and that played a different role in overall policy, even while the details of how war was waged remained similar.[6]

With the accession of Henry II in 1154, the cross-Channel obligations of the king's military forces were restored, but the Continental possessions were so vastly greater, with their center of gravity in Anjou rather than Normandy, that new systems and political structures were called for to meet these expanded needs. New systems led to new patterns of warfare. Thus despite the return of strong leadership to the military system, the changes set in

---

[6] I shall be publishing elsewhere a study of warfare under Stephen which will highlight the important transformations of political structure which resulted from the warfare of Stephen's reign.

motion in 1135 had by Henry II's reign ushered in a new period of English royal warfare. I have therefore terminated this study at 1135.

There has been an explosion of Anglo-Norman studies in the past fifteen years. The Battle Conference, the child of R. Allen Brown, is held virtually on the battlefield of Hastings and has stimulated much of this scholarship.[7] Inevitably, much of this recent work has dealt with military matters, either with castles, with the organization of military institutions, or with the actions of war.[8] It builds on earlier work in Anglo-Norman history in particular and medieval military history in general, work to which this study is much indebted. In the Anglo-Norman field, the work of John Prestwich and Warren Hollister on military institutions[9] has been of fundamental importance. In medieval military history, this study owes much in its approach to the pioneering work of R.C. Smail on crusading warfare[10] and to John Keegan's now classic *The Face of Battle*.[11]

Yet there is still no satisfactory study of the subject of Anglo Norman warfare as a whole.[12] Valuable as the research on castles and organization

---

[7] The *Proceedings of the Battle Conference*, now *Anglo-Norman Studies*, has been a most valuable forum for Anglo-Saxon, Anglo-Norman and Angevin historians. Cited hereafter as *Battle*. The Haskins Society, American sister to the Battle Conference and child of Warren Hollister, has ensured the trans-Atlantic character of the Anglo-Norman field. The *Haskins Society Journal* has recently emerged as a companion to *Anglo-Norman Studies*.

[8] Prominent in this respect is the work of Allen Brown himself on castles: *English Castles* (London, 1976) and the fundamental *History of the King's Works*, vols 1 and 2, ed. with H.M. Colvin and A.J. Taylor (London, 1963); of John Gillingham on the patterns of warfare, especially 'Richard I and the Science of War', in *War and Government in the Middle Ages. Essays in Honour of J.O. Prestwich*, ed. Gillingham and J.C. Holt (Woodbridge, 1984), and 'William the Bastard at War', in *Studies in Medieval History presented to R. Allen Brown*, ed. C. Harper-Bill, C. Holdsworth and J. Nelson (Woodbridge, 1989); and of Richard Abels on Anglo-Saxon military institutions: *Lordship and Military Obligation in Anglo-Saxon England* (Berkeley, 1988). Many others, including Marjorie Chibnall, have also made valuable contributions too numerous to detail here. See the Bibliography in general and the notes on particular topics.

[9] Prestwich, 'War and Finance in the Anglo-Norman State', *TRHS* 5th series, 4 (1954), 19–43, and 'The Military Household of the Norman Kings', *EHR* 96 (1981), 1–35 (the latter's illumination of the central role of the royal household in military organization is, I believe, particularly important); Hollister, *Anglo-Saxon Military Institutions on the Eve of the Norman Conquest* (Oxford, 1962) (but see the work by Abels cited above), and *The Military Organization of Norman England* (Oxford, 1965).

[10] R.C. Smail, *Crusading Warfare, 1097–1193* (Cambridge, 1956).

[11] Keegan, *The Face of Battle* (London, 1976).

[12] The only survey of the subject, John Beeler's *Warfare in England 1066–1189* (Cornell, 1966), is in need of fundamental revision and suffers from an unnatural geographical limit on its scope.

has been, it should be fitted into a complete study of Anglo-Norman royal warfare. Only then, I think, can the relative importance of these aspects of the military system be assessed, and only then can the actual performance of the system in the field be included in our view of the system. Likewise, the work on patterns of warfare needs to be set against the institutional background which produced and supported the armies. For the Anglo-Norman military system and Anglo-Norman warfare should not be viewed in isolation from each other. Bringing the two topics together, and thus I hope shedding new light on each, is one of the purposes of this study.

The problems raised by an incomplete view of military systems or warfare is illustrated by two aspects of the subject which have received considerable attention, but which have been somewhat misunderstood or been exaggerated in importance as a result. The first of these aspects is feudalism. Defining the word 'feudalism' is the first problem, as any student of the middle ages knows.[13] For the purposes of this study, I have adopted a simple, functional definition. A 'feudal' soldier is a soldier serving a defined (and usually limited) term of service in exchange for possession of a fief, a landed estate which provides him with his support. From this military historian's point of view feudalism is thus a system of maintaining a reserve of trained manpower owing certain specified terms of yearly service.

This is an intentionally limited definition, and is not meant to imply that broader definitions are wrong. Anglo-Norman England was a feudal society, and feudalism more broadly construed clearly was more than military service for fiefs.[14] But such a limited definition is necessary if the functional distinctions between various types of soldiers serving in the Anglo-Norman army are to be clearly discerned. This is because little of the literature on the subject of 'feudalism' (broadly defined) concerns itself with the military uses of the feudal system. This is not unexpected, for the military face of the feudal system was only one – and not necessarily the most important – of many, though it was the basic one. The purpose of my definition is to isolate the military element, and to distinguish it from other terms of service such as paid, mercenary service. It is thereby hoped to make the place of feudal service (narrowly defined) in the overall scheme of

13 Elizabeth A.R. Brown, 'The Tyranny of a Construct: Feudalism and the Historians of Medieval Europe', AHR 79 (1974), 1063–1088, explores this topic. I have, in effect, followed her advice to use of the word 'feudal' only with specific reference to fiefs (p. 1086).

14 I explore the problems of feudal society and the broad definitions of feudalism at length below, pp. 19–28.

military obligation clearer, and come to a more balanced assesment of its importance.

The study of battle tactics is the aspect of Anglo-Norman warfare, after feudalism, which has received most attention.[15] Specifically, the battle of Hastings continues to be fought by academic Anglo-Saxons and Normans with almost as much fervor as was shown in 1066.[16] Was the Norman victory the inevitable result of superior military technology, the mounted knight bound to ride down the outmoded Anglo-Saxon shield-wall? Or was a superior Anglo-Saxon army simply asked to do too much in too little time? I shall address such questions myself in the proper place. What is important here is that all too often modern historians have looked no further than Hastings, or no further than the assumed dominance of the knight in medieval warfare generally, to answer these questions. The action at Hastings must be compared with the other major battles of the period, as well as with the more numerous minor actions of which we have details. And even more importantly, it must be remembered that battle tactics constituted only a small proportion of the actions required of an Anglo-Norman army, and that its other tasks necessarily influenced the type of soldier it contained, and thus influenced its battle tactics. This will become clearer in the course of this study.

The primary sources for a study of English royal warfare fall into two categories, the narrative and the documentary.[17] Each of these groups presents the historian with different problems. With the narrative sources, the contemporary chronicles and histories, the major problems are lack of detail and uncertain reliability. The two problems are often related. The writers of eleventh and twelfth century histories were pre-dominantly religious men who often had little personal experience of or interest in military affairs.[18] They depended on secondhand accounts for news of campaigns outside their immediate locale. Distant campaigns were therefore often reduced to a brief notice that in such a year king so

15 This reflects and has its roots in an older tradition of military history which concentrated on the 'Art of War', and above all on battle tactics. See Keegan, *Face of Battle*, pp. 35–44, 53–60. The *pater familias* of this type in English studies of medieval war is Sir Charles Oman's A *History of the Art of War in the Middle Ages*, 2 vols (London, 1924).
16 See below, pp. 22–23 (incl. n. 26), and 163–65 and the literature cited there, for the connection of interpretations of Hastings to 'pro-Norman' and 'pro-Saxon' views of history.
17 See the Bibliography for a list of sources.
18 The division between the clerical and secular worlds was not nearly so sharp as is sometimes thought, however. See M. Chibnall, 'Feudal Society in Orderic Vitalis', *Battle* 1 (1978), 35–48, on the close connection of the warrior and monastic worlds.

and so raised a large army and marched with it against his enemies. This is helpful only in establishing a chronology of campaigns. The questions with which I am concerned – how was the army raised? how was it housed and fed as it marched? and so on – are unanswered in such outline accounts. To find answers, it is necessary to search out the strong points in the sources, where a writer had access to reliable details of military action either by witnessing the action himself or talking to trustworthy eyewitnesses, and at the same time had the interest to record what he knew.

It is obvious that some sources will have more strong points than others. Writers like William of Poitiers, whose background and training were secular (and military), and whose subject is military events are likely to provide far more information than Eadmer, say, whose training and, even more, interests were in religious affairs. The warrior/historian, if we may call William of Poitiers this, is not necessarily the ideal source. His and his audience's very familiarity with the subject may let him take for granted a knowledge of the nuts and bolts behind his story, the very nuts and bolts we wish to get at. He is concerned with what happened, not necessarily with the details of how it was done. But at least he is interested. And in general, the more in depth a writer tends to be on any subject, the more likely he is to reveal details of military practice, often by using analogies to well-known military customs. Orderic Vitalis, maddening as his lack of dates and erratic organization can be if a chronological history is one's goal, is one of the most valuable of the narrative sources for this subject because of his untiring attention to detail, as well as his acquaintance with members of Henry I's military household.[19] It is worth noting that useful detail may be found not only when Orderic (or any other source) is writing about military actions, but also in anecdotes of everyday life, for many of the Anglo-Norman military system's less visible details – camping practices, or transport of supplies, for example – may be revealed on such a level.

The documentary sources present different problems for the military historian. These sources' reliability is perhaps less open to question (given that one is not examining a forged charter), though a source of uncertain origin such as the *Leges Henrici Primi* must be approached with the same caution a narrative demands. But the evidence of genuine charters and writs, Pipe Rolls, and tracts such as the *Constitutio Domus Regis* is as factual as we could hope for. The question is how much of this

---

[19] Chibnall, 'Feudal Society' and *The World of Orderic Vitalis* (Oxford, 1984) are invaluable as background to Orderic's writings.

information is about military organization and operations? Unfortunately, not much in a direct way. Of course it is possible to extract from such evidence much that is useful: lists of officers in the king's household, regulations of the household; much, in fact, on the side of organization. This is because the military system shared its officers and some of its hierarchy with the legal and financial systems of Anglo-Norman government. It is the latter that are recorded, and it is through them that we see the military system. It is probably this legal and financial overlap, and the sources' consequent bias, which accounts for a good bit of the overemphasis on the feudal aspects of military organization. On the side of military practice, however, we get little. It was not an age of written orders, even if such could have survived for us to see. In general, military operations fell outside the sphere of recorded governmental activity by their nature: they were neither routine, nor subject to legal dispute and its call for hard evidence. Financially, their immediacy and mobility took them away from the county accounts of the Pipe Rolls and into the as yet unrecorded regions of the royal chamber. They generated, therefore, little paperwork, and so are the more difficult to get at today.

A problem shared by both narrative and documentary sources is uncertain military terminology, particularly in distinguishing different types of soldiers. Terms of classical origin were used, but not always in the classical sense, beside terms of more contemporary origin. How the historian interprets these terms can have a great bearing on what the Anglo-Norman army looks like, so it is important to approach them with an open mind, and arrive at meanings based as much as possible on context. Further, it must be borne in mind that the meaning of any one term may not be consistent over the period, from source to source, or even within the same source. This inconsistency reflects the fact that words for military personnel often reflected not military duties, but legal and social standing, especially conditions of landholding; and that this period saw much change and development in legal and social structure.

The problem of confused terminology extends to the present literature. Not only have the Latin and Anglo-Saxon terms often been approached loosely or with conventional translations too easily accepted, but modern English military terms have been used imprecisely or inappropriately. The problem with 'feudal' is only the best known example.

Given the critical importance of terminology in the interpretation of sources and the presentation of results, it is necessary to discuss the most important terms individually and where possible to provide fairly precise definitions, which will be used throughout this study. This, I hope, will prevent confusion, if not controversy. I shall discuss the modern terminology first, to provide a basis for interpreting the Latin and Anglo-Saxon words.

First, my use of the words 'infantry' and 'cavalry' is simply another way of saying 'unmounted soldier' and 'mounted soldier', but with the understanding that this refers to a changeable, operational posture on the part of the soldiers referred to. This follows from the fact that the horse in medieval warfare was used for two very different purposes: as a means of strategic (large scale, campaigning) transport; and as a weapon in battle. Thus, a soldier who rode to battle but fought on foot would, in my terms, have operated first as a cavalryman, then, in battle, as an infantryman. In this usage I am in fact following the medieval sources. Making this distinction avoids the anachronistic and silly practice, common to much of the present literature, of calling the Anglo-Saxons who rode to battle and fought on foot 'mounted infantry' while Anglo-Normans who rode to battle and fought on foot become 'dismounted cavalry'.

Archers and crossbowmen usually operated as footsoldiers, though they could be horsed for rapid marches if the force were small. But their different weaponry and generally lighter defensive gear makes it more accurate to treat them as a third category of soldiers, as the chroniclers do, and I have been careful to distinguish between archers and other infantry where necessary.

The word 'knight' presents a greater problem, because it is loaded with non-military meanings, and because changes in the institution of knighthood during this period created changes in the meaning of the Latin *miles*, for which it is the common translation. It is variations in the social status of knighthood which generates distinctions between 'belted' and 'common' knights, for example,[20] not distinctions in military function. Because of the irrelevant confusion the word can cause, I have tried to avoid using it where possible. When I do use it, it is with the military meaning of a soldier who was relatively well equipped and well trained to fight on horseback – that is, it is a military class distinction denoting what might be called elite troops. Although the training and ability of a knight to fight on horseback is important to this definition,[21]

[20] S. Harvey, 'The Knight and the Knight's Fee in England', *P&P* 49 (1970), 29.
[21] But see J. Gillingham, 'The Introduction of Knight Service into England', *Battle* 4 (1981), 53, who says that only possession of a horse, not fighting on one, is necessary in defining 'knight', because cost and not tactics set a knight apart. This is in fact a reasonable way to put the issue; but cf. R.A. Brown, 'The Status of the Norman Knight', in *War and Government in the Middle Ages*, ed. Gillingham and Holt, p. 20 and *passim*, who thinks that tactics is important. Brown, though, is also using a specifically social definition of knighthood, though one rooted in the function of fighting. I do not necessarily disagree with such a definition but simply use a narrower definition for the sake of clarity. The problem is parallel and related to the broad and narrow definitions of 'feudal'.

that he actually did so is not. Thus I do at times refer to 'dismounted knights'; in such cases it is the professional training and superior equipment of the soldiers referred to which are important.

Finally, it should be noted that the word 'mercenary' carries none of the negative connotations it has gained from later centuries. It is essentially the equivalent of 'professional', that is one who is paid for his work, and is thus contrasted with words denoting different bases of service, such as 'feudal' or 'territorial'. And like 'infantry' and 'cavalry' it is a definition of operational mode, not strict classification: an enfeoffed soldier, if paid for his service, is a mercenary, not a feudal soldier.

Of the Latin terms for soldiers, *equites* and *pedites* present the least problem, for they may be interpreted precisely as 'cavalry' and 'infantry' respectively. As I mentioned above, the medieval sources use these terms in the sense I have defined: *pedites* for soldiers fighting on foot, whether they had dismounted to do so or not; *equites* for soldiers fighting on horseback.[22]

Miles, on the other hand, varies in meaning in unpredictable ways. The classical meaning, *miles*, 'soldier', was used in England throughout the eleventh and into the early twelfth century,[23] covering footsoldiers and horsemen. Even when it has this general sense, though, it tends to refer to the better equipped and trained soldiers unless modified by *rusticus* or some such term. Because the better equipped and trained soldiers after 1066 were often knights, i.e. trained as cavalry, *milites* began to acquire in England the meaning it had already gained on the Continent, as a synonym for *equites*. We can be sure of this when it is used in the common phrase *milites peditesque*; and in this sense can cover troops who would probably be *servientes* or *vavassores* in charters and official records, as these latter terms refer imprecisely to differences in conditions of land tenure or social position rather than military practice.[24] At least by Stephen's reign *miles* has taken on the stricter legal definition (which affected its use by chroniclers to some extent) of 'holder of a *feudum militis*, or knight's fee', and it is in this legal and social meaning (established, of course, on military duty) that the word is best known, and commonly translated as 'knight'. Yet it is clear that 'knight' would be a confusing translation at best in many cases. I have attempted no general interpretation of *miles*. I have considered it safest

22 OV, 6:xxi.
23 Hollister, A-S Mil. Inst., p. 6.
24 OV, 6:xxv; M. Chibnall, 'Mercenaries and the Familia Regis under Henry I', History 62 (1977), 18–19; F.M. Stenton, The First Century of English Feudalism 1066–1166, 2nd edn (Oxford, 1961), p. 23.

to approach each source, and each occurrence within a source, separately, and decide whether 'soldier', 'cavalryman', or 'knight' (in the legal sense) is meant, based on context.

The Latin for archer was *sagittarius*; by this was meant users of the short bow. Crossbowmen, less common but still regularly used, were referred to as *arcuballistarii*, or, rarely, simply *ballistarii* – a term more often used for the operators of siege engines such as the ballista. The long bow was not yet in use.

Two Anglo-Saxon words for soldiers are fairly straightforward. 'Housecarl' was a general term for mercenaries, as well as designating the royal guard troops who were the core of the Anglo-Saxon army.[25] It is the latter meaning, equivalent to the household knights of the Anglo-Norman army, that I have used in this study. 'Butescarl' could also mean mercenaries in general, but was used particularly of troops who fought on shipboard.[26]

No doubt some of the definitions I have chosen are open to argument: certainly no social historian would adopt the purely military sense for 'knight' that I set forth, for example. But my purpose is not so much to give definitive meanings as to point out the lack of precision inherent in the medieval terminology, and to provide a modern vocabulary as free as possible of extraneous implications or assumptions. I hope thus to provide better tools for portraying the Anglo-Norman soldier, his activities, and the system within which he worked.

Such tools are necessary because the Anglo-Norman military system was an odd construction by modern standards. It existed in a long transition period between government by personal bonds and government by impersonal institutions. It thus shows characteristics of both. There were institutions, but they were malleable, subject to much more shaping by individual wills and personalities than our modern bureaucracies, and they were held together in large part by personal bonds of lordship and dependence, of friendship. They were personal institutions. On the other hand, their institutional character was increasing, because a new bond between men was assuming greater importance: money. And England's cash economy, though still primitive, was precocious for the times. It is impossible to separate these two strands, the personal and the

25 Hollister, *A-S Mil. Inst.*, pp. 17–18.
26 N. Hooper, 'Some Observations on the Navy in Late Anglo-Saxon England', in *Studies in Medieval History presented to R. Allen Brown*, pp. 206–7, where they are linked to a proto-Cinque Ports scheme of service; *lithsmen* was also a term for professional mercenary soldiers who fought on ships (pp. 205–6).

professional. In short, friendship and money were the twin pillars of the Anglo-Norman military system and the army it produced. It was an odd combination, perhaps, but William the Conqueror and his sons made it work. How they did so is the subject of this study.

The Anglo-Norman Realm and its Neighbors

CHRONOLOGICAL TABLE

William I, the Conqueror, 1066–1087

1066 Campaign and Battle of Hastings; William crowned king on Christmas day at Westminster.

1067–71 Campaigns to secure England, including

  1068: Siege of Exeter; revolts in the north of England.

  1069: Campaigns around York; revolt in Maine.

  1070: 'Harrying of the North': devastation of Yorkshire to prevent further revolt and hinder Scandinavian invaders.

  1071: Last Anglo-Saxon revolt suppressed; Scandinavian raids.

1072 Invasion of Scotland.

1073 Reconquest of Maine.

1075 Revolt of Earls Roger and Ralf; Scandinavian invasion repelled.

1076 Campaigns in Normandy and Brittany; William defeated in battle at Dol.

1078 Revolt by William's eldest son Robert Curthose; campaigns in Normandy and Maine.

1079 William defeated in battle at Gerberoy; Scottish invasion.

1081 Campaigns in Normandy and Maine against count of Anjou.

1083 Second revolt by Robert Curthose.

1085–86 Threat of major Danish invasion; Domesday inquest held and Domesday Book compiled.

1087 Campaigns in the Vexin; William mortally wounded while sacking Mantes. Robert Curthose succeeds to Normandy, William Rufus to England.

William II Rufus, 1087–1100

1088 Baronial rebellion against Rufus suppressed, including sieges of Tonbridge, Pevensey and Rochester, and naval battle off Rochester.

1089–91 Campaigns in Normandy against Robert Curthose, who loses Maine.

1092 Invasion of Scotland.

1093–94 Campaigns in Normandy against Robert Curthose.

1095	Second baronial rebellion suppressed, including campaigns in north England, Wales, and siege of Bamburgh.
1096	Robert Curthose pawns Normandy to Rufus to go on Crusade.
1097	Campaign in Wales.
1098	Campaigns in the Vexin; reconquest of Maine.
1099	Campaign in Maine against count of Anjou.
1100	Rufus killed in hunting accident in New Forest; succeeded by his younger brother Henry. Robert Curthose returns from crusade and resumes rule of Normandy.

Henry I, 1100–1135

1101	Invasion of England by Robert Curthose and baronial rebellion neutralized by negotiation.
1102	Campaign against Robert of Bellême in England, including siege of Bridgnorth. Last significant campaign in England.
1105–06	Conquest of Normandy from Robert Curthose, including
	1106: Siege and battle of Tinchebrai.
1109–14	Campaigns in defense of Normandy, including
	1109–11: Campaigns in the Vexin against king of France.
	1111–13: Campaigns in Maine against count of Anjou.
1116–19	Campaigns in defense of Normandy, including
	1118: Henry's army defeated in battle by count of Anjou at Alençon.
	1119: Henry defeats king of France in battle at Brémule.
1123–24	Campaigns in Normandy against baronial rebels and invasions from Anjou and France, including
	1124: Rebel forces defeated by king's forces at battle of Bourgthérolde.
1135	Henry dies.

Chapter Two

CONTEXTS: THE WORLD OF ANGLO-NORMAN WARFARE

THE INSTITUTIONAL CONTEXT: THE MILITARY SYSTEM AS A BRANCH OF GOVERNMENT

The combination of the personal powers of the duke of Normandy and the chief Norman families who were his supporters with the institutional strength of the Anglo-Saxon monarchy which William acquired was a formidable one.[1] William guided this fusion to his own advantage during the years of settlement following the campaigns of 1066, putting the stresses of a continuing crisis to good use. The crown gained dramatically in demesne lands as a result of the conquest, and gained in being able more effectively to exploit the wealth of England and Normandy through taxation. In sum, the English government that emerged from the conquest was, by the standards of the time, unusually strong and rich. This is reflected in the structure and composition of the army.

The institutional strength of the government may be seen in the control the kings had over their military resources, and in fact in the scale of these resources. English kings had two territorial systems of service available to them in England, the Anglo-Saxon fyrd and the imported feudal assessments.[2] Both were royal forces exclusively. That is, they could be called out only by the king or his subordinates acting on his behalf, and every soldier's overriding allegiance was explicitly to the king. The assessments for feudal service in England were such that very few knights were maintained, either in households or on fiefs, who were not owed to the king's service. This was not true in Normandy,

---

[1] For recent syntheses of the general course of the Norman settlement and the institutional arrangements which resulted from it see, among others, Barlow, *Feudal Kingdom of England*; M. Chibnall, *Anglo-Norman England* (Oxford, 1986); D. Bates, *William the Conqueror* (London, 1989).

[2] See below, Ch. 3, for a detailed discussion of the various forces available to the Norman kings.

where only a small proportion of all the knights enfeoffed in the duchy were owed to the duke's service. But private warfare, in which the excess enfeoffed knights would have been used, was illegal in England and Normandy (and pretty successfully prevented, especially in England, except in time of rebellion), another sign of the effective control exercised by the royal government over military affairs and resources.

Castles as well as soldiers were subject to royal control. There were, of course, many private castles in both parts of the realm. But a castle had to be licenced by the king before it could be built; 'adulterine' castles (built without licence) were subject to destruction. And any castle could be forfeited or destroyed in case of rebellion.

The institutional strength of the government was in large part responsible for its wealth, and the influence of money on the military system is clear. Mercenaries appear in most episodes of Anglo-Norman warfare, and military institutions to which money was originally foreign, such as the knight's fee, were influenced by it at an early date: scutage was collected regularly under Henry I and probably under his father and brother before him, for instance; likewise *fiefs rentes* were used from 1066 on.[3]

Money was, in fact, the fuel that made the military machinery run.[4] Wages for troops formed only part of vast expenses including wages for officers, payments for castle-building and repair, for the provisions which stocked the castles and supplied field armies, for diplomatic support for allies, for the bribes which so often eased the course of military confrontation, and for the upkeep of the government itself.[5] And the money was available. England was a rich country with a strong, developed, specialized economy; efficient management of their finances and exploitation of native Anglo-Saxon and imported Norman institutions gave to the Conqueror and his sons more ready cash than their rivals ever had.[6] The Anglo-Norman military system, then, was built on a large supply of money put to use by an efficient,

---

3 M. Powicke, *Military Obligation in Medieval England* (Oxford, 1962), p. 3; Hollister, *Mil. Org. Norman England*, pp. 169–70, 199, 187; B.D. Lyon, 'The Money Fief Under the English Kings, 1066–1485', *EHR*, 66 (1951), 181.

4 Cf. the comments of Richard fitz Nigel in 'The Dialogue of the Exchequer': 'The abundance of resources, or the lack of them, exalts or humbles the power of princes'. *EHD* 2:524; and Wace's comments on the role of money in successful war, cited in M. Bennett, 'Wace and Warfare', *Battle* 11 (1988), 47. Both are writing in the second half of the twelfth century, but their comments apply to the earlier period as well as their own.

5 J.O. Prestwich, 'War and Finance in the Anglo-Norman State', p. 36.

6 WP, p. 156; Prestwich, 'War and Finance', p. 35; D.J.A. Matthew, *The Norman Conquest*

powerful government. The army depended on both: one was useless without the other. Efficient administration ensured the workings of the fyrd and feudal systems and the existence of logistical support for the army. Money ensured the workings of the administration and the army it raised.

Just as the power and wealth of the government shaped the military system, use of the military system shaped the development of the government. The demands of a military machine that runs on money tend to increase with time, and the sources are full of references to the costs of warfare and the oppressions used to meet them.[7] J.O. Prestwich was the first to point out that 'the whole history of the development of Anglo-Norman administration is intelligible only in terms of the scale and the pressing needs of war finance.'[8] It was the cost of war that led to 'the government reforms, precocious centralization, harsh exploitation of financial rights and ferocious justice' which characterize Henry I's reign in particular,[9] but whose beginnings go back into the Conqueror's reign.

While it is possible to see the reciprocal influence of government strength and wealth and of the military system on each other, it is important to see that in many cases the division of administration implied by such wording is misleading. That is, military institutions or officials had non-military functions and vice-versa, so that it would be possible to say that waging war was simply one of several functions performed by the same administrative machine. The most obvious case of this is the numerous non-military uses of castles. They were always places of residence, often centers of local government, and almost always prisons. They sometimes served as treasuries and even mints. But perhaps the most important case of overlap between military and non-military is seen in the *familia regis*, the king's military household. This constituted the administrative and fighting core of the Anglo-Norman army. Its officers were also some of the highest 'civil' officials of the realm, and Prestwich has pointed out that the role of members of the household in the administration of the kingdom looms large throughout this period.[10]

The sharing of military and civil duties may also be seen in the use of

---

(London, 1966), pp. 18–20, 53; Hollister, *A-S Mil. Inst.*, p. 18; J. Beeler, *Warfare in England*, p. 307; OV 5:232; Chibnall, *Anglo-Norman England*, chs 4, 5.

[7] E.g. HH, pp. 232, 240.

[8] Prestwich, 'War and Finance', p. 36.

[9] F. Barlow, *Feudal Kingdom of England*, p. 192.

[10] Prestwich, 'The Military Household of the Norman Kings', pp. 18–22.

non-military officials for military duties. The sheriff certainly had civil and military powers,[11] and many bishops and abbots did as well, either on a local level – directing castle ward, for example – or as commanders of field forces.[12] Once again we see how an efficient and well-developed administrative system was really a military resource, emphasizing the point that waging war was a task performed by the same machine that raised money and dispensed justice (two functions whose connection is unquestioned). But we should not push this point too far, because there were military specialists – the household knights of the *familia* – just as there were financial experts in the Exchequer. The more important point to stress is that the military specialists worked within a structure whose form was not dictated by military necessity alone. The institutional overlap of military and non-military in the Anglo-Norman government must be kept in mind when we examine the organization of the military system later in this study.[13]

THE SOCIAL CONTEXT:
'FEUDAL SOCIETY' AND A WARRIOR ARISTOCRACY

Medieval Europe has rightly been called a society organized for war. But a society organized for war is not the same thing as a state organized for war (as almost all states have been). The states of medieval Europe conducted warfare constantly, but were not particularly organized for anything, especially in the early middle ages. They lacked developed powers of taxation, they lacked much of an educated elite outside the church, and thus they lacked the bureaucracies which allowed many other pre-industrial states in the rest of the world to conscript large numbers of the lower classes into military service. Therefore for most of the middle ages, European states did not depend primarily on their own resources – on what we would call public powers – to raise military forces. Instead, they drew on, used and tried to shape the military communities of the societies over which they ruled. This meant that, in practice, most of them drew on the elite class of the society which had emerged in the

11 *RRAN*, 2: no. 563.
12 *RRAN*, 2: no. 725. Along similar lines, see E. Searle, 'The Abbey of the Conquerors: Defensive Enfeoffment and Economic Development in Anglo-Norman England', *Battle* 2 (1978), 156–7, for a discussion of Battle Abbey's place in the defensive scheme for south-east England; and Elizabeth van Houts, 'The Ship List of William the Conqueror', *Battle* 10 (1987), 160 on clerics owing military service.
13 See below, Ch. 3.

centuries after the breakup of the western Roman Empire, an elite class made up of warrior aristocrats.[14]

This characteristic of European states had a number of consequences which form an important part of the context of Anglo-Norman warfare. To begin with, it accounts for the very blurred line between 'public' and 'private' warfare,[15] as is illustrated by the fact that the central institution of Anglo-Norman warfare, the *familia regis*, grew out of the king's personal (private) household organization. Second, it helps explain the small scale and limited territorial ambition of warfare in this era: states simply could not raise or support the sort of forces needed for large scale conquest. In this context, it also accounts in large part for the dominance of mounted soldiers in most medieval armies, a much misunderstood topic which I shall discuss in detail below.[16] Finally, that it was society and not the state providing much of the organizational impetus behind war meant that warfare was a common, everyday feature of early medieval life, and above all, that it was the central feature of the lifestyle of the elite.

One of the features of medieval state building after c.1000 was the attempt by princes to limit private warfare and turn the waging of war into more of a state monopoly. States' resources were still too weak to eliminate the warrior function of the aristocracy. Rather, princes attempted to bend the energies of the elite to their own uses. This stimulated an ongoing creative tension between princely power and aristocracy, as the two tried to balance their sometimes different interests within an overall framework of cooperation. If the balance between the two interests in the Anglo-Norman realm was more on the royal side[17] than it was in most other contemporary states, it was still very much a matter of balance and not dominance. That cooperation rather than opposition was the keynote of royal-aristocratic relations should not be surprising, since the two were in partnership in governance and shared a common cultural outlook.

---

14 The fundamental work on the emergence of this society is still Marc Bloch, *Feudal Society*, trans. L.A. Manyon (Chicago, 1961). In the mediterranean world, especially Italy and the Christian kingdoms of the Iberian peninsula, the stronger survival of towns provided an alternate societal source of military organization, town militias. See the superb study by James F. Powers, *A Society Organized for War. The Iberian Municipal Militias in the Central Middle Ages*, 1000–1284 (Berkeley, 1988).

15 A line which this study has cautiously sharpened with respect to non-royal warfare for the sake of space.

16 See below, pp. 23–24, and Ch. 5.

17 As in the Anglo-Saxon kingdom, and in Normandy just before 1066, though more tenuously than in England.

This cultural outlook arose out of what may be called 'feudal society'.[18] Given that fighting was so closely bound up with status, the structure and culture of feudal society clearly influenced the conduct of warfare under the Anglo-Norman kings, beyond the major structural limitations mentioned above. The most important influences for a study of Anglo-Norman warfare were what may be called, for the sake of convenience, the dynamics of class and ethnicity.[19] Both exerted influence primarily over codes of battlefield behavior, especially with regard to killing versus the taking of prisoners in war.

As members of a privileged warrior elite, the aristocracy was proud of its position and jealous of its function. The development of a code of chivalrous behavior for this class,[20] influenced by the Church's attempts to limit violence between Christian and Christian,[21] meant that when members of this class met in combat, prisoners were more common on the losing side than deaths.[22] Since this class was international, covering at least the lands of the Carolingian Empire, the influence of chivalry was wide. But it was not, in this period, very deep. Non-knightly soldiers, especially infantrymen, even if they should have fallen under the same codes, in practice did not. Aristocratic contempt for those of lower status is clear from the boasting of the rebels at Bourgethérolde. Referring to themselves as 'the flower of knighthood' they refused to consider letting members of Henry I's *familia*, whom they referred to as 'country bumpkins and common soldiers', intimidate them off their route, and vowed not to shrink from fighting them.[23] The result was that knightly combat with non-knightly troops was more likely to result in death on both sides.[24] Of course there was from the knights' point of view an economic element to this distinction: knightly opponents could be ransomed. But the depth of the class antagonism clearly went beyond immediate material calculation.

---

18 See Bloch, *Feudal Society*, especially Part II.
19 'Ethnicity' is a problematic term here, but one for which I can find no effective substitute. It is meant to cover differences not only of ethnic origin ('Scandinavians', for example), but also partly of cultural construction combined with political affiliation (as in the *gens Normannorum* – the Norman 'race', or people, who were not an ethnic group strictly speaking). 'Geographic origin' would do, but is clumsy.
20 Maurice Keen, *Chivalry* (New Haven, 1984) is now the standard work on this topic.
21 See C. Harper-Bill, 'The Piety of the Anglo-Norman Knightly Class', *Battle* 2 (1979), 63–77, for the influence of the church on the Norman elite.
22 See below, Ch. 5, for a discussion of prisoners and casualties.
23 OV 6:351. Though the king's *familia* does not exactly fit the description, the attitude of the rebels to social inferiors is clear.
24 Cf. J.F. Verbruggen, *The Art of Warfare in Western Europe during the Middle Ages, from the Eighth Century to 1340*, trans. S. Willard and S. Southern (Oxford, 1977), pp. 51–2.

The class dynamic was often combined with an 'ethnic' one. If knights felt contempt for townsmen and country bumpkins, the feeling deepened when the non-knights were foreigners as well. Welsh, Scots other than that country's emerging Norman nobility, Flemings, and Scandinavians certainly qualified for mistrust and slaughter. The cultural role of feudalism is strong here, for these were peoples without feudal social structures. That the cultural construct took precedence over the ethnic distinction is demonstrated by the Norman 'race': Normans and French, however much the former tried to distinguish themselves as a people apart, shared a culture and therefore took prisoners.[25]

Did the Anglo-Saxons count as foreigners? Certainly in the first years after the Conquest the Norman magnates mistrusted their new subjects, and Hastings was as bloody a battle as one could find. But were the Anglo-Saxons foreign to the Normans in social structure like the other peoples mentioned above, or was the hostility in this case a political phenomenon and the blood at Hastings a result of high-stakes gambling on both sides? I would suggest that it was more a case of the latter. To support this contention, we must examine the question of the coming of feudalism into England.

The social and legal contexts of feudalism and feudal society clearly have a huge bearing on the question of feudalism in England. No other topic in Anglo-Norman history has stimulated such heated (if not always well lit) debate as the introduction of 'knight service', 'feudal tenure', 'military feudalism', or whatever one chooses to call it, into England by William and his successors.[26] The questions involved in this debate, not always clearly separated or defined, would seem to be the following.

---

[25] On the gens Normannorum see R.H.C. Davis, The Normans and their Myth (London, 1976), and G.A. Loud, 'The Gens Normannorum – Myth or Reality?', Battle 4 (1981), 104–116. Similar feudal cultures did not necessarily prevent antoagonism between neighbors: the mutual hostility of Normans and Angevins was deep. But it did tend to mitigate its effects. Clearly, the greatest cultural/ethnic gulf lay between the Christian and non-Christian worlds.

[26] There is a huge and contentious historiography to this question. The debate, still colored at times by 'pro-Norman' (often = pro-aristocratic) and 'pro-Saxon' (often = pro-democratic) sentiment, has usually been cast primarily as a question of continuity versus revolution. Continuity meant the transformation of the five-hide fyrd into the feudal host: e.g. E.A. Freeman, History of the Norman Conquest of England (Oxford 1867–79); Marjory Hollings, 'The Survival of the Five-Hide Unit in the Western Midlands', EHR 63 (1948), 453–487; Eric John, Land Tenure in Early England (Leicester, 1961); D.J.A. Matthew, The Norman Conquest. Revolution meant the introduction of a system – knights owing service for fiefs – completely unlike anything in Anglo-Saxon England: e.g. J.H. Round, 'The Introduction of Knight-Service into England', EHR 6 and 7 (1891, 1892), (the origin of this school and a bitter attack on Freeman); F.M.

What did William introduce into England? Why did he introduce it? Did the introduction of whatever it was constitute a revolution for English society?

The answers to these questions will depend in large part on what definition of feudalism is adopted. At the broadest level, Bloch summarises the characteristics of European feudalism as a subject peasantry; widespread use of the service tenement instead of a salary; the supremacy of a class of specialized warriors; ties of obedience and protection which bind man to man; fragmentation of authority; and the survival within this of state and family as alternate forms of organization.[27] This may be called the social definition of feudalism. A stricter military definition would include only military service rendered in exchange for a fief.[28] Allen Brown would add to the military definition the necessity that the soldiers rendering service be 'knights' and that castles be a part of the system.[29] Castles were certainly a common part of the feudal landscape, but Brown's claim that they were necessarily part of the 'system' of feudalism may be excused as special pleading for one of his favorite topics.[30] What about 'knights'? Once again, definitions are necessary.

The military definition of 'knight' adopted for this study is 'well armed and trained soldier', well-armed including hauberk, sword, helmet and horse.[31] The social definition would be as simple as 'member of the warrior elite'.[32] But between these poles lies an explosive problem:

Stenton, *First Century of English Feudalism*; R.A. Brown, *The Origins of English Feudalism* (New York, 1975) (as well as most of Brown's other work on the topic). Others have taken a more balanced approach: see J.O. Prestwich, 'Anglo-Norman Feudalism and the Problem of Continuity', *P&P* 26 (1963), 39–57; Hollister, *Mil. Org. Norman England* and *A-S Mil. Inst.* Few now hold to the continuity view in its strict formulation, but for a recent and provocative reformulation of the view along slightly broader lines see John Gillingham, 'Knight Service', pp. 53–64. But the revolution view should no longer seem as revolutionary in light of better understandings of Anglo-Saxon military institutions (see especially Abels, *Lordship and Military Obligation*) and Norman military practices, as explored below. Recent work on the topic includes J.C. Holt, 'The Introduction of Knight Service in England', *Battle* 6 (1983), 89–106; Chibnall, *Anglo-Norman England*, pp. 9–10; R.A. Brown, 'The Status of the Norman Knight'; Elizabeth van Houts, 'The Ship List of William the Conqueror', *Battle* 10 (1987), 159–83.

[27] Bloch, *Feudal Society*, 2:446.

[28] The definition adopted for this study for the sake of clarity. Cf. Elizabeth A.R. Brown, 'Tyrranny of a Construct', p. 1086.

[29] Brown, *Origins of English Feudalism*, pp. 23–24, 31–32.

[30] And both conditions may be attempts to exclude Anglo-Saxon England from the feudal world by definition.

[31] Cf. Gillingham, 'Knight Service', p. 53; Brown, 'Status of the Norman Knight', p. 28.

[32] Cf. Brown, 'Status of the Norman Knight', pp. 19–20; Bloch, *Feudal Society*, passim. As

tactics. Did one have to fight on horseback (or at least be trained to do so) to be a knight?[33] The problem with this condition is that it is simply arbitrary. Many warrior elites of the pre-industrial world were mounted;[34] this was a natural consequence of the desire to display wealth and status (horses of any type being expensive, warhorses especially so) and of the advantages to any individual of campaigning and fighting on horseback.[35] Why insist on one particular tactic – the charge with couched lance[36] – as necessary to knighthood? If we reject tactical considerations as part of knighthood, are knights a necessary part of feudalism? Militarily, not really: the principle of service for fiefs was used to maintain vavasours and serjeants as well as the better armed *miles*; but to say yes does not really damage the sense of the definition. Socially, the answer is obviously yes: a warrior elite is inherent in the social definition of feudalism. But what does this mean for William and England?

Did William introduce feudalism into England? Pretty clearly he did, by either the social or military definition, introduce the Norman-French version of feudalism into his new kingdom. The more interesting questions are why did he, and did he thereby revolutionize England?

It is easy to assume that military necessity prompted William to impose *servitia debita*, quotas of knightly service, on his barons and on religious houses in the early years of his reign. There are several reasons, though, why we should question whether this was the sole reason operating at the time.

First, it should be noted that knightly quotas were only the first step in the introduction of a feudal system.[37] The barons met their obligations initially by the use of household knights – mercenaries, in other

---

noted above, there are also socio-legal definitions of knighthood that do not concern this study; see above, p. 10.

33 Gillingham maintains that 'it was equipment, not battle tactics, which determined cost': 'Knight Service', p. 53. But Brown points out that horses trained for combat were more expensive than lesser mounts ('Status of the Norman Knight', p. 28; see also R.H.C. Davis, 'The Warhorses of the Normans', *Battle* 10 (1987), 67–82).

34 E.g. the Persian cataphracts, the Macedonian Companions, the Roman *equites*, the Shang aristocracy, the Japanese samurai. The list could easily be extended.

35 See below, pp. 160–62.

36 A tactic which was not universal even among those capable of delivering it, as the dismounting of knights shows. See below, pp. 156–57.

37 Elizabeth van Houts has suggested that the quota system arose out of ship and manpower negotiations between William and his magnates during the preparations for the 1066 campaign: 'The Ship List of William the Conqueror', pp. 171–172. But cf. Gillingham, 'Knight Service', p. 63 on a broader European context for quotas.

words. Subinfeudation, the establishment of knights on knights' fees by the barons in return for service that helped meet the barons' quotas, was a gradual process.[38] So this question now is split in two: why were the quotas imposed? and why subinfeudation?

Military necessity certainly was one reason for the quotas: forced to maintain a relatively large army in the field for several years after 1066 to pacify a country which would not have been yielding its usual revenues to him yet, William probably used the quotas to spread the cost of mercenaries. That is, the quotas initially were a form of direct military taxation, taxation that shifted the administrative chores as well as the financial liability onto the taxpayers. The arbitrariness of the quotas imposed by the king on his major barons has struck many writers as looking like the result of political deals of the sort associated with taxation.[39] Indeed, this view of feudal quotas probably applies well beyond the initial period of conquest. David Crouch examined the feudal obligations of the twin brothers Robert of Leicester and Waleran of Meulan in Henry's reign and beyond, and concluded that, 'We can fairly assume that the Beaumont twins hired knights when they needed to make up a quota.'[40] Even after subinfeudation had progressed, the quotas probably continued to function as a form of indirect taxation, a way of maintaining a trained reserve of manpower on the land. The questions of supporting manpower on the one hand and the terms of service by which that manpower is used on the other are separate.[41] So quotas certainly had military necessity behind them, at least in part. What about fiefs and subinfeudation?

Given the limited use of this element of the feudal system,[42] and given that William encouraged and supervised the subinfeudations that complicated the system and perhaps made it less useful, we should look beyond strictly military reasons for the introduction of knight service (as distinct from quotas) into England.[43]

The numerous non-military reasons for many cases of subinfeudation,

---

[38] Hollister, *Mil. Org. Norman Eng.*, pp. 49–50.
[39] J.C. Holt, 'The Introduction of Knight Service into England', pp. 99, 105.
[40] D. Crouch, *The Beaumont Twins* (Cambridge, 1986), p. 132.
[41] See below, pp. 47–51.
[42] See below, pp. 51–57.
[43] Failure to do so leads to what one authority has called the 'mystery of the purpose of the imported military feudal institutions', and we may question whether his answer to that military mystery – that they helped consolidate the conquest and then became obsolete (E. Miller, review of Hollister, *Mil. Org. Norman Eng.*, *EcHR*, 18 (1965), 417) – is any more satisfactory than saying that money made English feudalism 'bastard' from the start

from the social and political to the personal and nepotic, have been pointed out by several scholars.[44] The process of subinfeudation was easily encouraged even within the context of more precise definitions of feudal military obligations that emerged after 1066,[45] for landholding by homage and 'knight's service' – however its obligations were defined, and of which military service in the field was perhaps the least used – was a major form of legal and social contract among the upper classes. Inheritance and marriage were the only other forms of contract having equal or greater importance.[46] The importance of homage and knight's service as a legal form in landholding is emphasized by its parallel use in monetary contracts: specifically, the only real difference between a fourteenth century indenture contract and a twelfth century *fief rente* was the legal formality in the latter of rendering homage as if for a landed knight's fee.[47] Obviously, on the broader social level, Norman feudalism had to come to England with the Norman warrior elite.

The above must be borne in mind when we come to examine the actual military use of the feudal system and the overall composition of the Anglo-Norman army, for it warns again that there could be an important difference between military obligation and military practice.[48] This difference resulted not only from the overlap of military and non-military officials, functions and institutions in the Anglo-Norman government, but from the overlap of social and military customs of landholding.

The last question here, however, is how revolutionary the introduction of Norman feudalism was in Anglo-Saxon England. Once again, our answer depends on the terms of the question. Was there a tenurial

---

and doomed it to a slow death from the moment of its birth: Hollister, *Mil. Org. Norman Eng.*, pp. 278–9. Cf. Gillingham, 'Knight Service', p. 53 for the distinction between *servitium* and knight service.

[44] Harvey, 'Knight and Knight's Fee', pp. 7–9; Richard Mortimer, 'Land Tenure and Service: The Tenants of the Honour of Clare', *Battle* 8 (1985), 197.

[45] Chibnall, 'Military Service in Normandy before 1066', p. 75.

[46] Eleanor Searle, *Predatory Kinship* and 'Emma the Conqueror', in *Studies . . . to R. Allen Brown*, points out the close links to lordship and homage of marriage, inheritance, and kinship, and shows that the women in such a system were far from passive pawns in marriage diplomacy. As members of the knightly class, they shared its ethos and lifestyle, even if they rarely if ever engaged in actual fighting. But see below, p. 96, n. 11, for wives as their husbands' lietenants in castle guard. Marjorie Chibnall, 'Women in Orderic Vitalis', *The Haskins Society Journal* 2 (1990), 105–121, also discusses the role of women in the feudal world.

[47] B.D. Lyon, *From Fief to Indenture* (Harvard, 1957), p. 263.

[48] Cf. Prestwich, 'Anglo-Norman Feudalism and the Problem of Continuity', *P&P*, 26 (1963), 53; and M. Powicke, review of Hollister, *A-S Mil. Inst.*, *Speculum*, 39 (1964), 160.

revolution, a change in the personnel of the ruling class in the kingdom? Unquestionably. Normans replaced or were inserted over Anglo-Saxons in the landholding hierarchy, and even the Anglo-Saxons who survived suffered loss of status.

Was there a social revolution? Recent work on the Anglo-Saxon kingdom, especially Richard Abels' work on Anglo-Saxon military institutions, suggests that there was not.[49] In the general terms laid out by Bloch, Anglo-Saxon England was clearly a form of feudal society, even if the terminology and legal technicalities of land tenure differed from those of Norman feudalism: subject peasantry; widespread use of the service tenement instead of a salary; the supremacy of a class of specialized warriors; ties of obedience and protection which bind man to man; fragmentation of authority; and the survival within this of state and family as alternate forms of organization. This is not to deny that the legal differences in the long run may have had a revolutionary effect on the political structure of the realm, nor that the effects of the tenurial revolution contributed mightily to that long run change. But in the context of 1066, one warrior elite had been replaced by another.

Was there a military revolution? Once again, the answer almost has to be no. There was, undeniably, a shift in tactical tradition from fighting on foot or shipboard to fighting on foot or horseback. It is one of the central contentions of this study, explored at greater length later,[50] that this change did not mean all that much in the context of overall patterns of eleventh and twelfth century warfare.

But let us look at the question outside the area of tactics for a moment. The Anglo-Saxon and Norman armies were in almost every way nearly identical. The arms and armor of each side are indistinguishable in the Bayeux Tapestry.[51] Both armies had at their core a group of paid household warriors, the housecarls and the *familia* knights.[52] Both surrounded this core with forces of a rural warrior elite, owing service out of a combination of lordship and land tenure.[53] Both systems and their associated warrior classes drew comparable sustenance from underdeveloped agrarian economies ruled by similar and similarly primitive governments – with the Anglo-Saxons probably having the edge in sophistication, the

---

[49] Abels, *Lordship and Military Obligation*; 'Bookland and Fyrd Service in Late Saxon England', *Battle* 7 (1984), 1–25; see also Gillingham, 'Knight Service', pp. 63–4.

[50] See below, pp. 150–162.

[51] Ian Peirce, 'Arms, Armor, and Warfare in the Eleventh Century', *Battle* 10 (1987), 237–257.

[52] Cf. Hooper, 'Some Observations', p. 206.

[53] See below, pp. 51–57.

Normans perhaps in vigor. Should we expect one side or the other to have some vast military advantage arising out of this uniform social and institutional background? The notion seems implausible.

In fact, the Anglo-Saxon and Norman armies were not all that different tactically. And if we compare the Anglo-Saxon army and the Anglo-Norman army, there is almost no difference: commonly, both armies rode to battle and fought on foot. Hastings was as close a battle as one can find,[54] demonstrating that the effectiveness of the Anglo-Saxon and Norman systems was similar.[55] Even the combined Anglo-Norman system, with all its wealth and institutional backing, did not decisively outclass its main continental opponents. The Anglo-Norman kings were generally successful, but not universally: there was nothing inevitable about their victories any more than the outcome of Hastings was inevitable. The success in war of the Anglo-Norman kings required hard work, good leadership, and the skillful use of tools other than war to further royal policy aims. It is this last subject that will now be examined.

THE POLITICAL CONTEXT: WARFARE AS A TOOL OF POLICY

The aims of warfare, and thus the way war is waged, are a result of the policy that warfare is intended to implement. Medieval policy almost never called for a complete, Clauswitzian overthrow of the enemy.[56] As a result military historians have often found medieval warfare indecisive, devoid of strategic skill, and lacking in the military historian's treat, the 'decisive battle'.[57] Such a view is unfair to medieval generalship and misunderstands not only the prevailing strategy of medieval warfare but also the policy behind medieval wars, policy that was generally quite

---

[54] See below, pp. 163–68 on the battle; the general connection between governmental strength and tactics explored in Chapter 5 is also relevant in this context.

[55] Similarly, David Bates places the Normans against a wider northern French background and concludes that such a view 'requires the rejection of the specific notion that the Normans possessed a special and exceptional aptitude for war.' *Normandy before 1066* (London, 1982), p. 245.

[56] Given the level of resources available to medieval rulers and the prevailing class and religious ethics of the time complete overthrow of the enemy was both discouraged and usually unrealistic. But when warfare crossed cultural boundaries (as it did in some ways in 1066), especially the boundaries of Latin Christendom (as in Spain, the Holy Land and eastern Europe), warfare could assume a more 'Clausewitzian' form, at least in the long run.

[57] Oman, *Art of War in the Middle Ages*, *passim*, for the seminal version of this view of medieval warfare.

limited in terms of territorial ambitions. The policy of the Anglo-Norman kings was in this sense typically medieval: limited and for the most part defensive.

Having said this, we are faced with the campaign of 1066 and with Hastings, one of everybody's 'decisive battles of the Western World'. It does not really disguise the nature of the campaign to say that William was simply claiming what the papacy regarded (thanks to skillful diplomacy) as his by hereditary right. This was a pretext, albeit a crucial one, for every other campaign of this period whose design was conquest had such a pretext: Henry I justified his conquest of Normandy in 1105–6 to the Pope in the following terms, according to Orderic: 'I did not deprive my brother of the duchy of Normandy, but laid legal claim by battle to the just inheritance of our father', the right to which Robert had forfeited by mismanagement.[58]

But the offensive aims of the 1066 campaign were not what set it apart. For although offensive campaigns were rare at the level of royal (or comital) warfare, they were not unknown. More importantly, the lifestyle and power structure of early medieval rulers and warriors had been based on aggression – or predation, as it has also been called – if not always for conquest, then at least for plunder.[59] Such aggression and predation were becoming rarer by 1066 as secular princes harnessed their aristocracy's energies to their own ends (as William did so spectacularly well), and soon the church would succeed in redirecting even more of that energy into the Crusades. The general growth of the ideology of legitimacy and lineage also limited opportunities for predation, and brings us back to the pretexts for offensive warfare mentioned above. But the spirit of an aggressive warrior aristocracy was alive and well in 1066.

What set the campaign of 1066 apart from the normal territorial aggressiveness of warrior society was partly scale, and above all that it was literally – and so crucially – decisive. Within two months, William had completely destroyed any immediate resistance, and within a few years had consolidated his conquest at the expense of the existence of an entire ruling class, the Anglo-Saxon thegnage. Yet it may fairly be said that the decisiveness of the campaign was largely a result of accidental factors: Harold's death at Hastings, and the lack of any other viable

---

58 OV, 6:284.
59 For Europe generaly, see G. Duby, *The Early Growth of the European Economy. Warriors and Peasants from the Seventh to the Twelfth Century*, trans. Howard B. Clarke (Ithaca, 1974); on the particular pattern of Norman expansion see Eleanor Searle, *Predatory Kinship and the Creation of Norman Power, 840–1066* (Berkeley, 1988), though cf. Bates, *Normandy before 1066.*

claimants to the throne. Without Harold's death, particularly, William might have won the battle but not the war, or even won the war but not all of England. The point is that the totality of the initial victory could not have been planned. Nor, if most of William's biographer's judgements are correct, was the revolutionary course of the settlement planned.[60] William's claim to be legal heir to England may have been a pretext for the invasion, but it seems to have guided William's conservative attitude towards his new kingdom, at least at first. If he did not succeed in simply replacing one king with another, as Henry replaced one duke with another in 1106,[61] then it was circumstance and not policy that decided the result.

In its generally defensive nature and in the legal support arranged for offensive measures, the policy of the Anglo-Norman kings conformed to the prevailing morality of warfare, a morality reflecting the strong influence of the church on diplomacy – and by extension on warfare as a tool of policy – in the twelfth century. The bishop of Oporto, addressing the crusaders who were to take Lisbon, cites Isidore of Seville on the church's doctrine: ' "A war is just," says Isidore, "which is waged after a declaration, to recover rights or repulse an enemy." '[62] War, in the church's view, should be declared and defensive, whether in direct response to an attack or to reclaim lost rights and possessions.[63] For the most part, the Anglo-Norman kings conformed to the church's teaching.

Indeed, the efforts of William to obtain the papacy's support for his planned invasion in 1066, and Henry's justifications in 1106, show that the Anglo-Norman kings regarded the church's approval and support as important to the lasting success of their wars. And in 1066, the pope's support may have had immediate benefits in terms of attracting mercenary soldiers to William's cause.

The church usually had less influence on the actual conduct of warfare once it was underway, however. The bishop of Oporto went on to say that 'it is not a sin to wage war, but it is a sin to wage war for plunder.'[64] Nonetheless, plundering was one of the most frequently performed acts

---

[60] D.C. Douglas, *William the Conqueror* (London, 1964), pp. 305–10; Bates, *William the Conqueror*, pp. 126–8.

[61] Though see Hollister, 'Henry I and the Anglo-Norman Magnates', *Battle* 2 (1978), 93–107 for Henry's manipulation of the baronage after his conquest of Normandy.

[62] *De Expugnatione Lyxbonensi*, ed. C.W. David (New York, 1976), p. 80.

[63] See Frederick H. Russell, *The Just War in the Middle Ages* (Cambridge, 1975), for a thorough treatment of this subject. See also C. Harper-Bill, 'The Piety of the Anglo-Norman Knightly Class' on the effect of church teaching on the warrior class.

[64] *De Expugnatione Lyxbonensi*, p. 82.

of war on all sides in twelfth century warfare,[65] though more as a means than an end in itself.

The church was not completely powerless in enforcing its views, however. The church viewed rebellion as a clearly unlawful form of warfare, as Archbishop Lanfranc informed Roger, earl of Hereford, in 1075. As one of the king's chief lieutenants in England, Lanfranc directed the king's forces against the rebel; as archbishop, he excommunicated him.[66] Thus when the moral force of the church worked with the temporal power of the government, each reinforced the other and became that much more effective.

Further discussion of the influence of the church on warfare – including, for example, the Peace of God and the Truce of God – is beyond the scope of this work, although it should be noted that in the hands of a strong ruler such as William I, the Truce of God formed an important tool in the suppression of private warfare.[67] But the role of the church in the forms and function of diplomacy, and thus in defining the objects for which rulers could go to war, is clear.

To restate the main themes of Anglo-Norman policy then, it was generally defensive. William, as Orderic has it, expressed this side of war policy on his deathbed: '[Henry of France] often invaded my land with a huge army, but he never succeeded in carrying off booty or plunder or capturing my men.'[68] Defense of the kingdom was one of the king's duties as king. When policy called for offensive campaigns, it did so either with the pretext of defending or recovering territory which legally belonged to the king or his vassals (the county of Maine was the arena for several such campaigns), or it contemplated only intimidation for the purpose of keeping peace, not permanent conquest (Wales was frequently subjected to such campaigns). In the former case, it should be noted, a well-founded and often sincerely believed pretext could usually be discovered, for if no legal foothold existed in a strategically important border area, a few well-arranged marriages or induced rebellions could usually create one.[69]

---

[65] See below, p. 98.
[66] *The Letters of Lanfranc Archbishop of Canterbury*, ed. and trans. H. Clover and M. Gibson (Oxford, 1979) no. 33A.
[67] P. Contamine, *War in the Middle Ages*, trans. M. Jones (Basil Blackwell), 1984, p. 52. The Christianization of the warrior class and the limits on killing that this encouraged was noted above.
[68] OV, 4:87.
[69] Searle, 'Emma the Conqueror', for the potential long term as well as short term diplomatic effects of marriage alliances. The judgement that Anglo-Norman policy was

Indeed, as a method of gaining territory conquest by warfare was expensive, dangerous and of more uncertain duration than expansion by legal means.[70] And after William I, his sons were constrained by a limited range for new conquests and stronger opposition of a reformed church to wars of conquest.[71] Even in defense war was expensive and dangerous, a tool to be used as a last resort when other means failed. What were the other means available to the kings of England for expansion and defense of the realm?

One of the most effective, given the wealth of the Anglo-Norman government, was bribery. In 1090, for instance, Philip of France joined Robert Curthose to besiege the castle of a supporter of William II. William crippled the alliance by bribing Philip into going home, and repeated the trick in 1094 when Philip joined Robert to besiege Eu.[72] Robert himself had his price in the right circumstances: needing money to go on Crusade, he in effect pawned the duchy to William in 1096. And he allowed Henry to buy off his claim to the throne of England in 1101 for a yearly pension of £2,000. Henry I split Robert of Bellême's league with the Welsh in 1102 with bribes to the latter.[73] And though bribery was unused against rebellion, for obvious reasons, it could induce rebellion in others' vassals, either to distract a potential invader or to prepare the path of invasion. Henry's gold won much of Normandy from Duke Robert before a blow was struck, as the Worcester chronicler vividly describes:[74]

Henry, king of England, crossed the sea; on his arrival, nearly all the Norman barons, deserting the count their lord and the fealty they owed him for the king's gold and silver, which he had brought from England, rushed to him and handed over their castles, walled towns and cities to him.

---

generally defensive is based on the actual results of warfare and policy between 1066 and 1135. The 'culture' or tradition of Norman policy was probably more offensive minded, but was restrained in practical terms after 1066 by the size of the united realm and the number of enemies it faced. On the offensive character of the Norman polity, see Searle, *Predatory Kinship*; though she carries the story only up to the conquest, the implication of Searle's model is that the Anglo-Norman polity would have continued to be offensive, or predatory, after 1066.

70 The impermanence of William I's conquest of Maine should be noted in this context.
71 Matthew, *Norman Conquest*, p. 222; Hollister, 'Henry I and the Anglo-Norman Magnates', p. 98.
72 Florence, 2:27; HH, p. 217.
73 Florence, 2:50.
74 Florence, 2:53–4; cf. Wace, cited in Bennett, 'Wace and Warfare', p. 47.

Money was undoubtedly helpful, too, in the diplomatic moves which isolated Robert before the invasion. The Flemish money fief agreement of 1101, renewed in 1103, by which Henry bought the friendly neutrality if not the support of the Count of Flanders, illustrates this clearly. Even when it could not replace warfare, diplomacy – alliances and negotiated settlements – made warfare easier and less costly. Allies like the count of Blois could threaten an enemy from a different quarter and thereby draw off a threat, and in actual hostilities occupy at least a portion of enemy forces. All three of England's kings during this period were adept diplomats, Henry above all.

Not just money but the threat of war at times encouraged the progress of diplomacy. Henry needed do no more than raise an army to bring the Welsh to terms in 1121, for example.[75] And once again the wealth of the Anglo-Norman kings, and thus their greater ability to bear the costs of a war than their neighbors, backed up such a threat – as William II made explicit to Helias, count of Maine, in 1096. He warned Helias of the money the count would have to spend repairing the walls of his chief city, 'for at the earliest opportunity I will visit the citizens of Le Mans; I will show them a hundred thousand lances with banners before their gates, and will not leave you unchallenged in the enjoyment of my inheritance.'[76]

Bribery, diplomacy and alliances, and the threat of warfare; all were employed instead of or in addition to warfare in the execution of policy towards external enemies. If an invader could be turned back or land could be won without the use of force, so much the better. None of these tools, however, was useful against internal enemies. In dealing with rebels and rebellion, the policy of the Anglo-Norman kings was harsh and generally unforgiving, and thus their means of dealing with them were more forceful than with foreign threats. On the other hand, the goal of the kings was to use as little force as necessary, and to apply that force as much as possible through legal process rather than militarily. To this end, rebellions might be settled through negotiations in the first place, particularly if they coincided, as they often did, with foreign invasions. Later, at a time and place more advantageous to the king, the rebel would be arrested and either imprisoned or exiled, and his land would be confiscated and redistributed to more loyal subjects, all this occurring on some good legal pretext.[77] In rebellions after 1071, which

[75] Symeon, HR, pp. 268–9.
[76] OV, 5:232.
[77] The best example is Henry's dealings with Robert of Bellême in 1101–2: Hollister, 'The

were all raised by Anglo-Norman barons as opposed to by Anglo-Saxons, the kings were encouraged in their harshness by the native population of England; whatever restraint they exercised was a result of the influence of the 'loyal' baronage. For example, as Henry I pressed his campaign against the rebel Robert of Bellême in 1102, 'the earls and magnates of the realm met together and discussed fully how to reconcile the rebel with his lord.' But the common soldiers (*pagenses milites*) in the army urged harshness:[78]

> . . . they shouted out to the king, 'Henry, lord king, don't trust these traitors [the barons]. They are out to deceive you and undermine your royal justice. Why do you listen to men who urge you to spare a traitor and let a conspiracy against your life go unpunished? See, now, we all stand loyally by you and are ready to obey your least command. Storm the fortress, press the traitor relentlessly from all sides, and make no peace with him until you have him in your hands, alive or dead.'

The lack of a popular balance to baronial power may account in part for the greater frequency of revolts in the Norman half of the realm, in addition to the greater proximity of potential allies for rebels in the duchy. This last factor brings us to a consideration of the strategic surroundings of royal warfare.

THE GEOGRAPHICAL CONTEXT:
THE STRATEGIC MAP

Though England was the wealthier, more prestigious half of the Anglo-Norman realm, Normandy was the homeland for the first generation of conquest kings and barons, and exerted an emotional hold even over their English born successors.[79] It commanded more of their attention politically and militarily because of this, and because the graver threats to the kings' security bordered Normandy, at least after 1085, when the last real Scandinavian threat dissipated.

Campaign of 1102 against Robert of Bellême', in *Studies . . . to R. Allen Brown*, pp. 193–202.

[78] OV, 6:26–7, and n.2 on the various interpretations of *pagenses milites*. While it probably did include Norman soldiers of lesser status than the barons and earls, the presence of large numbers of infantry in the army (p. 28) indicates a healthy contingent of Anglo-Saxon soldiers as well. Cf. the composition of the forces loyal to Henry I against his brother Robert in 1101: Malmesbury, GRA, 2:472.

[79] Cf. J. Le Patourel, 'Normandy and England 1066–1144', in *Feudal Empires, Norman and Plantagenet* for the strategic and political unity of the realm.

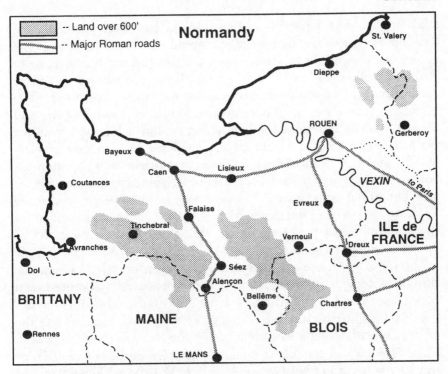

The most important trouble spots on the Norman border were the district of the Vexin, which separated Normandy from the Ile de France and its Capetian kings, and the county of Maine, between Normandy and the county of Anjou.

The area of the Vexin lay in the Seine valley between the Andelle and the Oise rivers. The original Norman settlement had cut the Vexin in half at the river Epte, and this made the most natural border between Paris and Rouen. But the Normans had received legal title to the entire Vexin from Henry I in the 1030s, while Henry and his son Philip I were able to reexert French influence during Duke William's stormy minority, and Philip finally took over the area while William campaigned in Maine in 1077. The area remained in dispute throughout the period of this study, for the Capetians' policy was consistently hostile to a strong Normandy united with England, and the problem of trans-border lordships dominated this area.[80]

Anjou was an even stronger rival to the Norman dukes than the Capetians were, and Maine was their point of conflict. A more recent

---

[80] Judith A. Green, 'Lords of the Norman Vexin', in Gillingham and Holt, *War and Government in the Middle Ages*, pp. 47–61.

feudal unit than its powerful neighbors, Maine had developed under the lordship of Anjou; the diocese of its capital, Le Mans, lay within the ecclesiastical province of Tours. Duke William had taken advantage of Angevin weakness in the 1050s to seize Maine, but a hostile populace and a resurgent Anjou made his grasp of the county precarious. The Normans surrendered it during the weak rule of Duke Robert, and though William II regained it briefly, Robert lost it for good to direct Norman control before Henry I had completed his conquest of Normandy, and Fulk V of Anjou inherited it outright in 1110 from his father-in-law, Helias of la Flèche. Maine remained a disputed border area, but Anjou would be the dominant power within the county. Henry was fortunate to have the steady friendship of Blois during his reign, for this counterbalanced to some extent the increased danger created by Angevin control of Maine.

The other borders of Normandy were less consistently troublesome. Brittany accepted Norman suzerainty with only occasional protest, and Bretons are found in the Anglo-Norman government, the kings' household, and among the baronage throughout the period. Flanders was the other power whose influence impinged on the Norman sphere of action. Duke William had conquered England with Flemish help; Count Baldwin VI was his brother-in-law, received from William a 300 mark money fief, as his father Baldwin V had, and was a firm friend. But dynastic struggles after his death in 1070 produced a hostile Count, Robert 'le Frison'. The Anglo-Flemish alliance was not renewed until 1090, between Rufus and Count Robert II, and again in 1101 between Henry I and the same count; but the most Henry achieved for much of his reign was unfriendly neutrality from Flanders. Fortunately, most Flemish military activity looked eastwards, towards vassals of the German Emperor.

The military character of the Norman frontier made decisive action difficult. It was heavily castellated, and a maze of vassalage which knew no borders created a political quicksand of conflicting loyalties in the most vulnerable regions. Decisive action was not impossible. Le Mans, for instance, was the key to Maine: if it fell, castles which had been bypassed on the way then gave in without a fight. But if there were no key point like a Le Mans, reducing several minor castles could be a long and tedious process, for defensive techniques were generally well matched against offensive tactics.[81] Yet the nature of the frontier helped the Normans defensively as much as it did their enemies.

[81] See below, p. 144.

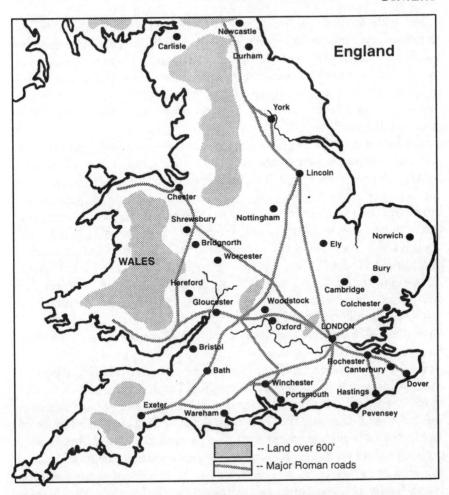

As for the other features of Norman military geography, three deserve
mention. First, roads were important in warfare. The road systems, the
Roman roads in particular, were perhaps less important than in other
ages, because armies were smaller and depended less on wheeled transport of supplies and equipment during campaigns. Thus small roads and
tracks could serve where larger roads did not go. But roads were still
necessary. Second, the rivers of the province, running parallel rather
than perpendicular to likely invasion routes, provided no real barrier or
natural border, especially as the Epte in the Vexin had been breached by
political manoeuvres. In fact, though the rivers themselves rarely served
as alternatives to roads for moving armies, river valleys, most importantly
the Seine valley, often marked the path of invasion. The only other
geographical feature which affected invasion routes and defenses was the

rough, hilly land of south-central Normandy. The gap in this difficult terrain created by the valleys of the Sarthe and Orne, and traversed by the Roman road from Le Mans through Alençon and Séez to Falaise, was the critical area of the Normandy-Maine border; while the area exposed to French threat began to the east of the massif at about Verneuil. I shall discuss all three of these features – roads, rivers, and rough terrain – in more detail later.[82]

The frontiers of the English half of the realm were less dangerous than those in Normandy for two reasons. First, the enemies – the Welsh and Scots – were less organized and less advanced militarily than those on the continent. Second, they were farther from the vital centers of the kingdom. The exception to this rule was the Scandinavian 'frontier': the threat of invasion by Norse or Danish armies. This threat persisted until about 1085, and until then caused great concern. The seaborne Scandinavian armies were capable of striking anywhere from York to Southhampton in force, and raiding virtually anywhere else on the coast. The magnitude of the threat may be gauged by the extremity of the measures taken to combat it, including the infamous 'harrying of the North' in 1070 and the housing of masses of mercenaries which may have led in part to the Domesday inquest in 1085.[83]

The Welsh frontier consisted of two strips of relatively flat, easy terrain, a narrow one along the north coast and a broader region along the south coast, separated by the rough, mountainous land that dominates the interior of the country. The coastal flatlands were the avenues of Anglo-Norman encroachment into Wales from Chester and Shrewsbury, pushed forward under baronial initiative with the blessing but only rarely the support of royal forces. The Welsh themselves were fierce fighters, but as likely to be fighting each other as unified to face the Anglo-Normans.

The Scottish kingdom, on the other hand, was from early in the twelfth century achieving a sort of feudal unity based on the Anglo-Norman model. The Anglo-Scottish rulers held important English fiefs and created a force of mounted knights to spearhead their armies. They kept their political position vis á vis the kings of England conveniently fuzzy: they did homage for their English fiefs and generally acknowledged the supremacy of the English kings, while at the same time maintaining

---

[82] See below, pp. 113–16.

[83] For a gateway into the vast and complicated subject of Domesday, see David Bates, A Bibliography of Domesday Book (Woodbridge, 1986), and the review article by William Kapelle, 'Domesday Book: F.W. Maitland and His Successors', Speculum 64 (1989), 620–40.

independence of action and, effectively, independence of title. This un-defined relationship benefitted both sides, for the English were in no position to enforce claims of complete suzerainty, but the Scots could not defend a complete independence which would have jeopardized their valuable English fiefs anyway.

The final 'frontier' of the Anglo-Norman realm was the internal one, for the threat of rebellion – by Anglo-Saxons in the early years of the Conquest, by Norman magnates in England and Normandy as soon as the Anglo-Saxons were pacified – often constituted a greater danger than that posed by external enemies. Indeed, the two dangers were almost always linked. The Danelaw was the region most dangerous for Scandinavian invasion due to the potential support of the Anglo-Danish population living there, for example. And Robert of Bellême was a most dangerous rebel in Normandy because his familial lands and castles were scattered along the border and controlled some of the most important routes into Maine. The threat is summed up by the report of Henry I's attitude towards his enemies in the war of 1123–4: he was more con-cerned by the treachery of his own men than by the invasions of external foes.[84]

The danger of rebellion increased dramatically when England and Normandy were under separate rule, as they were from 1088 to 1096 and again from 1100 to 1106, for the many Norman magnates who held land on both sides of the Channel were then put in a position of owing divided loyalty. This accounts for the urgent effort devoted by William II and Henry I to winning the duchy from their elder brother Robert. The magnates, too, saw advantage in a united kingdom, but many promoted the ineffectual Robert as likely to be the easier master. In the event, the king of England reunited the realm in both cases. The divided loyalties of lords who held lands of both the French and English kings admitted of no such solution. Neither king contemplated the complete conquest of the other's kingdom, nor would such a conquest have been likely had it been envisioned. As a result, the vassals of two kings took their men and castles to whomever the moment favored.[85]

The major problem presented by the three groups of frontiers – Norman, English and internal – was one of time and distance. In an age when communications were slow at best, the effective distance between Scotland and Maine was vast. The Channel presented the major barrier to communications and the movement of armies; to kings with lands on

84 Symeon, HR, p. 274.
85 OV, 5:214.

either side of it, straddling the Channel was thus their major problem.[86] In practical terms this meant a need to prevent multiple threats widely separated, or to deal quickly with such threats, without the king's presence if necessary, when they arose. What this problem called for was a combination of three things.

First, in the cause of preventing threats from materializing, means other than warfare were needed. These means were discussed above; their importance as necessary alternatives to warfare, not just as options available in case of crisis, is to be stressed.

Second, the king needed forces which could meet any threat fairly quickly. In effect, this meant maintaining some forces on both sides of the Channel at once, and ensuring free roads and friendly castles within each part of the realm to facilitate the gathering and movement of these forces.

Third, the king needed reliable subordinate commanders. He could not be everywhere at once; if the more dangerous enemy required his presence in Normandy, for instance, he had to entrust royal forces in England to a loyal and competent subordinate and let him deal with the enemy there.

How the Anglo-Norman kings prepared for these needs and how they met them in the field between 1066 and 1135 is the subject of the next three chapters of this study. I have approached these subjects topically rather than chronologically, for they changed very little over the course of this period. The lack of change reflects in large part the consistency of the contexts of royal warfare discussed in this chapter. Institutionally, socially, politically and geographically, the world shaped Anglo-Norman royal warfare as it took place.

---

[86] Matthew, *Norman Conquest*, p. 223. It is probably more accurate to view the Channel not so much as a barrier but as a dangerous highway, risky yet well-travelled: cf. Le Patourel, 'Normandy and England 1066–1144', p. 9.

Chapter Three

THE ANGLO-NORMAN MILITARY SYSTEM

MANPOWER

The Leadership Pool

The military organization, like the rest of government in an age before the dominance of the written word, was less a staffed machine than a collection of leaders ruling personally over their spheres of responsibility. Thus, finding leaders was the first step in raising an army.

The leadership pool available to the Anglo-Norman kings for military leaders was basically the same as the non-military leadership pool of Anglo-Norman society. The greater and lesser magnate families of Normandy – the *omnes primi Normannorum* of the sources[1] – made up the bulk of this pool. Members of similar families from Brittany and to a lesser extent from elsewhere in France (Blois and Flanders, predominantly) and Europe also came to the service of the Anglo-Norman kings. A few survivors of the pre-Conquest Anglo-Saxon leadership class, mostly ecclesiastics such as Wulfstan bishop of Worcester and Aethelwig abbot of Evesham, held positions of military command after 1066,[2] as at times did members of the Scottish royal family.[3] But particularly after the Anglo-Saxon survivors died out, the leadership pool came almost exclusively from the continent, and from Normandy above all. The men of these magnate families, and in some cases the women,[4] staffed the government at every level, and filled the positions of authority in the Church. Men from the same families, indeed often the same men, lay or ecclesiastic, led the army. A few examples will illustrate this.

As William I secured the conquest of England in the campaigns of 1067 and 1068, he entrusted key castles to some of the most important of

---

1 Florence, 2:54–5.
2 Florence, 2:11; Douglas, *William the Conqueror*, p. 232.
3 Symeon, *HR*, p. 222.
4 On women see Chibnall, 'Women in Orderic Vitalis', pp. 111–16. As she points out, Orderic 'took for granted that [women] were cooperators with their husbands, perhaps almost partners, in the duties that lay upon members of the military order' (p. 116).

Norman magnates: Hugh of Montfort-sur-Risle; Robert, count of Eu; Baldwin of Meules, brother of Richard fitz Gilbert; William fitz Osbern.[5] William of Warenne and Richard fitz Gilbert himself were two of William's most important lieutenants throughout the reign, as was William's own half-brother Odo of Bayeux before his arrest for treason; Geoffrey bishop of Coutances, a member of the Mowbray family, also exercised military authority under William I.[6] Under William II, we find royal soldiers and castles entrusted to, among others, William Peverel, Stephen of Aumale, and Robert of Bellême; the king's brother Henry also received a royal commission.[7] Henry as king drew his commanders from the same pool: William II of Warenne held high commands, as did Robert count of Meulan and the king's illegitimate son Richard.[8]

The Anglo-Norman kings could draw on a large pool of potential leaders, given the military character of the ruling class: most sons of landed families grew up experienced in arms. Warfare in the eleventh and twelfth centuries was not a complicated art, so that personal character and natural ability to lead counted for more than schooling in the art of war in the making of a commander. Thus finding men of ability proved not too difficult a task. The major limit on the leadership pool was not overall numbers or even military ability. Rather, the trustworthiness of the men capable of military command seems to have been the great problem for a king selecting lieutenants.

The career of Robert of Bellême provides an excellent illustration of the complex problem of loyalty.[9] Robert was the eldest son of Roger of Montgomery, one of the Conqueror's closest supporters. He was heir to the family's continental estates, which formed an important bloc in south and southwest Normandy and Maine, and his chief motive (as for most magnate families) was to maintain and expand his own holdings. This task was complicated first by the cross-border nature of the family's holdings on the Norman marches, and second by the division of the Anglo-Norman realm in 1087–96 and 1100–06. The most recent study of Robert's career divides it into four phases. 'Firstly there were the years of stability under the Conqueror, then the disorders of Curthose's rule in Normandy from 1087–1096, thirdly another, shorter period of

---

5   Douglas, *William the Conqueror*, p. 217; Le Patourel, 'Norman Barons', in *Feudal Empires*, p. 7.
6   OV, 2:316; *RRAN*, 1:no. 82; Florence, 2:11.
7   Symeon, *HR*, p. 224; OV, 4:214; 5:234; HH, p. 218.
8   OV, 4:88; 6:246.
9   Kathleen Thompson, 'Robert of Bellême Reconsidered', *Battle* 13 (1990), 263–86, reassesses and reviews Robert's career.

comparative stability when king William Rufus controlled both England and Normandy, and finally the years after 1100 during which Henry I established himself in England, took Normandy from Curthose in 1106 and eventually dispossessed and imprisoned Robert for life from 1112.'[10] Robert was loyal to the Conqueror. He reacted to the confusion of Curthose's succession in Normandy to assert his own power in the absence of ducal control, then became a loyal follower of Curthose. But Curthose never seems to have trusted his powerful subject, and relations between the two were uneasy. The ineffectiveness of Curthose's rule in protecting Robert's lands finally led to an abortive shift to Rufus in 1094, and when Curthose went on crusade Robert became a trusted and loyal supporter of Rufus. But after Rufus' death, Robert was again forced into supporting Curthose, who remained suspicious of him, against Henry, who was consistently and implacably hostile to him for reasons, perhaps purely personal, that remain elusive. Robert of Bellême was clearly a man of military ability, especially in designing fortifications, but could work successfully only for one of the three sons of the Conqueror. His career illustrates the role of trust and personal relations in the structure of the Anglo-Norman military system.

So loyal lieutenants were crucial because a royal castle or troop of soldiers placed in unreliable hands easily became a weapon of rebellion, while treacherous commanders within a royal army could severely limit the king's military options. Henry I faced this problem during campaigns in Normandy in 1117–18, when foreign threats coincided with baronial revolts; he was unwilling to conduct a long siege, says Orderic, because he could not trust his own men in the confusion of conflicts between kinsmen.[11] In the periods during which the realm was split, 1088–96 and 1100–06, divided loyalties in particular affected the leadership pool, as did the existence of an alternate candidate for the throne. But the problem of loyalty remained critical throughout the period.

The Anglo-Norman kings used a variety of measures designed to maintain the loyalty of their subordinates. The threat of punishment of course hung over those who offended royal power. Banishment and confiscation of lands, which left open the possibility of redemption through faithful service, was most common, but more serious offenses could lead to mutilation, especially blinding and castration, or even death.[12]

Of course, nothing could replace the trust of a close personal

---

10 Thompson, 'Robert of Bellême', p. 266.
11 OV, 6:200.
12 Chibnall, 'Feudal Society in Orderic Vitalis', *Battle* 1 (1977), 41.

friendship such as existed between William I and Roger of Beaumont, who, along with Roger de Montgomery, ran the duchy during the 1066 campaign,[13] and whose sons continued to serve William and his sons loyally. William also had complete confidence in the integrity of Archbishop Lanfranc, to whom the rule of England was often entrusted when the king went to Normandy; his handling of the revolts of 1075 justified William's faith in his ability to lead, as well.[14] William no doubt judged Lanfranc on his personal character, but as head of the Church in England, the Archbishop had an even greater stake in the maintenance of order and the royal power on which order rested. Extra insurance such as this was never unnecessary. The arrest for treason in 1086 of Odo of Bayeux – the king's own half-brother, a churchman, and long a trusted supporter of the king, who had been left in charge of England in 1067, for instance, and who had been richly rewarded with land in the kingdom – illustrates the magnitude of the problem faced by the Anglo-Norman kings.

Yet those chosen by the kings as military commanders stayed in fact remarkably loyal. In an age when personal ties were so important, we must attribute a large part of the Anglo-Norman kings' success to their ability to inspire friendship, affection and personal devotion in their followers.[15] To this they added several important inducements which formed part of the system of employing military leaders.

It may safely be said that any military leader of any importance retained by William I, Rufus or Henry became a member of that king's military household, the *familia regis*.[16] The household attracted men to its service from all over Europe as well as from the king's own lands. It offered the chance of service at perhaps the most famous and glamorous court outside of Constantinople, under kings known for their military prowess – an important point to men eager for adventure. It also offered financial benefits in the form of an annual retaining fee, plus wages for active service and compensation for losses on campaign.[17] The hope of even greater rewards from kings known for their generosity, Rufus especially, also encouraged long term service. Great magnates who served

---

13 Douglas, *William the Conqueror*, pp. 185–6.
14 *Letters of Lanfranc*, nos. 31–6.
15 Prestwich, 'Military Household', pp. 26–8; Hollister, 'Henry I and the Anglo-Norman Magnates', pp. 93–4.
16 Prestwich, 'Military Household', *passim*. This article is of great importance in understanding the leadership pool in Anglo-Norman warfare. The membership of the household is discussed there in greater detail.
17 See below, p. 60.

in the household could receive additions to their lands, appointment to influential positions, and even earldoms: William fitz Osbern (earl of Hereford in 1067), William Warenne (earl of Surrey in 1088), and Robert of Beaumont (earl of Leicester early in Henry I's reign) all were members of the *familia*.[18] The landless younger sons of great families could hope to be granted their own lands or an estate through marriage: Engenulf and Geoffrey of Laigle served in Henry's *familia* for this reason. The sons of rebels often served in the hope of regaining the family estates: Reginald and Roger, sons of the earl Roger of Hereford who rebelled in 1075, served Henry I throughout his reign and in the end received rewards for their loyalty.[19] Thus the military household was the key to tapping the Anglo-Norman leadership pool. It provided a loyal staff of men who were at the heart not only of the military system, but who filled important offices throughout the government.

The fact that many members of the king's military household held offices such as sheriff that went beyond the strictly military in their powers makes it difficult for the historian to establish a command hierarchy. No formal chain-of-command governed the Anglo-Norman military – military 'rank' did not exist as such. But if we consider just the military responsibilities involved in different assignments, several levels of command may be discerned.

At the highest level stood the king. Leadership began with the king, and throughout this period the king – whether William, Rufus or Henry – met the most important threats in person. The king's personal example as a military commander played an important part in attracting able subordinates. Or at least his reputation did: Rufus was at least as renowned a military leader as his father had been and his brother would be, despite a much more meagre record in the field, because personal style and boasting built his reputation just as effectively as actual campaigning.[20]

The king could not be everywhere at once, so when trouble arose in widely separated parts of the realm, he needed able lieutenants to deal with part of the enemy forces. The second level of commanders next to the king were these most trusted subordinates, who took over a wide field of operations – all of England, perhaps, if the king were in Normandy –

---

18 Prestwich, 'Military Household', pp. 13–15; Jennifer Ward, 'Royal Service and Reward: The Clare Family and the Crown, 1066–1154', *Battle* 11 (1988), 261–78 traces this relationship in detail for one magnate family.

19 Prestwich, 'Military Household', pp. 20–1.

20 Frank Barlow, *William Rufus* (London, 1983), p. 436; Prestwich, 'Military Household', p. 26.

and control of a great number of royal troops with their own lieutenants. Thus, under the overall leadership of Lanfranc, royal forces in England met the revolt of 1075 with William of Warenne and Richard fitz Gilbert at their head, assisted by Geoffrey of Coutances and Robert Malet in the east and Wulfstan of Worcester and Aethelwig of Evesham in the west.[21] In 1098 and 1099, Robert of Bellême commanded royal forces throughout Maine; Ralph of Bayeux commanded the royal army at Bourgthérolde in 1124.[22] When royal forces could be concentrated against a single foe, such lieutenants accompanied the king as his corps commanders, as it were. At Tinchebrai in 1106, divisions of Henry's army were led by Ralph of Bayeux, Robert of Meulan, William II Warenne, and Helias of Maine.[23] Helias illustrates the position of a 'subordinate ally' in the Anglo-Norman command structure – a foreign leader, sometimes hired with his troops as the Flemish Count Robert's money fief agreement with Henry specified,[24] serving not independently but as a high lieutenant.

The next level of command was more limited in its responsibilities. A commander in this group took control of a detachment of troops and a castle as a base of operations. His job was to defend the castle and the surrounding district. If circumstances dictated the gathering of a larger force under the king or one of his lieutenants, he led his detachment in the larger army. Robert Curthose attacked and captured two such commanders in Rufus' pay in 1094: Roger of Poitou and his troops at Argentan and William Peverel and his men at Hôlme; Ralph of Bayeux's army at Bourgthérolde consisted of several such detachments including that of Odo Borleng.[25]

The levels of command so far discussed rose from the leadership pool into the military household. At the lowest level of military responsibility the king tapped the leadership pool in a different way. Men already in positions of authority, lay or ecclesiastic but not necessarily military, executed military tasks, mostly of a local and routine nature. Such men – sheriffs, abbots, local lords – were not members of the military household except coincidentally (that is, a sheriff might be a member of the household, but not because of the military responsibilities of the office). The tasks they performed were primarily the supervision of castle ward and

---

[21] *RRAN*, 1:no. 82; OV, 2:316; Florence, 2:11.
[22] Prestwich, 'Military Household', pp. 17–18; OV, 6:348.
[23] OV, 6:88.
[24] Chaplais, no. 1.
[25] HH, p. 217; Symeon, HR, p. 224; OV, 6:348; see also the terminology of Wace for army commanders: Bennett, 'Wace and Warfare', pp. 49–50.

the gathering (and command, perhaps) of local contingents of the fyrd or feudal host.[26] There are suggestions that the incidental nature of the military authority exercised by such men, particularly the ecclesiastics, reduced their ability to enforce their authority: in 1105 Henry directed a precept to all the barons of the abbey of Abingdon, directing them to keep the king's ward at Windsor as before and as Faricius the abbot directed, and much regretting that they had not obeyed the abbot's commands as they ought.[27]

Manpower Pools

As Duke William planned his invasion of England, one of the fears his Norman supporters expressed concerning the adventure was England's greater *copia militis* – supply of soldiers – than Normandy's.[28] When he completed the conquest, this *copia militis* had passed, somewhat reduced but still intact, to the Conqueror. Added to his Norman resources and to the soldiers his newly increased wealth could attract from other provinces, William's supply of potential warriors was impressive. Three different pools of manpower made up the supply, each available in different ways and each providing different types of soldiers.

The first consisted of Anglo-Saxons owing service in the fyrd. The sources of obligation for fyrd service, as reconstructed by Richard Abels, were 'royal lordship, personal lordship, and land tenure.'[29] The fyrd

---

26 RRAN, 2:nos. 563, 649, 1606; W. Stubbs, *Select Charters, and other Illustrations of English Constitutional History, from the earliest times to the reign of Edward I*, 9th edn, revised by H.W.C. Davis (Oxford, 1921), p. 97.

27 RRAN, 2:no. 725.

28 WP, p. 156.

29 Abels, *Lordship and Military Obligation*, p. 181. Fyrd service has been thought, following Hollister (*A-S Mil. Inst.*, Chs 2–4), to have been divided into the 'great' fyrd and the 'select' fyrd, the former representing the Anglo-Saxon version of the ancient Germanic 'nation in arms', based on the obligation of every free man to defend king and country. Abels convincingly refutes the evidence for a 'great fyrd' (*Lordship and Military Obligation*, pp. 175–9), concluding 'The "nation in arms," like the Anglo-Saxon peasant commonwealth so dear to Victorian scholars, is a historical myth' (p. 179). The obligation of all free men to defend king and country certainly did exist: it is clearly stated in the 'Laws of William the Conqueror' (Stubbs, *Select Charters*, p. 98), and probably formed the basis for the Angevin reorganization of national service by the Assize of Arms in 1181, along with the corrolary service in Normandy: A.L. Poole, *Obligations of Society in the Twelfth and Thirteenth Centuries* (Oxford, 1946), p. 34; Hollister, *Mil. Org. Norman Eng.*, p. 232; F.M. Powicke, *Loss of Normandy*, p. 310. But the sort of men so obligated and the type of forces thus raised has to be reevaluated in light of Abels' work. The overall picture of Anglo-Norman military service is not much affected by such reevaluations, for even the scholars who argued for a great fyrd saw it as an insignificant

existed partly on the basis of a territorial obligation – one man owed from every five hides of land – which was organized for the support of these soldiers.[30] These soldiers, who would have been thegns and their commended men, were available to the Anglo-Norman kings either through their personal and territorial obligations or as mercenaries. The hiring of five-hide soldiers would have been used to extend their annual term of service, and perhaps when they served overseas, though the fyrd obligation may have been extended to such service. Using English soldiers as mercenaries may have become necessary by sometime in Henry I's reign if they were to be used at all, however, for competition from the feudal system of territorial obligation and the general lowering of status undergone by Anglo-Saxon landholders undoubtedly affected the ability of the five-hide system to support and supply its soldiers. Nonetheless, English soldiers regularly joined the armies of William I and his sons, even if the terms of service are not always clear, and their loyalty to the kings is well noted.[31] Failure to perform fyrd service was an offense that belonged to royal jurisdiction.[32]

Some of the fyrd soldiers may have had horses for transport, but they were not trained to fight on horseback, and the vast majority were simply spear-armed infantrymen; the level of defensive armoring probably varied, with shield, helmet and mail shirt protecting the best equipped.[33] The fyrd probably could produce some archers as well, but this is not clear. The number of these soldiers available was quite large – almost certainly outnumbering the number of soldiers owed through feudal obligation. We get some idea of the pool's potential from a call up in 1094 of the fyrd. The number reported is 20,000:[34] this is certainly an exaggeration, but the meaning – that a large number of infantry answered the call – is clear.[35]

---

force militarily, used basically in local defence: Hollister, *A-S Mil. Inst.*, pp. 28–31. That local townsmen and perhaps peasants at times defended their homes is certainly true; that they were obligated or called out to do so is another question entirely, and doubtful. See Abels' discussion of the sieges of Exeter in 1001 and 1068 (misstated as 1067): *Lordship and Military Obligation*, p. 178.

30 See below, p. 66.

31 Florence, 2:10 (1073); ASC (D) 1074 (1073); HH, pp. 235 (1106), 240 (1117); OV, 2:208 (1068), 308–12 (1078); 6:26 (1102); Symeon, HR, p. 233 (1101).

32 LHP, c. 10, 1; service in Normandy by Norman forces was also subject to royal jurisdiction: RRAN, 2:nos. 825, 905.

33 The Bayeux Tapestry shows some English soldiers with swords and horses but no hauberk: BT, pls 66–7, 73.

34 Florence, 2:35; ASC (E) 1094.

35 Compare Orderic's report that 30,000 Englishmen turned out voluntarily to support Rufus in 1088: OV, 6:126. Frank Barlow has calculated the potential strength of the fyrd

The second pool of manpower available to the Anglo-Norman kings consisted of soldiers enfeoffed in England and Normandy.[36] These soldiers were mounted, trained to fight on horseback, and armed with lance and sword. Almost all would have had horses, protective armor, consisting in the majority of cases of shield, helmet and mail hauberk.[37]

The king could obtain such soldiers in two ways. First, a portion of them owed the service of their feudal tenure to the king, either directly or as part of the contingent owed by an intermediate lord in the feudal hierarchy. This portion constituted a much larger fraction of the total number enfeoffed in England than it was in Normandy. Second, any enfeoffed soldier could be hired for service instead of or in addition to performing his feudal duties. The advantages for the king of mercenary service were a term of service limited only by his ability to pay, not by feudal custom, and avoidance of all the problems of liege homage and feudal loyalty raised by the tangled feudal hierarchy, not to mention the problems of calling out a force with such a confused line of obligation. Advantages existed for the enfeoffed soldiers, as well. In addition to the potential rewards for *familia* service mentioned above in the context of leadership, soldiers living on fiefs that may not always have been large enough to support them fully in knightly status might well have needed to supplement their income with paid service to make ends meet, particularly as costs rose in the twelfth century.[38]

Whatever their terms of service, the enfeoffed soldiers of the realm were, like the fyrd soldiers, consistent supporters of the king, especially in England. These two groups plus the clergy of the kingdom

---

as 14,000 (*Edward the Confessor* [Berkeley, 1970], p. 171); Contamine estimates 20,000, but this may be based on Florence: *War in the Middle Ages*, p. 51.

36 Once again bearing the social context of the military system in mind, it would be possible to see almost all non-Anglo-Saxon soldiers available to the king as 'feudal' in a broad sense. The distinction used here – feudal soldiers as those owing service for fiefs – is useful for distinguishing more finely between various soldiers based on their means of support (fief, wage, etc., in which feudal support was not uncommon), and on the basis of their obligation to serve (not necessarily identical with the means of support, and in which feudal obligations were less common).

37 R.A. Brown, 'The Status of the Norman Knight', p. 28.

38 Harvey, 'Knight and Knight's Fee', p. 15, argues that knights in Domesday were enfeoffed on an average of no more than one to one and a half hides each – clearly a level little above peasant existence. R.A. Brown, 'The Status of the Norman Knight', p. 23, warns against assuming that fiefs of such size were their holders' only means of support. See also D.F. Fleming, 'Landholding and *Milites* in Domesday Book: A Revision', *Battle* 13 (1990), 83–98. Brown, using a broad (probably too broad) definition of feudalism, includes *familia* service as part of the feudal support of knights. While the definitions I have adopted make *familia* service mercenary as opposed to feudal, the difference is one of definition, not of disagreement over how knights lived.

stood firmly by Henry I in 1101 when Duke Robert invaded, for example.[39]

The size of this pool of manpower depended partly on how it was utilized. It was noted above that the *servitium debitum*, the number of soldiers owed to royal or ducal service, did not necessarily include the entire pool. Furthermore, the pool itself grew between 1066 and 1135: initially the number of enfeoffed soldiers in England was very small, as the barons and abbots who owed contingents to the royal host hired household knights to meet their obligations, using the next pool of manpower to be discussed just as the king would. The number of enfeoffments in Normandy, where the system was older, was probably more constant. Nonetheless the total *servitium debitum* probably gives a good idea of this manpower pool's potential. In England it has been generally calculated at between 4000 and 6000;[40] the total in the duchy was somewhat less, and the ducal *servitium* made up perhaps only a fifth of that total.[41]

The third and possibly largest of the manpower pools available to the Anglo-Norman kings was the stock of potential mercenaries within reach of the king's silver. It is difficult and pointless to generalize about the members of this group, for their nationality, training, social standing and terms of service varied greatly, as a few examples will show.

The kings hired some on a more or less permanent basis as members of the *familia regis*, and drew them from the same source as the Anglo-Norman leaders discussed above: landless adventurers, second sons of magnate families, sons of rebels hoping to regain their patrimony. In fact those chosen as leaders were often soldiers who had worked themselves up through the ranks of the *familia*. Such soldiers of the *familia* joined individually on more or less standard terms.[42] On the evidence of the Flemish money fief of 1101, these terms extended to mercenaries hired en masse;[43] and were probably usual for most hired troops. The overlap between this pool of manpower and the feudal pool should be stressed again: a large and important part of those soldiers hired as mercenaries undoubtedly came from Normans settled in the duchy and the kingdom on land that owed military service anyway. The role of feudal assessments and enfeoffment as an indirect military tax, or

---

[39] Florence, 2:49; Symeon, *HR*, p. 233. Some enfeoffed soldiers undoubtedly followed their immediate lords against the king, but on the whole the group seems loyal.

[40] E.g. Beeler, *Warfare in England*, p. 266.

[41] Douglas, *William the Conqueror*, pp. 282–3.

[42] See below, p. 62.

[43] Chaplais, no. 1.

means of supporting a reserve of soldiers, was central. Whether feudal obligations as the basis for service were as important is very much open to question.[44]

After the English and Normans, the most frequently used groups of soldiers were Breton and Flemish, but there are also references to troops from Maine and Anjou, the whole of France, and Wales.[45] With such a wide field to draw from, the types of soldiers available included all possibilities: heavy armed infantry; archers and crossbowmen; mounted troops; and any of the specialists of medieval warfare, including artillerists, miners and engineers. Potentially at least, this clearly formed the largest pool of manpower available to the Anglo-Norman kings.

The Composition of Armies

The composition of royal armies in the field was thus a result of selection from these pools by the various means indicated. But assessing the relative importance of these three sources of manpower is difficult, because documentary evidence for army composition is scarce, while narrative sources mostly offer little more than that the king raised an army of *Normannos et Anglos, milites peditesque* – Normans and English, horse and foot – a phrase from which it is dangerous to draw too many conclusions. When more detail is forthcoming about who the troops were, their basis of service may remain unclear; if we know that they were mercenaries, we may not know which pool they were hired from. Furthermore, the composition of royal armies varied quite naturally with the circumstances: whether it was a major campaign or a minor one, whether the campaign took place in England or Normandy, whether the campaign was planned in advance or a rapid reaction to emergency; for some troops were available in greater numbers, some at shorter notice, and so forth. Finally, this is where the distinction between military obligation and actual army composition must be especially borne in mind, since even troops who owed feudal or fyrd service might in fact serve as mercenaries, as mentioned above. In discussing the composition of royal armies I shall try to answer three questions: under what terms of service did the soldiers in the army serve; what pools of manpower provided the soldiers; and what types of soldiers did armies include.

The core of the army in England and Normandy consisted of the mercenary troops of the *familia regis*, and in some cases this force was the

---

[44] Cf. Prestwich, 'Military Household', p. 32.
[45] HH, pp. 235, 240; OV, 6:24, 190; ASC (E) 1085; Florence, 2:18, 64.

only one necessary: the entire royal army at Bourgthérolde was made up of household troops, for instance.[46] That mercenaries, rather than the territorial soldiers produced by the fyrd and feudal systems of obligations, created the foundation of the military forces of the Norman kings should not be surprising. Only mercenaries could be used all the year round, and thus provide the permanent corps of leaders and soldiers essential for meeting emergencies and maintaining a structure within which temporary soldiers – mercenary or territorial – could be employed in an organized way. And being paid professionals, mercenary troops were of high quality and trustworthiness, even exhibiting a sense of professional pride. One of the best examples of this spirit comes from Henry's siege of Bridgnorth in 1102. Robert of Bellême's garrison was made up of a mix of mercenaries and feudal vassals. As Henry's pressure on the castle increased, the feudal vassals, unbeknownst to the mercenaries, cut a deal with the king to surrender the stronghold. The mercenaries tried by force to prevent the peacemaking, but were shut up in part of the castle by the feudal troops, who admitted the royal forces. Orderic's account of the aftermath is revealing:[47]

> The king allowed the mercenary troops to leave freely with their horses and arms, because they had served their master as was right. As they rode out through the beseiging forces they bewailed their fate, loudly complaining that they had been unfairly let down by the deceit of the garrison and their masters, and called the whole army to witness the tricks of these plotters, so that their downfall might not bring contempt on other mercenaries.

That mercenaries were employed in the king's *familia* should not be surprising, either. Household organization of military forces was standard in the eleventh and twelfth centuries. This had been true of Anglo-Saxon armies with their corps of housecarls,[48] and held for all Normans of importance, as the use of the Anglo-Saxon *cniht*, meaning servant or retainer, as the vernacular for *miles* indicates.[49] The king's household was simply a larger, more organized, and probably more monetarized version of the baronial *familia*.

As I indicated in the discussion of the three pools of manpower, the permanent members of the *familia*, both leaders and soldiers, were drawn

[46] OV, 6:348–50.
[47] OV, 6:28–9.
[48] Hollister, *A-S Mil. Inst.*, pp. 17–18.
[49] Stenton, *English Feudalism*, pp. 139–40; CDF, no. 1326.

primarily from the third pool, the potential mercenaries serving for no other reason. Many undoubtedly also came from the pool of enfeoffed soldiers.

The household soldiers all served mounted, as one would expect of an elite force responsible for meeting emergencies quickly. Most were knights: well equipped and trained to fight on horseback. But the household also included archers, and the knights were by no means horse-bound: they had to dismount when defending or attacking a castle, and also dismounted for battle when the circumstances called for such tactics.[50]

The permanent forces of the household were not always sufficient to handle the king's enemies on their own. In some minor campaigns and virtually every major one the king supplemented the *familia* in several ways. The *familia* was itself capable of rapid expansion by the inclusion of short term mercenaries.[51] Large groups of mercenaries, as well as territorial soldiers, also were called on to serve under the leadership of (but not as part of) the *familia*. The nature of the usual extensions differed from England to Normandy, so I shall discuss the two areas separately.

In England, the Anglo-Saxon foot-soldiers of the fyrd were a constant part of royal forces. They were called out by William I as early as the spring of 1068, less than a year and a half after Hastings, to help besiege Exeter.[52] The foot-soldiers' usefulness in siege warfare encouraged their continued use once baronial revolts became a problem. English soldiers helped suppress the Earls' rebellion of 1075, stormed Tonbridge for William II in 1088, besieged Robert of Mowbray's strongholds at Tynemouth and Bamburgh for William in 1095, and enabled Henry I to take Arundel from Robert of Bellême in 1102.[53] Their effectiveness in this work was such, and their hostility to the barons so strong,[54] that Bellême's resistance in 1102 was the last baronial revolt in England for the rest of Henry's reign. But Anglo-Saxon infantry was not restricted to siege warfare, forming a significant portion of royal forces prepared for battle, for instance, in 1075, 1097, 1101 and 1102.[55] No wonder the Anglo-Saxon Chronicle complained

---

[50] HH, p. 241; *Constitutio Domus Regis*, in *EHD*, 2:427; OV, 6:348. See below, p. 000, for a discussion of dismounting as a battle tactic.

[51] See below, pp. 156–57.

[52] OV, 2:212.

[53] Florence, 2:11, 38; Symeon, *HR*, p. 216; OV, 6:20.

[54] OV, 6:26.

[55] OV, 2:316; 5:222; Florence, 2:49; OV, 6:28.

that Rufus 'was always harassing this nation with military service'.[56] Local defense forces may also have participated with the fyrd in some actions, as when *provinciales* are said to have repulsed a Danish fleet at Ipswich in 1069.[57]

Next to the fyrd, the *familia* was most crucially supplemented by extra mercenaries, especially to meet particularly dangerous threats. The types of troops raised included cavalry, archers, infantry, and operators of siege engines, as for instance, William's army at Hastings, itself a largely paid force, did.[58] The importance of infantry forces to Anglo-Norman armies is shown by William's use of mercenary infantry at Hastings and in the northern campaigns of 1068–9, when Anglo-Saxon infantry was unavailable or not to be trusted.[59] And the use of mercenaries in large numbers as a supplement to the *familia* to meet extraordinary threats is clear from several examples. Threatened by mass rebellion and Scandinavian invasion, especially in the north of England, in 1069, William I built castles which he filled with a strong and select force of stipendiary soldiers.[60] The great invasion scare of 1085 moved William to bring to England 'a larger force of mounted men and infantry from France and Brittany than had ever come to this country';[61] the costs of supporting this force may have prompted the Domesday survey. Finally, Duke Robert's planned invasion in 1101 formed the background to Henry's agreement with Robert of Flanders, calling for 1000 *equites* to serve in England, under the count's command, should Henry need them.[62] There is no evidence that Henry invoked the treaty at the time, but a similar agreement had been used by the Conqueror in 1066.[63] Less notable mercenary forces appear regularly in England throughout the reigns of the Conqueror and Rufus;[64] the peace of Henry's reign made forces beyond the *familia* unnecessary in the kingdom, it seems.

Though there is more evidence for the existence of the feudal system of enfeoffments and obligations than for any of the other manpower pools, evidence for military use of the system is somewhat rare, especially

56 ASC (E) 1100.
57 OV, 2:226.
58 Florence, 1:227; WP, p. 150; OV, 2:196.
59 C.H. Lemmon, 'The Campaign of 1066', in Whitelock et al., *The Norman Conquest* (London, 1966), p. 93; OV, 2:237.
60 . . . *quae militum electissimo robore uberrimaque stipendiorum copia munivit.* WJ, p. 142.
61 ASC (E) 1085; Florence, 2:18, calls them *solidariis, pedonibus, et sagittariis* drawn *de tota Gallia.*
62 Chaplais, no. 1.
63 Prestwich, 'Military Household', p. 9; also by Rufus in 1093.
64 E.g. OV, 2:220 (1069), 358 (1079); 5:234 (1098), 292 (1100); WJ, p. 140 (1068); Florence, 2:9 (1071).

where host duty (service in the field, as opposed to castle ward) is concerned. J.H. Round, the great scholar of the knight's fee, was 'only able to find three instances of the summoning of the feudal host', including the much cited writ of summons William I issued to Aethelwig, abbot of Evesham in 1072, presumably for the campaign waged in Scotland that year.[65] Indeed some of the evidence for the existence of the system inspires little confidence that it was used militarily: the many cases of fractional enfeoffments in the charters indicate the regular collection of scutage from early in Henry's reign at least, and probably earlier.[66]

Before we reduce the role of the feudal host too far, however, the meaning of the phrase 'Normans and English', which describes many of the armies gathered in the kingdom during the period, should be examined, for it may indicate the participation of feudal troops.

Florence uses such a phrase – *magna copia, tam Anglorum quam Nortmannorum* – of the royal force raised to meet the rebellion of earls Roger and Ralph in 1075; Orderic calls it simply the army of England.[67] The Anglo-Saxon Chronicle, though, reports that 'the castle garrisons which were in England and also the local people came against them and prevented them all from doing anything.'[68] It seems safe to equate the Chronicle's 'local people' with Florence's English and to conclude that the region's fyrd contingent joined the campaign. If we equate the Normans with the castle garrisons, on the other hand, we cannot be sure whether the Normans are in fact feudal troops, for castle garrisons could be formed in several ways. At royal castles, mercenary service was probably more important than feudal service.[69] And while the rebels claimed that the greater part of William's army (*maior pars exercitus*) was fighting overseas when they rebelled, referring presumably to the *familia*, the presence of William de Warenne and Robert Malet, both *familia* members, among the royal leadership indicates some *familia* presence among

---

[65] Prestwich, 'War and Finance', p. 22; Stubbs, *Select Charters*, p. 97. The instances would be reduced to two, and the most famous example eliminated, by David Bates' preliminary suggestion (in 'Some Observations on the Rule of William I, as seen through his Charters', paper presented at the American Historical Association Annual Meeting, December, 1987) that the writ of summons to Aethelwig is a forgery. John Gillingham sees all of Round's evidence for the introduction of knight service as very suspect or useless: J. Gillingham, 'The Introduction of Knight Service into England', pp. 55–8. On the general scarcity of evidence for the feudal system in operation even at the baronial level, see Crouch, *Beaumont Twins*, p. 132.

[66] *RRAN*, 2:nos. 831, 1203, 1872, e.g.; Stenton, *English Feudalism*, p. 190.

[67] Florence, 2:11; OV, 2:316.

[68] ASC (E) 1075.

[69] See below, pp. 74–7.

the royal troops.[70] Thus mercenaries probably formed a large proportion of the Normans in this army of Normans and English, and it seems reasonable to assume that this gathering was representative of royal armies of Normans and English in England.

So feudal troops serving as such, though undoubtedly present, were by no means the majority even of the Normans in armies of Normans and English; in addition, the English contingent probably regularly rivalled or outnumbered the Norman.[71] Loyal *milites gregarii* joined royal forces when it was convenient – i.e. when a campaign was nearby – or under extreme necessity, as in 1101,[72] and thus formed a regular part of the royal armies usually raised in England. The fyrd dominated numerically in these armies in most cases, but the elite of the army were mercenary, and in emergencies mercenaries – including enfeoffed soldiers serving for pay – probably outnumbered the fyrd.

The troops used to supplement the *familia* in Normandy have a longer history, for warfare broke out regularly in the duchy throughout the period, while warfare virtually ceased in the kingdom after 1102. They also differed in some ways from those used in England, though the differences may be in their terms of service rather than who they were.

English soldiers served as regularly in Normandy as at home, providing a loyal mass of infantry for major campaigns. But while we may be fairly sure that English soldiers serving in England were called out under their fyrd obligation, we cannot be as sure when they served overseas. If the fyrd did owe overseas service, use of it, if not the obligation itself, was a Norman innovation. The evidence is scarce, but the fyrd probably served as such in Normandy under the Conqueror and Rufus, and did part of its service for Henry I as such. Thus William II called out the fyrd for overseas service in 1094, though in the event only the money which identifies the soldiers as fyrdmen crossed the Channel;[73] there are hints of overseas obligations in the charter evidence.[74] On the other hand, English mercenaries are specified, with Breton mercenaries, in 1118, though as a castle garrison rather than in field service.[75] Whatever their terms of service, English infantry appear in force for campaigns in 1073, 1079, 1106, 1117 and 1118.[76]

---

[70] OV, 2:310–12; RRAN, 1:no. 82.
[71] E.g. Florence, 2:22–3: *Normannorum, sed tamen maxime Anglorum* (1088).
[72] Florence, 2:49.
[73] Florence, 2:35.
[74] RRAN, 2:no. 1428.
[75] OV, 6:190.
[76] ASC (D) 1074 (1073); Florence, 2:10 (1073); OV, 3:110 (1079); 6:208 (1118); HH, pp. 235 (1106), 240 (1118).

Mercenaries of other nationalities campaigned regularly beside English troops and the *familia*. Breton troops provided a regular source of aid. In addition to the example cited above, Breton forces are mentioned at Tinchebrai in 1106, in 1117, 1123 and probably in 1079.[77] Flemish forces – 1000 knights in Normandy, 500 in Maine – were stipulated in the money fiefs of 1101 and 1110; a similar agreement may have been behind Robert of Flanders' intervention in the duchy in 1094 (paid for, possibly, by the money collected from the fyrd).[78] But for many of the armies raised by the Norman kings during this period in Normandy, descriptions such as 'Normans and English and many others'[79] leave us as unsure of an army's composition as it does in England.

Once again it must be noted that feudal service undoubtedly played some part in the raising of Norman armies, and probably a greater part in the duchy than in the kingdom, but the part may have been modest. As we saw above, only a small fraction of the duchy's military tenants owed service to the duke. The mass of Norman *milites*, unlike those in England, were quite accustomed to following their immediate lord in his private wars against other lords or against the duke himself.[80] It was Henry's suspicions concerning the loyalty of these Normans that led him to hire an English and Breton garrison for Bures in 1118.[81]

In general, the *familia* was probably a larger part of armies in Normandy than in England, partly because the fyrd was used only in major campaigns, when it was worthwhile transporting it cross-Channel. Temporary mercenaries were just as important as in England, supplementing the permanent *familia* in times of need. Feudal forces as such were present but not in the majority.

The Size of Armies

I have tried to indicate the relative proportions of different types of troops in Anglo-Norman armies in the preceding sections. Evidence for the total numbers in these armies is scarce and not always reliable, but some estimates may now be made.

Figures of twenty-, thirty-, and sixty-thousand given for gatherings of English infantry in 1094, 1088 and 1102 respectively,[82] are clearly

---

[77] HH, pp. 235, 240; Symeon, *HR*, p. 274 (1123); OV, 2:358 (1079).
[78] CDF, no. 1325.
[79] *Normannos et Anglos aliosque multos*; OV, 6:208.
[80] E.g. Symeon, *HR*, p. 274.
[81] OV. 6:190.
[82] ASC (E) 1094; OV, 4:126; 6:28.

exaggerations, off by an order of magnitude, one supposes. In fact, we are told that in the 1102 campaign Henry had 3000 rural *milites* in his army[83] – a much more believable number – who may well be the same soldiers as the sixty thousand *pedites* of a few weeks later. Even 3000 is at the upper limit of the reasonable figures in the sources. The Flemish money fief of 1101 called for forces of 1000 or 500 to join the *familia*; in 1110 these figures were cut in half. Five hundred is in fact the most common number used of both field armies and castle garrisons; and most figures fall between 100 and 800.[84] Given that some of these are only for parts of armies, it seems reasonable to estimate the usual size of Anglo-Norman armies at between 300 and 3000 depending on the importance of the campaign and how much time there was to gather troops.

We have what might be called an official figure which falls in the same range: Henry I wrote to Anselm after Tinchebrai in 1106, reporting that he had defeated his brother's army, capturing 'four hundred *milites*, and ten thousand infantry'.[85] The number of infantry seems large, though we are told elsewhere that Robert had gathered a large force of infantry;[86] but there is no need to take it at full value. British estimates of Argentine prisoners taken on the Falklands in 1982 were initially high by thirty to forty percent;[87] the less numerate English commanders of the twelfth century may be excused a similar exaggeration. If Robert's army totaled about 6000 of all types, and Henry's was the same or slightly smaller, then the armies in this critical campaign for the conquest of Normandy would have just about matched those at that other extraordinary gathering of military might, Hastings, where the best estimates of army size are between 5000 and 7000.[88] These figures should be considered the upper limit for the size of Anglo-Norman armies.

If the usual Anglo-Norman army numbered fewer than 3000, it is clear that none of the manpower pools had to be stretched to meet the needs of the Norman kings. Taken all together, only a small proportion of the total available manpower needed to be called out at any one time. Given the abilities of the supply, transport and communications systems, which

---

83 *pagensium militum*; OV, 6:26.
84 OV, 2:212 (500), 220 (500); 6:194 (500), 218 (100), 236 (400 and 500), 348 (300); Florence, 2:2 (500); Symeon, *HR*, pp. 187 (500 and 700), 224 (800, 700 and 1400).
85 Eadmer, p. 184.
86 OV, 6:84–6.
87 Initial reports were of about 15,000 prisoners: *The New York Times*, June 16, 1982, 1:1; the final estimate after all prisoners had been returned was just over 10,000: *The New York Times*, July 15, 1982, 3:4.
88 Lemmon, in Whitelock et al., *Norman Conquest*, pp. 112–14.

I shall discuss later, it is probable that only a small proportion could be called out. It was these factors, not the available manpower, which limited the size of Anglo-Norman armies.

Ships and Sailors

The final part of the military system requiring a manpower pool was the navy. It is convenient to include the potential 'ship pools' available for naval service, either for transport or combat, in this section as well, for raising a navy involved finding not only sailors but ships for them to sail. There is very little evidence for the naval system or its activities, but certain conclusions may be drawn.

Naval combat, which I shall discuss in more detail later,[89] was a simple affair and occurred only rarely. 'Marines' – men trained to fight on shipboard – were therefore a luxury in the Anglo-Norman system. The 'butescarls' who helped William I assault the isle of Ely in 1071, and perhaps those assigned by Henry I to guard the Channel in 1101,[90] could thus have been survivors or descendants of Anglo-Saxon mercenaries, trained in the Anglo-Danish tradition to fight on land or sea.[91]

Necessary in far greater numbers and far more frequently were sailors, men who could handle ships but who did not need to fight. We must assume that the manpower pool drawn on to supply the navy consisted of the experienced non-military sailors – merchants and the men they regularly employed – who worked out of the coastal towns, especially in England. That the kingdom could supply more sailors than the duchy is probable. Before the invasion of 1066, while Harold kept his fleet mobilized off the Isle of Wight, the Norman nobles worried whether enough trained oarsmen could be found in the space of a year to take the invaders over.[92] What the terms of service were for sailors taken into military duty is completely unclear, but naval forces were usually needed only for a short time – perhaps only one crossing of the Channel – so

---

[89] See below, p. 174.
[90] Florence, 2:9, 48.
[91] Cf. Hooper, 'The Navy in Late Anglo-Saxon England', pp. 206–7 on *butescarles* and their possible link to a proto-Cinque Ports system (see n. 95 below). Hooper argues (pp. 205–6) that the professional Danish-Saxon fleet, largely disbanded in 1051, is identified by the term *lithsmen* in the sources.
[92] WP, p. 156. On the other hand, the duchy did in the end manage to supply enough sailors and ships, indicating a substantial marine establishment. See also the important article by C.M. Gillmor, 'Naval Logistics of the Cross-Channel Operation, 1066', *Battle* 7 (1984), 105–131, on requisitioning and hiring of ships and esp. p. 125 for arguments that William's fleet was predominantly sail-driven.

sailors may have been simply commandeered with their ships, or hired at rates standard for non-military transport.

The king requisitioned ships occasionally, as we know from efforts by the owners to have them returned: the abbot of St Augustine's, Canterbury, seems to have lost a ship at Sandwich to a royal crossing between 1116 and 1118, for example.[93] When ships and sailors or marines served for pay, this may be considered mercenary service. The Norman kings obtained ships and sailors in three other ways. The first, building ships in any number, was only resorted to in extreme circumstances. The prodigious effort of the Norman carpenters illustrated in the Bayeux Tapestry in fact went unrepeated and could only have accounted for a small part of the Norman fleet.[94] The combined naval resources of England and Normandy made it unnecessary to build quickly on a large scale.

Two other systems allowed the king to draw on the resources of England, both originating in the Anglo-Saxon kingdom. First, there was a ship fyrd, a territorial obligation based on hidage; but the operations of this system and whether it survived to be used by the Normans is unclear.[95] Second, specific town duties, arranged probably under Edward the Confessor, formed the rudiments of a proto-Cinque Ports system, providing fifty-seven ships for fifteen days a year.[96] The term of service could be extended at the king's expense, so the pool of Cinque Ports ships and sailors, whether serving by obligation or as mercenaries, undoubtedly formed the most important and most used source of Anglo-Norman navies.

ADMINISTRATION

The *Familia Regis*

At the core of army organization was the *familia*. The military system was built around its officers, regulations, operational divisions, and capabilities. Indeed in many ways the *familia* was the military system, for the

---

[93] *RRAN*, 2:nos. 1189–91; cf. no. 694. The quotas of ships owed by the magnates of Normandy to William in 1066 (see E. van Houts, 'Ship List', *passim*) would presumably have been requisitioned or hired from the areas under the magnates' control.

[94] Gillmor, 'Naval Logistics', 114–119 on the logistical impossibility of the Normans building the entire fleet; *BT*, pls 38–9; van Houts, 'Ship List'.

[95] Hollister, *A-S Mil. Inst.*, ch. VI; Hooper, 'The Navy in Late Anglo-Saxon England', pp. 210–12.

[96] Hollister, *A-S Mil. Inst.*, ch. IV; Hooper, 'The Navy in Late Anglo-Saxon England', pp. 206–7; K. M. E. Murray, 'Shipping', in A.L. Poole, ed., *Medieval England* (Oxford, 1958), pp. 170–6.

influence of its members, if not its actual structure, reached into every aspect of the Anglo-Norman military machine.

At the head of the *familia* were the officers and commanders who ran the system. The officers of the *familia* kept track of its scattered detachments and managed the administrative tasks that kept the *familia* and its extensions in being. The most important of the military officers of the *domus regis*, the smaller body which was at the center of the entire government and whose members included the chancellor and chamberlain, were the constables, the master-marshal, and the deputy marshals. The master-marshal was paymaster of the royal army, while the constable probably acted as quarter-master-general,[97] though the commander of an independent detachment probably took charge of the pay, supply and housing of the troops under his command. Just as important as the constables and marshals, however, were the commanders without title, the barons and 'officers of the *familia*'[98] who executed the king's orders, led in his army and took charge of his castles. Some order of precedence undoubtedly existed among such men, based on seniority, office, or title – the latter two including non-military honors – but what it was we can only speculate. Certainly, as noted earlier, no such thing as strict military rank existed. The only indication of anything resembling it outside of the offices of the *domus* is the title *princeps militiae* bestowed occasionally on some independent commanders. Robert of Bellême was Rufus' *princeps militiae* for several years during operations in Maine, and the title is used at times of castle commanders.[99]

The regulations of the *familia* concerned terms of service and discipline. While the latter, though backed by the force of law, varied in severity according to the judgement of each king, the former were so widely known as to be customary.

At the highest level, we know the compensation due to the officers of the household from the *Constitutio Domus Regis*. The constables and the master-marshal received two shillings a day, one salted simnel loaf, one sextary of ordinary wine, one small wax candle and twenty-four pieces of candle if they were outside the king's household; if within the household, they received fourteen pence, half a sextary of ordinary wine and a candle at discretion. The marshals received eight pence a day, a gallon of ordinary wine, and twelve pieces of candle when outside the king's

---

[97] *Const. Domus Regis* in *EHD*, 2:426; G.H. White, 'The Household of the Norman Kings', *TRHS* 30 (1948), 150; *RRAN*, 2: no. 961.

[98] *magistratus familiae*; *RRAN*, 2:no. 713; OV, 6:88.

[99] Prestwich, 'Military Household', p. 17; OV, 2:218.

household; three pence a day and a candle when within. The serjeants of the marshals received three pence a day when they were on the king's business.[100] At a lower level within the *domus*, the bowmen of the royal hunt received five pence a day each, which may represent the wages of military bowmen, as well; the figure is at least indicative of the range of compensation for common soldiers.[101]

But most of the members of the *familia* would have served under terms closely resembling the indenture contracts used by Edward III. Individual recruits received an annual retainer fee, put by one source at a minimum of £5 a year,[102] though the fee may only have been paid to recruits from outside the realm. When called to active service, the knights of the household were paid a daily wage, provided with food and compensated for the loss of horses or equipment in action: *ad victum regis et ad perdita reddenda sicut mos est familie regis*.[103] Orderic was familiar with these terms of service: he has Odo Borleng warn the *familia* before Bourgthérolde that if they fail to fight, 'we shall deserve to forfeit both our wages and our honour; and, in my opinion, we shall never again be entitled to eat the king's bread.'[104] In fact the only thing we do not know precisely about the terms of *familia* service is the daily wage paid to knights on campaign. It is not specified in the Flemish money fief of 1101: it was too well known for this to be necessary. The rate paid to Anglo-Saxon mercenaries has been calculated at 4d. a day, and this rate may have held for Norman knights around the time of the Conquest, as well.[105] The knightly rate prevalent early in the Angevin period had risen to 8d. a day, and there is a notification by Henry I quitclaiming the abbey of Ely a custom of 8d. per day *et solidatis et perditis unius militis*,[106] which looks like the cost of the service of a knight on the usual terms. This appears to support 8d. as the rate under Henry I. Hollister has argued, using scutage rates, that an intermediate figure of 6d. held between the Anglo-Saxon 4d. and the Angevin 8d.,[107] but the evidence is not clear.

Finally, members of the *familia* received bonus payments and even greater rewards – estates, earldoms, offices – as rewards for long and loyal

---

100 *Const. Domus Regis* in *EHD*, 2:426.
101 *Const. Domus Regis* in *EHD*, 2:427.
102 Prestwich, 'Military Household', p. 8.
103 Chaplais, no. 1.
104 OV, 6:350.
105 Hollister, *Mil. Org. Norman Eng.*, p. 212.
106 *RRAN*, 2:no. 685.
107 Hollister, *Mil. Org. Norman Eng.*, p. 212.

service.[108] There was no set scale of reward and the king's generosity varied, but it was the hope of such reward which attracted many men to service in the *familia*.

Regulations concerning discipline were more variable than those relating to terms of service. We know that William I laid down laws to keep order in his army soon after his coronation; these may be reflected in the *Leges Henrici Primi*, where we find that murder and breach of the peace committed in the king's *familia* put the offender at the king's mercy with respect to his property and limbs.[109] Rufus' *familia*, though, gained infamy for its lack of discipline on the march, plundering like an enemy army in the king's progresses through England.[110] In reaction to the excesses of Rufus' *familia*, Henry instituted a series of reforms after his victory at Tinchebrai. Regulations prohibited looting and plundering; required the taking and buying of goods at set prices; and restricted billeting.[111] Serlo, bishop of Séez, set the tone of the reforms in an Easter sermon to the *familia* delivered at the start of the campaigns which led to Tinchebrai. An exhortation to good morals culminated in the Bishop's cutting the long hair of Henry and his entire *familia*.[112] A more austere style in dress, diet and conduct prevailed thereafter – Prestwich calls it a 'strain of puritanism'[113] – which enhanced the good reputation of Henry's court, and not incidentally reduced the cost of maintaining the *familia*.

The scope of Henry's reforms should not be exaggerated though. They dealt mainly with external discipline, that is the *familia*'s relationship with the outside world.[114] There is nothing to show that Rufus' *familia* was internally undisciplined – seditious, lax in its duties, or unwilling to fight – even if it was reputedly immoral. All the Norman kings seem to have been effective disciplinarians in this sense, using the carrot of future reward and the stick of legal punishment as set forth in the *Leges* to keep their military forces in line. No doubt too their ability to succeed in military enterprises helped

---

108 Prestwich, 'Military Household', pp. 13–15; Jennifer Ward, 'Royal Service and Reward', p. 277.
109 WP, p. 232; *LHP*, c. 10, 1; c. 80, 1; Chibnall, 'Feudal Society in Orderic Vitalis', p. 41 for types of punishment.
110 HH, p. 230.
111 Eadmer, *HN*, pp. 192–3; Malmesbury, *GRA*, 2:487; *RRAN*, 2:no. 713; Prestwich, 'Military Household', p. 30.
112 OV, 6:66.
113 Prestwich, 'Military Household', p. 29.
114 Chibnall, 'Feudal Society in Orderic Vitalis', pp. 45–6, argues that the reforms were aimed at increasing his support from the church, and points out that long hair remained in fashion for knights long after 1106.

maintain discipline; good discipline in turn made continued success more likely.

The *familia regis* originated as part of the personal retinue of the king, his attendants and guards. By this period, however, it had long outgrown these personal roots. Contingents of the *familia* could be stationed far from the king; and of course many of the men regularly with the king were not members of the *familia*. Nevertheless, there seems to have been an operational division of the *familia* based on attendance on the king.

The distinction between the *familia* as a whole and the king's personal troop is made explicitly in the *Leges Henrici Primi*, where the term *hosticum* is used, it seems, with this meaning.[115] For example, among the crimes subject to royal jurisdiction are fighting in the king's domus or *familia* and breaking the peace in the *hosticum*.[116] It must be admitted that the *Leges* are not the clearest source in the world, but that the Norman kings had a bodyguard of trusted soldiers seems plausible. The *hosticum* may have been an extended bodyguard, more a personal troop such as kings and emperors have often maintained. Unfortunately, no other source offers any clues as to the size of the *hosticum*. It is tempting to speculate based on the number of ships used in Channel crossings – more than eight were gathered for a routine crossing in 1133, for example[117] – that the *hosticum* was a significant troop of men. But in fact we can never be sure and indeed the troop's size may have varied widely.

We have no way of knowing whether the king's personal troop had a stable membership, inclusion in which was a privilege, or whether it changed regularly depending on the king's needs and whims. Detachments of the *familia* as a whole operated independently when necessary and received reinforcements when crises loomed; the *hosticum* probably showed similar flexibility.

Taking the king's troop and the detachments garrisoning important forts together, the *familia* was 'a formidable force in war, prominent at Tinchebrai and Brémule, decisive at Bourgthérolde and controlling a network of castles from Carlisle to Le Mans and from Cardiff to Gisors.'[118] A few examples will illustrate the range of the *familia*'s capabilities.

We find the *familia* in action on its own as early as 1069: a unit of the

115 *LHP*, ed. note, p. 325.
116 *LHP*, c. 10, 1; see also c. 13, 8; c. 68, 2; c. 80, 1.
117 John of Hexham, pp. 295–6.
118 Prestwich, 'Military Household', p. 29.

familia regis sallying from Lincoln intercepted and largely destroyed a foraging party led on a raid by Edgar Atheling.[119] Detachments of the *familia* took part in raids on the French Vexin in 1097, both taking and losing prisoners in local fighting.[120] The next year, led by Robert of Bellême, it conquered Maine; when Fulk of Anjou counter-attacked the next year, the *familia* held the county's castles against him while William gathered reinforcements to come to their aid.[121] The role played by the *familia* in the battles of Henry I's reign has already been noted.

It was not just when campaigning on its own that the *familia's* capabilities were vital to the Anglo-Norman military system. Its regulations concerning terms of service formed the basis for the employment of any mercenary forces, and thus provided the king with the power rapidly to expand his military forces without sacrificing organization. The Flemish money fiefs of 1101 and 1110 were based on and organized into the established methods of the *familia*; they show that expansion of the force by the addition of 500 or 1000 knights within a month was quite conceivable. The only difference in organization introduced by a large scale money fief such as this was in the means of paying the annual retaining fee: the 'fief', accepted with the rendering of homage. Whereas an individual recruit's fee might be paid directly from the Exchequer or wardrobe, money fiefs of this size (£500 in 1101, reduced to £400 in 1110) were drawn on county farms.[122] Otherwise, whether the mercenaries hired became members of the *familia* or not, they served on its terms and under its orders. Furthermore, it cannot be stressed enough that only the permanent structure and full-time commanders provided by the *familia* enabled less formally organized territorial troops like the fyrd and the feudal host to be used effectively. Finally, specialists such as engineers and artillerists could be retained within the *familia*. When William de Warenne and Robert Malet captured Norwich castle from Earl Ralph of Norfolk in 1075, they occupied it with 300 men at arms, *ballistarii* and many siege engineers.[123] Robert of Bellême himself was skilled in the machinery of siege and defense.[124] In an age when castles played a dominant role in the course of warfare, such men were vital to the success of the military system.

The structure, capabilities and discipline of this full-time, professional force should be borne in mind when we examine the strategic abilities

119 OV, 2:226.
120 OV, 5:216.
121 OV, 5:256; HH, 231.

122 Lyon, 'Money Fief', pp. 170–1.
123 *Letters of Lanfranc*, no. 35.
124 OV, 4:232.

and tactical successes of Anglo-Norman armies in the field, for they were at the root of these abilities and successes.

The Fyrd and the Feudal Hosts

When the Anglo-Norman kings wanted to raise troops other than mercenaries, whether for reasons of economy, expediency or dire need, they had two choices. First, there was the fyrd, inherited from the Anglo-Saxon kingdom. Second, there was the feudal host, still developing in Normandy when it was abruptly expanded to England in the years immediately following the Conquest. Both of these forces were territorial: that is, their service was tied to land-holding.[125] The feudal host also became, like the fyrd, territorial in another sense, in that its organization became linked to the territorial units of government, especially the shires in England, as well as being part of the honors and family lands of great lords which themselves became territorial administrative units. These territorial forces, though subordinate to the *familia* operationally, existed separately: each had its own organization.

I

The starting point in the sources for an investigation of the late Anglo-Saxon fyrd comes from Domesday Book, Customs of Berkshire:[126]

> If the king sends an army anywhere, one soldier goes from every five hides, and 4s. are given to him from each hide for his food and pay (*ad victum vel stipendium*) for two months. This money is not sent to the king but given to the soldiers.

This describes concisely the fyrd obligation and the method of its operation. Most of England was hidated, and when the king called out the fyrd, one soldier went from every five hides. Each of the five hides contributed four shillings to the representing soldier, making a total of twenty shillings. It is because this money was not sent to the king, but given to the soldiers, that we happen to know a bit more about this mechanism. In 1094, Rufus, in Normandy, found himself in need of

---

125 The service of both forces was also tied to lordship, as discussed above, Ch. 2.
126 Stubbs, *Select Charters*, p. 107. The fundamental secondary works on Anglo-Saxon military obligations and systems are Abels, 'Bookland and Fyrd Service' and *Lordship and Military Obligation in Anglo-Saxon England*; and Hollister, *A-S Mil. Inst.*, chs III–V. This section owes much to the work of both of these scholars.

money at short notice. Therefore, according to the Worcester chronicler, 'he ordered that 20,000 footsoldiers be sent to his aid in Normandy. When they had gathered at Hastings to cross the sea, Ranulf Flambard took at the king's command the money which had been given them *ad victum*, that is, 10s. from each, and ordered them to return home; the money he sent to the king.'[127]

It will be noticed that Flambard collected only ten shillings from each soldier, and that this had been given them *ad victum*, whereas the Berkshire customs specify twenty shillings *ad victum vel stipendium*. From this it may be inferred that fyrd soldiers received 10s. on departure *ad victum* on campaign (they were not, like the soldiers of the *familia*, *ad victum regis*) and 10s. on return *ad stipendium* for their services.

What the above account leaves out is the crucial role of lordship in conjunction with the territorial obligations. In fact, Abels shows that the thegns of the fyrd were of two types.[128] First were those thegns commended to the king, who owed service in respect of lordship, and owed only themselves. Second were those who held bookland of the king, who owed service in respect of their land: it was on bookland that the five hide obligation fell.[129] Clearly if a thegn held more than five hides, he owed the service not only of himself, but of enough additional men to meet the land's quota. The free men commended to him served under him and fought at his side in the fyrd; their service arose from the obligation on the land but was owed through their lord.

The normal service limit of the fyrd was two months a year, served in wartime only.[130] For comparison with the mercenaries of the *familia*, this term and the above monetary compensation comes (given that two months equals 60 days) to a 'wage' of 2d. a day if support *ad victum* is calculated separately, 4d. a day if not. This would have been quite a good wage at the beginning of our period, comparable with mercenary wages. But by sometime in Henry I's reign, as we saw above, mercenary wages had risen to 6d. at least, probably 8d., and this may indicate a decreased ability of the fyrd to support itself adequately. Furthermore, hidage assessments tended to be reduced as time went on,[131] either out of

---

127 Florence, 2:35. Cf. ASC (E) 1094.
128 Abels, 'Bookland and Fyrd Service', pp. 7–14 for the following.
129 And the services of bridge- and fortress-work, which was owed by the thegn but performed by peasants: Abels, 'Bookland and Fyrd Service', p. 5.
130 Hollister, *A-S Mil. Inst.*, p. 86.
131 E.g. *RRAN*, 2:nos. 650, 1011.

political favor or because of the land's reduced ability to supply the fyrd's soldiers.[132]

The fyrd had surely also suffered in 1066. Many of its leading thegns must have died in the campaigns of the summer. Others may well have been among those Anglo-Saxons who left England and ended up in the service of the Byzantine Emperor.[133] And even those thegns holding bookland who survived would have suffered loss of lands or status as Normans became the leading landholders of the realm. But many of the lesser fyrdmen commended to the thegns must have survived, and transferred their service to their new Norman masters. So as Abels says, 'England's Carolingian-style government was not only capable of taxing its subjects and creating a unified currency, it was also able to exploit the wealth of the kingdom systematically for its defense.'[134] And even in reduced form, the system continued to work well enough to supply a significant number of soldiers regularly throughout most of the period 1066–1135.

Other aspects of fyrd service are built around the basics of the lordship and five-hide system. A number of penalties for failure to perform fyrd service are evident. In the Anglo-Saxon period at least, a thegn holding bookland was subject to forfeiture, while his commended retainers owed him 40s. if they failed to show up.[135] The Leges Henrici Primi gives a heavy 120s. fine for failure to perform fyrd service; but some service could be commuted in advance for 20s., the exact cost of a replacement.[136] The severity of the punishment for failure to perform fyrd service reflects that it was, with fortress work and bridge repair, one of the trinoda necessitas, the three most nearly universal obligations on the land. These services were occasionally lifted from some holdings, but more often formed the exception in charters of liberties – 'free of all burdens save fyrd-service, bridgework and burh-work' – even in

---

132 This may support the observation of M. Powicke that 'this [five-hide army] was an assessment, and an old one at that, rather than a fully effective scheme of service. There was surely a hugh gap between intention and result.' M. Powicke, review of Hollister, A-S Mil. Inst., 160. But cf. Abels, 'Bookland and Fyrd Service', p. 16 and the tables on pp. 19–25 on the correlation of land value and hidation.

133 John Godfrey, 'The Defeated Anglo-Saxons Take Service with the Eastern Emperor', Battle 1 (1977), 63–74.

134 Abels, 'Bookland and Fyrd Service', p. 18.

135 Abels, 'Bookland and Fyrd Service', pp. 10–11.

136 LHP, c. 13, 9; Hollister, A-S Mil. Inst., 160. It has been suggested that the latter provision influenced both the rate and the early introduction of scutage into Anglo-Norman feudalism: Hollister, 'The Significance of Scutage Rates in Eleventh- and Twelfth-Century England', EHR 75 (1960), 577–88.

spurious ones.[137] Failure in fyrd service was also, not surprisingly, an offense subject to royal jurisdiction; the royal nature of the fyrd is also reflected in the custom that the king had to be present to call the fyrd, though this did not always happen in practice.[138]

Land and lordship also governed the organization of the fyrd once raised. At the lowest level, it seems that the fyrd served by lordship, with commended men fighting beside their lords.[139] The service of such lesser men was also apparently organized by 'neighborhood' or village groups. The *Leges Henrici Primi* requires neighbors to be called in clearing a man of failure to perform fyrd service, 'since his absence alone from such a gathering would not go unnoticed' and decrees that the property of a deserter from the fyrd was forfeited to his comrades; similarly, the army of London was organized by wards.[140] At a higher level, the fyrd was often organized by hundred and shire, that is called out shire by shire under the direction and command of the sheriff, with the hundreds as sub-groups of the shire.[141] Between the local lordship and the sheriff, organization and command probably depended on the political geography of the shire. Before the conquest, bishops had played a minor role in calling out and leading the fyrd, and they undoubtedly continued to afterwards, alongside abbots and other local lords.[142]

The regular shire organization of the fyrd may have made it possible for the king to call out fyrd contingents in rotation when he needed a force for more than the two months of regular fyrd duty, or to call out a fyrd force in almost any part of the country where he happened to need it. The Danelaw was one area in which the local fyrd could not be used, at least as long as a threat of Scandinavian invasion remained, because the loyalty of the native Anglo-Danish population was highly suspect.

---

137 *RRAN*, 1:nos. 5, 23; 2:no. 1382.
138 *LHP*, c. 10, 1; Hollister, *A-S Mil. Inst.*, p. 91; Abels, 'Bookland and Fyrd Service', p. 10.
139 Abels, *Lordship and Military Obligation*, p. 184, where he suggests the similarity of such lordship groups tactically to the conrois of knights on the continent (see below p. 70 and n. 145 for further discussion of tactical groupings of feudal troops).
140 *LHP*, c. 66, 66; c. 13, 12; Stenton, 'Norman London', in G. Barraclough, ed., *Social Life in Early England* (London, 1960), p. 185.
141 Abels, *Lordship and Military Obligation*, pp. 182–3; Hollister, *A-S Mil. Inst.*, p. 92.
142 Powicke, *Mil. Obl. Med. Eng.*, p. 12; Hollister, *A-S Mil. Inst.*, pp. 93, 96. In fact it may well have been the loyalty of the church to the new king after the conquest that allowed the fyrd to be used so soon by a ruler it had fought only months earlier. The authority of the bishops and the sheriffs within the fyrd may have increased after the conquest, for the great earls and important thegns who led the fyrd prior to 1066 had been largely eliminated.

II

The organization of the Anglo-Norman feudal host is actually the organization of two feudal hosts: that in England and that in Normandy; on two different levels: operational, or organization in the field, and territorial, or the organization of the enfeoffments and feudal obligations which produced some of the troops of the feudal host. (Some were household mercenaries hired by the lords to fill their quotas.) It is on the latter level that the feudal systems of England and Normandy differed, though they naturally influenced each other in important ways. I shall therefore discuss the two territorial systems separately after looking at the operational organization of both.

Whether the troops a lord brought with him to the host were mercenaries or were enfeoffed and owed him the service, they served as members of his military household.[143] Baronial *familiae* were not nearly as developed, extensive, disciplined, or particularly, monetarized as the royal military household, but their structure, coming from the same roots as the royal *familia*, paralleled it. Some of the same officers, the constable above all, appear in baronial *familiae*; the constable usually led defense of baronial castles,[144] and undoubtedly had some role when the baron's *familia* served in the field. Therefore when the feudal host came out to supplement the royal *familia*, a hierarchy of *familiae* was formed in the field. This probably created the basis for tactical division of the host, with a small *familia* gathered around a lord and his banner making up what became known in the vernacular as a *conroi*.[145]

Soldiers not only served under their lord, they were in his surety, and forfeited their holdings to him in case of desertion.[146] And like the fyrd

---

[143] CDF, no. 714.

[144] See below, p. 96.

[145] The *constabularia* of ten knights of which so much has been made (e.g. Beeler, *Warfare in England*, p. 277), in my opinion never existed. It was not an age prone to detailed, orderly organization on the Roman model: leadership was personal and organization thus variable. Cf. Chibnall, who claims 'that knights would tend to become organized in groups of five or ten was, in the long run, inevitable; it was a fact of military tactics.' ('Military Service in Normandy before 1066', p. 72.) I see nothing inevitable about decimal organization for small groups of cavalry (the Roman cavalry was organized in regular groups, but not of five or ten: E.N. Luttwak, *The Grand Strategy of the Roman Empire* [Baltimore, 1976], p. 43), and in fact the political geography of feudal and *familial* obligations would seem to make non-decimal organization likely if not inevitable. This is not to say that there were not small groups – small groups were tactically inevitable. But that 'the strength of the conroi or unit varied according to the power of the liege lord' (Verbruggen, *Art of Warfare*, p. 75) cannot seriously be argued with. See also Abels, *Lordship and Military Obligation*, p. 184, on the small units of the fyrd.

[146] Hollister, *Mil. Org. Norman Eng.*, p. 89; LHP, c. 8, 2a; c. 13, 12.

the soldiers of the feudal host were probably called out through their lords, while the enforcement of feudal obligations at least in England fell under the shrieval organization usual for such legal matters.

The sources we have make it somewhat difficult to imagine exactly how the feudal host was called out, especially once the number of household knights maintained by the baronage had been reduced by subinfeudations. In the first place, it seems that rather than sending writs directly to the barons who owed contingents to the host, the king had his sheriffs spread the call: thus Ranulf sheriff of Huntingdonshire was informed by Rufus of a reduction of the service due from Abbot Aldwin of Ramsey.[147] The writ of summons from William I to Abbot Aethelwig of Evesham shows the same thing: Aethelwig is ordered to advise all those who are under his *ballia et justitia* to have the *milites* they owe before the king at Clarendon by a set date; Aethelwig himself is also to appear with the five *milites* he owes.[148] But who exactly did Aethelwig, or a sheriff, summon? All those who happened to be resident under his *ballia et justitia*? Or only those whose *caput honoris* lay in the district? Who summoned barons not resident at their *caput*, if the latter? What if a baron were overseas? Did his steward or constable take the summons? The sources leave us to guess at the answers to such questions.

Furthermore, the major barons rarely enfeoffed their soldiers directly.[149] Rather, they enfeoffed each other for social, economic and political reasons, or granted manors out of nepotism or other personal reasons, all of which tends 'to undermine the notion of land always held and distributed at this social level in return for military service.'[150] How did the king collect the actual soldiers at the bottom of this tangled hierarchy? Were all enfeoffed soldiers in a district summoned by the sheriff – and if so, how were household knights accounted for? If the barons were summoned, did they then send summons to all their sub-tenants all over the country? One can imagine a baron receiving a summons from the king for his own contingent, and then receiving a summons from another baron for the knights of a subinfeudation, and then sending another baron – perhaps the same one who had summoned him – a summons for a subinfeudation he had made. But how long would such a process take? The feudal host that emerges from the sources for feudal military obligation does not look like a useful field force.

147 *RRAN*, 1:no. 462.
148 Stubbs, *Select Charters*, p. 97. See above, n. 65, concerning the authenticity of this writ.
149 Harvey, 'Knight and Knight's Fee', pp. 7–9.
150 Richard Mortimer, 'Land and Service: The Tenants of the Honour of Clare', p. 197.

But the system had to have worked in some way. Part of the problem is in imagining a feudal host strictly in terms of fiefs with defined incidents of service. It seems most probable that the more defined the terms of service in a feudal host were, the less militarily useful the force was – that in fact defined terms of service are characteristic of feudalism as a legal rather than a military system.[151] This is because most definitions of service would in fact have limited the fief holder's obligations. An effective feudal host would have been a far more informally regulated body, with service governed by the 'Let's go, boys' rule: when service was needed, it was rendered. And such a host would of necessity have included many household soldiers (those to whom a lord could most easily say 'Let's go, boys') and probably other mercenaries (depending on the leader's financial resources) in addition to those owing service for land. In other words it would not have been a purely 'feudal' host.[152] It is in fact doubtful whether an effective army composed only of soldiers rendering defined terms of service in exchange for fiefs was ever raised in the middle ages. But feudal elements, especially with less defined terms of service, were of course a major part of medieval military resources.

The feudal systems underlying most host service differed from England to Normandy in two respects. First, the quotas of knight's service were significantly different in average size, and had been imposed in different ways. Second, the military obligations of feudal tenants differed slightly.

In Normandy, military fees had developed slowly, and at the time of the Conquest were not yet fully defined. Under the influence of developments in England and of general trends in in the late eleventh and twelfth centuries, the duties and legalities of Norman feudalism crystallised.[153] The main points include the following. Quotas of service for the barony were fairly small – almost never more than ten knights – and usually formed a third to a fifth of the total number of knights enfeoffed on a baron's estates.[154] The excess was available for the baron's private

---

151 Or perhaps as a legal as well as a military system, with the legal element tending to restrict the military.
152 Cf. Chibnall on the host in Normandy before 1066: 'Any evidence that the duke exacted a minimum period of service is sadly lacking; service was governed by need, and household troops and more casual mercenaries were both prominent.' She therefore characterises military service in the duchy before 1066 as 'pre-feudal'. 'Military Service in Normandy before 1066', p. 72.
153 Chibnall sees fixed terms of service and set aids and reliefs developing between c.1070 and 1140, with the definition of family lineage and hereditary rights playing a large role: 'Military Service in Normandy before 1066', pp. 74–5.
154 Douglas, *William the Conqueror*, pp. 281–2; E. van Houts suggests that the quota system evolved from the ad hoc arrangements in 1066 whereby the magnates of Normandy

use. Field service came to be defined as forty days a year in war time served at the knight's own cost;[155] service was probably not owed overseas.

In England feudalism narrowly defined arrived with William I after the Conquest.[156] The quotas of service were arbitrary and quite large: 'not less than eleven lay lords owed sixty or more knights, and at least twenty-seven more owed a service of twenty-five knights or over, whilst six bishoprics and three abbeys owed forty knights or more.'[157] Because the quotas were so large, the total number of enfeoffments usually ended up about the same as the total *servitia debita* (remembering that the process of subinfeudation took some time), leaving the baronage with no excess for their private use, though some barons eventually enfeoffed more knights than they needed, while some enfeoffed fewer. The military obligations for field service were also a bit more onerous than in the duchy. It seems that under the influence of the fyrd's term of service, two months per year may have been customary in war, forty days in peace; but overseas service was not owed.[158] Once again knights performed all service at their own cost: feudal forces were not *ad victum regis*.

In both the duchy and the kingdom service could be commuted for the cost of a replacement knight. Scutage probably was collected in England before it was in Normandy, based on the model of fyrd commutation.[159] Both scutage and commutation helped the government pay for the *familia* and reinforcement mercenaries. It was perhaps as much by providing money as by field service that the feudal host, in particular, supplemented the *familia*.

The apparently relatively minor use of the field service aspect of feudal military obligations should not, however, obscure the overall importance of such obligations to the Anglo-Norman military system.

In the first place, the *servitium debitum* combined with subinfeudation created an efficient system of maintaining a manpower pool, as noted earlier.[160] This manpower pool was self-supporting, and in fact contributed to the stability and governance of the realm. Furthermore, it was

agreed to minimum contributions in men and ships to the planned expedition: 'Ship List', p. 172.
155 CDF, no. 714.
156 See above Ch. 2 for a discussion of the functional similarities of continental feudalism and Anglo-Saxon military arrangements.
157 Douglas, *William the Conqueror*, p. 282.
158 Hollister, *Mil. Org. Norman Eng.*, pp. 94–5, 103.
159 Hollister, 'The Significance of Scutage Rates in Eleventh- and Twelfth-Century England', pp. 577–88.
160 See above, p. 49.

a pool readily called on – whether by feudal obligation or, perhaps more importantly, mercenary service – and loyal when called. For even if an enfeoffed soldier received pay for his service, the legal and moral obligations of his acceptance of a fief with homage could not have been forgotten. There were, as this study suggests, probably more 'paid feudal soldiers' than the strict meaning of the term 'mercenary' may reveal. Furthermore, scutage and paid feudal service could have combined to effect a form of rotation of service by feudal forces that rotating call ups by geography or lordship could not. The scutage of one enfeoffed knight may well have paid for the service of another.

In the second place, feudal soldiers owed – and regularly performed – other services than field service, services which formed an important part of the military system. Castle ward was probably the most important and most used of these, and will be discussed shortly. Attendance at court, given the close relationship of government and military systems, had political, and thus military, significance. The service of riding with the king (or lord), though not strictly field service, also was important militarily. Thus the *servitia debita* of England and Normandy and the feudal forces they created were important to Anglo-Norman military organization despite being probably less used in the field than has usually been thought.

Castle Ward

A special aspect of army organization was the provisions made for ward of royal castles. We may distinguish three levels of garrisoning. In peacetime skeleton crews, consisting of some *janitores* and *vigiles* – non military personnel, really – and a minimum of knights or other soldiers, staffed most castles.[161] In wartime the garrisons would be expanded significantly, but the numbers involved remained under a hundred,[162] sufficient for defense of a good castle, but too small for independent offensive action save perhaps foraging raids. Royal and baronial castles shared these two levels of garrisoning, though the terms of service of royal and baronial garrisons might not be exactly the same. The most important royal castles, however, were garrisoned by detachments of the *familia regis*

---

[161] Brown, *English Castles*, p. 185; *PR 31 HI*, p. 138.

[162] E.g. OV, 6:24 (80 *stipendiarios milites* at Bridgnorth in 1102), 220 (30 *equites* each at Le Sap and Orbec in 1118).

numbering in the hundreds rather than the tens.[163] The organization of such garrisons followed the lines discussed above for the *familia*. It is with the smaller garrisons, whose job was primarily castle ward, rather than the latter, to whom a castle was a base of operations, that we are now concerned. As with the territorial armies, the fyrd and the host, castle ward fell under the operational command of the *familia*, even when the *familia* did not make up the garrison, but had an organization of its own. This organization varied with the means used to obtain the ward service, of which there were two.

The first was feudal. Castle ward was one of the regular duties attached to knights' fees. Most fees owed castle guard at a royal or a baronial castle, but not at both. Since castle guard was served yearly in war or in peace, it could be a greater burden than host service,[164] especially as host service was more likely to be commuted for pay. A vassal might also be asked to provide a larger contingent for castle ward than for host service.[165]

It was in the organization of feudal duty at royal castles that the feudal system was most closely tied to territorial administrative units such as the shire. This was due to the limitations of feudal service. Each fee owed castle ward for a limited period only, so to provide a year-round garrison some wider arrangement had to be made; this arrangement often fell under the direction and enforcement of a sheriff. Fees were grouped and each group assigned a portion of the year in which to do its service; several such groups in the vicinity of a royal castle would between them provide a small garrison for the year.[166] The primary responsibility for directing and enforcing such an arrangement fell to the castellan. The archbishop of Canterbury made such arrangements at his castle at Rochester under Henry I, choosing from among his own men and compelling others, who were not his men, to do ward at the accustomed times; abbot Faricius of Abingdon directed ward at Windsor early in Henry's reign, but apparently had trouble enforcing obedience.[167] In such a case the power of the sheriffs backed up the authority of the castellan.

---

163 E.g. Symeon, *HR*, pp. 187 (500 Normans in two castles at York in 1069), 224 (DCC. *milites regis Willelmi, cum bis totidem scutariis et castellanis* at Argentan and DCCC. *homines* at Hôlme, both in 1094).

164 Stenton, *English Feudalism*, p. 192.

165 *CDF*, no. 714.

166 Hollister, *Mil. Org. Norman Eng.*, pp. 150–1; Frederick Suppe, 'Castle Guard and the Castlery of Clun', *The Haskins Society Journal* 1 (1989), 123–34, for such arrangements at a Welsh border castle later in the twelfth century.

167 *RRAN*, 2:nos. 1606, 725.

Michael de Hameslap had the keeping of Rockingham castle early in Henry's reign. The barons and vavasours owing ward there were under his direction, and he or the sheriffs where the soldiers held land enforced obedience.[168]

The second means of obtaining ward of royal castles was through mercenary service. Assessing the relative importance of feudal and mercenary service is difficult. If we include garrisons of *familia* detachments as mercenaries, paid garrisons certainly vastly outnumbered feudal ones, especially in Normandy. There, key castles always stayed under *familia* control, and feudal garrisons at royal (ducal) castles were probably rare: the number of feudal troops due to the duke was small, so fees could less easily be organized along the above lines than fees in England; and the loyalty of Norman feudal forces was sometimes suspect.[169] In England, the comparison depends on chronology. Mercenaries dominated castle ward for much of William I's reign, for the subinfeudation upon which feudal castle ward depended took place gradually through the reign. Feudal ward may have played as large a role as it ever did under William II, for the peace maintained under Henry I could have encouraged the commutation of ward and the use by the king of small paid crews. In any of the reigns, mercenaries would have reinforced feudal or paid garrisons in time of need: the rotating service of normal feudal ward left no room for expansion of feudal garrisons.

The organization of paid watch crews (they barely qualify as garrisons) used at royal castles, mostly in England, was a financial matter, and not surprisingly was included in the normal functions of the Exchequer and county farms. Expenses were paid by the sheriff or his designated subordinate and account was rendered at the Exchequer.[170] If a baron's estates fell for some reason into royal custody, the baronial castles were staffed in the same way, though the account was rendered by the farmer or custodian of the estate: thus in the Pipe Roll of 1130, the lands of Roger of Mowbray are administered by Henry de Montfort, who accounts for porters and watchmen at four of Roger's castles.[171]

A final aspect of the royal military system relating to castle guard concerns transfer of ward from royal to baronial castles. This was naturally subject to royal approval, and was a privilege paid for by the favored

---

168 *RRAN*, 2:no. 563.
169 It was the policy of both William Rufus and Henry 'to insist on castellans occupying the major number of Norman castles as royal officials rather than holding them in fee.' Chibnall, 'Feudal Society in Orderic Vitalis', p. 40.
170 *PR 31 HI*, pp. 76, 128, 141, 142, 143, 152.
171 *PR 31 HI*, pp. 137–8.

baron. Both Hervey Bishop of Ely and Alexander Bishop of Lincoln obtained the service of their own knights, who had owed ward at royal castles, for their own castles in this way.[172] The dates of these transfers – 1130 and 1133 (probably) respectively – may indicate the decreasing importance to the king of feudal castle ward in England under Henry, though they may be merely expensive personal favors. Whether the provisions made for castle ward at baronial castles was subject to royal control or approval is doubtful. The king exercised control rather through licencing of baronial castles and the right of confiscation on grounds of treason.

Supply

Supply in the Anglo-Norman military system operated on two levels: the supply of an army in the field; and the administrative arrangements for the provisioning of castles as permanent depots and for supplying the army in the field. It is the latter I shall discuss now. This is the 'logistical tail' of the army, the system that kept the army in being. I shall include in this discussion a brief examination of the production of materials of war which fell at times outside of government control.

Purchase and distribution of supplies fell under the direction of the *familia*. The constables were probably in command of this function, acting as quartermasters-general, though the master-marshal was the accountant for costs of *familia* supplies as well as for wages.[173] Merchants of the king's household, who travelled with the king's writ and were free of tolls and passage-money, were under the officers' command.[174]

Ducal officers directed the purchase, storage and guarding of supplies of fodder in the duchy. These included a 'Maréchal de Venoix' at Caen and a 'Maréchal de Prés' at Le Vaudreuil; corvées imposed on villages in the districts of the central depots ensured regular harvest and transport.[175] Interestingly, there is no evidence of depots in England specifically for fodder. Arrangements were certainly made for the supply of cavalry in the kingdom, not only in castle depots but at royal breeding farms. The system in the duchy probably reflects the greater importance of cavalry in Normandy before 1066; 'la Prairie [at Caen] toujours exis-

---

172 *RRAN*, 2:nos. 1656, 1791; *PR 31 HI*, p. 44.
173 White, 'Household', p. 150; *Const. Domus Regis* in *EHD* 2:427.
174 *RRAN*, 2:no. 705.
175 L. Musset, 'Une institution peu connue de la Normandie ducale: les prés et le foin du seigneur roi', *Annales de Normandie* (1979), 375–6.

tante, est attestée depuis 1027.'[176] After the conquest, whatever increase in cavalry supplies needed to be made in England, if any, was handled within the framework of *familia* and county farms which ensured other supplies.

The system of supply also included arrangements for transport of the supplies purchased. The corvées attaching to the administration of *le foin du roi* were mentioned above. In England, carrying service apparently was one of the most common obligations on the land, and in charters of liberties appears in close conjunction with the usual military obligations of fyrd service and castle- and bridge-work. Thus an early charter of Henry frees St. Pancras and the monks of Lewes of a series of burdens including scutage (the earliest mention by name of this institution), bridge building, castle building, and carrying service, ship-service, and transport of treasure.[177] A charter from later in the reign frees the Canons of the Holy Trinity, London, of military service on foot or horseback and of cart- or packhorse- or ship-service.[178] The latter charter shows the variety of means of transport which the king could demand. Royal control of shipping and cartage is further illustrated in a precept by Henry to Hervey bishop of Ely forbidding any ship to put in at any strand (*litus*) in Cambridgeshire except at the strand of the king's borough of Cambridge. Nor were carts to be loaded or toll to be taken anywhere but there.[179]

The cost of purchasing supplies for an army on the march was met out of the king's chamber. But when the supplies were bought for the provisioning of castles, especially routine stocks in peacetime, some of the charges could be transferred to the county farms and the accounting to the Exchequer. The cost of transporting supplies to castles was also transferred in this way. When purchase and transport was handled on the Exchequer accounts, the sheriff took charge of the operations. In the Pipe Roll of 1130, wine and foodstuffs such as grain, oil and bacon made up the bulk of the supplies purchased and transported in this way: wine and grain were carried from Woodstock to Clarendon, for example; wooden building materials and pepper and other spices also appear, the latter probably for royal use rather than for castle garrisons.[180] Weapons were the other major item stocked in castles for the use of the garrisons

---

176 *Ibid.*, 375.
177 *RRAN*, 2:no. 510.
178 *RRAN*, 2:no. 1316; the charter is probably forged, but this simply reinforces the weight and importance of the obligation. See also nos. 520, 1334.
179 *RRAN*, 2:no. 1729.
180 *PR 31 HI*, pp. 1, 13, 77, 144; the total expenditure for purchase and transport of these items comes to £62 13s. 10d.

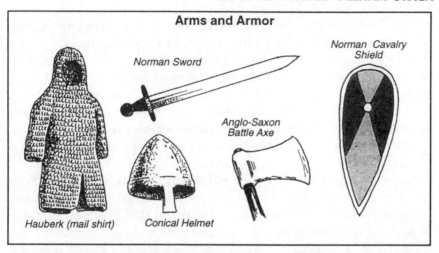

Arms and Armor

Norman Sword

Norman Cavalry Shield

Anglo-Saxon Battle Axe

Hauberk (mail shirt)   Conical Helmet

or a field army: arms, food and other necessary equipment made up the complete castle stores.[181] Armor and weaponry do not seem to have been purchased on the county farms. Outside both the *familia* and the county farms, castles obtained some of their stocks, food especially, locally from the district under the castle's control.

Food, wine, timber: such items made up the common goods of medieval trade and were therefore easy to obtain. Items particular to warfare – armor and weaponry – were rarer, more expensive, and harder to obtain, and thus deserve a bit more notice as to their manufacture and purchase. Though not exactly manufactured, warhorses may be included in items particular to warfare that required special arrangements to obtain.

The most important piece of defensive armor for Anglo-Norman soldiers was the hauberk, a shirt of chain mail. Mail required skill and a good deal of time to manufacture,[182] and was therefore not an item bought in bulk either on county farms or very often on the king's chamber account. In all likelihood the mail shirt and the conical iron helmet which complemented it were supplied not by the employer but by the employee in twelfth century warfare. That is, each soldier provided his own armor. Undoubtedly some professional soldiers did not own a mail shirt and wore only the quilted gambeson which normally went under the mail (though they would not then qualify as *milites*, or knights); some members of the fyrd were probably incompletely

---

[181] OV, 6:190; *RRAN*, 1:no. 83; Brown, *English Castles*, p. 190.
[182] J. Mann, 'Arms and Armour', in Poole, ed., *Medieval England*, p. 316; Ian Peirce, 'Arms, Armor and Warfare', pp. 239–40.

armored, for instance. But most would have counted mail among the necessary equipment, along with helmet, sword and horse, of a professional soldier. Mail was durable and was handed down from man to man, and could be repaired when damaged. It was repair and, for the other items mentioned, replacement that the government was responsible for. Replacement of losses was, as we have seen, one of the terms of *familia* service. The small size of armies meant that only small stocks of equipment needed to be maintained for this purpose, in a central depot like the Tower.

As for replacement of horses, royal breeding farms would have been maintained for the hunt as well as for wars.[183] We know of at least one: Swein, a shieldbearer of the king, appears in the 1130 Pipe Roll in charge of breeding the king's mares at Gillingham.[184] The king's own horses and replacement of casualties among *familia* horses came from such farms (as well as from monasteries, which frequently maintained breeding pens), many probably located in the Seine valley of Normandy, which was ideal horse breeding territory.[185] Good (well bred) destriers were expensive – £20–30 for the best, as compared to about 14s. for a common workhorse, and required regular supplies of oats and fodder, especially in winter.[186] The number of horses needed even for small Anglo-Norman armies should not be underestimated. Each knight would have needed, in addition to at least one good destrier, at least three lesser horses: a pre-battle riding horse, a squire's horse and a pack horse.[187]

In the case of armor, weapons, or horses the need for the government to maintain replacement stocks decreased with its ability simply to pay the replacement cost directly to the soldier, and leave procurement to him.

Engineering

Military engineering was as vital a part of the Anglo-Norman military system as arrangements for supply, for engineers, organized in various

---

183 Davis, 'Warhorses of the Normans', is a very important article on the breeding of warhorses by the Normans; he contends that the Normans were successful in warfare largely due to the quality of their destriers (p. 67). While that particular conclusion is open to dispute, the problems of horse breeding which he details are not.
184 *PR 31 HI*, p. 12.
185 Davis, 'Warhorses', pp. 74–5.
186 OV 5:242.
187 Davis, 'Warhorses', p. 79.

ways, built and maintained the castles in which stores were kept and armies fought, and built and repaired the bridges over which both supplies and soldiers moved.

I

The routine work of royal engineering, devoted mostly to castle building and repair, but also including bridge and road work and siege machine construction, 'was normally under the administrative control of the sheriff and the financial control of the Exchequer.'[188] Outlays for works on royal castles appear regularly throughout the one Pipe Roll surviving from Henry's reign, though at nowhere near the level of expense normal under Henry II. Henry I was not a great builder in any case, but most of his energy would have been directed to his Norman castles, and after nearly thirty years of peace in England the works carried on were in the nature of maintenance and routine repairs. Thus £17 0s. 6d. were spent on the Tower of London, £22 7s. 8d. at Arundel, and £7 6s. 2d. at Gloucester, to cite only three examples.[189] The total spent on works comes to somewhat more than £120.[190]

Of the labor force used in such works, the skilled artisans and engineers were paid workmen. The Anglo-Norman kings could expand the unskilled workforce without having to hire labor, however. The *trinoda necessitas*, of which fyrd service was one, included the burdens of *brigbot* and *burgbot* – bridge building and fortress building. Although the latter provided in Anglo-Saxon times only for town, or *burg*, defenses, it was very quickly used by the Conqueror and his supporters to speed the erection of royal and private castles. The organization of this service parallelled that of the fyrd, though it was performed by men lower on the social ladder, in that it was organized by village and lordship up through shire, and failure to perform the burdens was subject to royal jurisdiction and a 120s. fine.[191] A feudal obligation related to castle guard also existed by which some castle maintenance was done.[192]

The records relating to royal building activities in the Angevin period are much more extensive than for the Norman period. Working with these records, R. A. Brown saw the existence of what may be called a '*familia* for works':[193]

---

188 Brown, H.M. Colvin and A.J. Taylor, eds, *History of the King's Works*, 1:26.
189 *PR 31 HI*, pp. 144, 42, 78.
190 I calculate £122 18s. 10d. *PR 31 HI*, passim.
191 *LHP*, c. 10, 9; c. 13, 9; c. 66, 6b; *RRAN*, 1:no. 23; Brown, *King's Works*, 1:24–5.
192 Brown, *King's Works*, 1:26.
193 Brown, 'Royal Castle-Building in England, 1154–1216', *EHR* 70 (1955), 374.

The appearance of the small group of specialised craftsmen by name upon the records, their uniform and high rates of pay, together with occasional specific references to them as king's men, and above all the movement of the same individuals and groups of individuals from one work to another, all point to the existence of something like a small central engineering department . . . the task of this small corps of specialists was to direct and supervise the labour of the larger number of less skilled provincial workers which castle-building demanded. . . .

Although the scale of building under the Normans was not as large as under the Angevins, it is possible that a similar organization existed in the earlier period, at least for extraordinarily large works like the construction of the White Tower under William I and II. It would in fact be surprising if the branches of the *familia*, which reached into so many departments of royal activity, military and otherwise, did not appear at times in the organization of military engineering. We may perhaps interpret Rufus' preparations before invading Maine in 1098 in this light: he ordered Robert of Bellême to gather a large force of *familia* soldiers in his castles, and sent him copious supplies of money not only for the soldiers' wages but for improving the castles' defenses with walls, ramparts and towers.[194] The castle repairs certainly fell under the command of a *familia* officer, Robert of Bellême. But whether a true *familia* organization of the chief engineers existed is unclear.

Castle building of any kind was under royal jurisdiction: castles built without licence placed a man *in misericordia regis*.[195] Other legal regulations concerning engineering matters relate to roads. All highways were completely the concern of the king, and *stretbreche*, or interference to a royal road by blocking, digging, and so forth, was subject to royal jurisdiction and required a 100s. compensation at the least.[196] In fact we have the records of a case of *stretbreche* in which the steward of Alexander, bishop of Lincoln, was fined £15 and a mark of gold for the causeway he made blocking the king's highway.[197] The bishop apparently took the complaint to the king, for the king issued two notes to Richard Basset and Aubrey de Vere, the officials in charge, and to the sheriff of Nottinghamshire, permitting the bishop to divert the Fosse Way at Newark in order to make the causeway (*calceda*) for his fish-pond. The

---

194 OV, 5:234.
195 *LHP*, c. 10, 1; c. 13, 1.

196 *LHP*, c. 10, 1–2; c. 12, 2.
197 *PR 31 HI*, p. 117.

highway was to be diverted through the town in whatever way the bishop wished.[198]

That royal permission was necessary for the bishop to divert the road agrees with the definition of royal roads in the *Leges Henrici*: a royal road is always open, may not be blocked or diverted by anyone's walls, and leads into a royal city, *burg*, castle or port.[199] The emphasis on *burgs* and castles makes the military importance of royal roads clear. The military use of royal highways is further emphasized by the *Leges'* claim for the width of royal highways: they ought to be wide enough for two wagons to pass, for two herdsmen to touch with their goads outstretched, and for sixteen *milites* to ride abreast.[200]

But just as royal roads could in fact be diverted with the king's permission, they were not necessarily up to this legal standard of width. Sixteen armed knights abreast would take up almost twenty meters of road. This is not an impossible width; but the passage itself does not even seem consistent. A road wide enough for two wagons to pass, or for two herdsmen to touch with their goads outstretched, but no wider, would accommodate no more than six or eight armed knights abreast. This seems a more reasonable figure. Yet such is the allure of the word *milites* that it is the larger figure that has often been cited alone.[201]

II

Despite the regulations, roadworks were the least organized aspect of royal engineering activities. Bridgeworks and castleworks had their *brigbot* and *burgbot* burdens to provide maintenance labor; no 'stretbot' burden corresponded to these services. There was no clear system for road repair and maintenance, in fact. This relative lack of organization is reflected in the amount of roadwork done – or at least for which we have evidence. Compared to bridges and, especially, castles, roads were the neglected target of Anglo-Norman military engineering.

Most of the roadwork done under the Norman kings consisted of minor alterations or diversions to the existing network of roads. The diversion of the Fosse Way by the bishop of Lincoln, though not carried out by the king, typified this type of roadwork. Also typical was the diversion by the king of a road which passed close by the church of St. Mary's of Wymondham, in order that the monks would not be disturbed

---

198 *RRAN*, 2:nos. 1660–1.
199 *LHP*, c. 80, 3a.
200 *LHP*, c. 80, 3.
201 Stenton, 'The Road System of Medieval England', *EcHR* 7 (1936), 3.

by travellers, and of a road that ran through the grounds of Holy Trinity, London.[202] Such alterations had no military significance, but do illustrate that royal attention to the road system was not altogether lacking. Evidence of road making, that is the extension of the road system, however, is scarce; such activity was probably quite rare. Some road building took place locally – by a landowner on his own demesne, for instance – under royal jurisdiction.[203] The construction of small extensions by royal authority is indicated by land grants made in compensation for land taken to make roads.[204] But, we know of only one instance of extensive road building from the entire period. In 1102, Henry besieged Robert of Bellême's castle at Bridgnorth. When it fell, he then marched to Shrewsbury via a narrow, overgrown track which proved inadequate for his army. He therefore ordered the 'sixty thousand' foot-soldiers in the army to cut down the wood with axes and make a much wider road.[205] This may reveal why road building was an uncommon activity of royal engineering: it required a large number of workmen. In general the extant road system proved adequate, for the most part, to the needs of the relatively small Anglo-Norman field forces. The men who would have done roadwork, perhaps by some sort of 'stretbot' system, were better used (as Henry's infantry already had been) in the army, or in the construction of bridges and castles.

In fact, as Sir Frank Stenton has noted, 'it was not by the making of new roads, but by the building of new bridges, that the Englishmen of the Middle Ages set about the improvement of their communications'.[206] The Norman kings retained the Anglo-Saxon *brigbot* service, as noted above, for this purpose. Most bridges of the time were wooden, and so had to be repaired constantly, as well. The largest single expenditure on building in the 1130 Pipe Roll was £25 for building two arches of London Bridge, and 3s. 4d. were spent to repair the bridge at Rochester for the king's arrival.[207] Especially on works as large as London Bridge, rebuilt in stone at the same time as the Tower, between 1097 and 1099, under the direction of Ranulf Flambard,[208] paid skilled workmen directed the labor of the *brigbot* service.

---

202 *RRAN*, 2:nos. 1310, 1315.
203 *RRAN*, 2:no. 1304.
204 *RRAN*, 2:no. 1324.
205 OV, 6:28, and 30, n. 1; Hollister, 'The Campaign of 1102 against Robert of Bellême', p. 199, suggests this is 'the stretch between Harley and Cressage on the present A 458.'
206 Stenton, 'Road System', p. 6.
207 *PR 31 HI*, pp. 144, 64.
208 Barlow, *Feudal Kingdom*, p. 168.

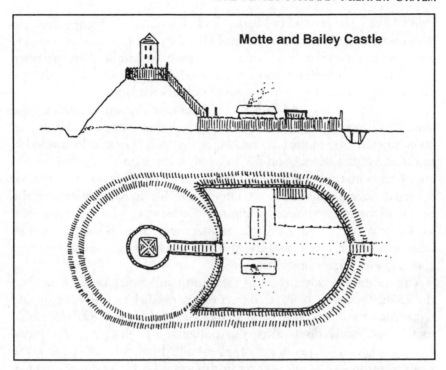

Motte and Bailey Castle

One final interesting piece of engineering work that received notice in Henry's reign involves not bridges but the actual waterway. In 1121, Henry cleared and improved the Fosse Dyke between Torksey and Lincoln and so 'made a way for ships.'[209] The military significance of this probably relates to transport of supplies by water to the castle at Lincoln.

Yet far overshadowing even bridge building among the activities of Anglo-Norman engineering was castle building. The conquest brought the private castle to England, and totally transformed the military geography of the realm within a decade. Building continued in Normandy at the same time, and the period saw significant developments in the design and construction of castles.

Fortifications in England before the conquest were limited to town defenses. These usually consisted of an earthwork rampart and ditch topped by a wooden palisade. The Normans introduced a new type of castle, the motte-and-bailey, which was private rather than communal and which thus soon existed in far greater numbers than town fortresses

---

[209] Symeon, *HR*, p. 260.

could have. The motte-and-bailey had originated in France and the Rhineland sometime before the mid-eleventh century, and was already widespread in Normandy in 1066;[210] it came to England in intimate connection with military feudalism, as feudal castle-ward shows, though technically not as part of the system of military feudalism.

The typical motte-and-bailey castle consisted of an enclosure (the bailey) of roughly oval shape, created by a ditch, rampart, and palisade; and a mound (the motte) at one end of the bailey, topped by a wooden tower and a palisade around the top rim of the mound. The motte was anywhere from five to at least ten meters in height.[211] It was a simple but effective design, difficult to assault directly or to sap because of the height of the mound, and having the permanence of any large earthworks. Its particular advantage in engineering terms was that it could be built very quickly – in as little as eight days – in almost any sort of country, with largely unskilled labor.[212]

The military disadvantages of the motte-and-bailey castle related to the timber portions of its construction: it needed constant repair and replacement just as wooden bridges did, and in defense it was vulnerable to fire and easily dismantled. But unlike the engineering of bridges, which remained predominantly timber-built throughout the period, the main trend in castle engineering in this period was the replacement of wood with stone.[213] This occurred mostly at already constructed castles; very few new castles appeared after the first half of William I's reign. The bailey palisade and the ring wall on the motte were the first components to be replaced by stone curtain walls. The motte tower usually could not be replaced, at least until late in Henry's reign, as the earth of the artificial mounds had not settled sufficiently to support the weight of a stone tower.

But the most characteristic stone element in twelfth century Norman castles, added within the bailey at some motte-and-bailey sites and forming the focus of defenses at new sites started in stone, was the great keep or *donjon*, of which the White Tower is the best known example. Keeps of this period, square in plan, depended on the thickness and height of their walls for their defensive strength. They were not designed so that the defenders could easily strike back at attackers from within the walls. Such buildings were stronger than the earth and timber

---

210 Hollister, *Mil. Org. Norman Eng.*, pp. 136–7; Brown, *English Castles*, p. 39.
211 Brown, *English Castles*, pp. 55–6.
212 A.J. Taylor, 'Military Architecture', in Poole, ed., *Medieval England*, pp. 103–4; Brown, *English Castles*, pp. 155–6.
213 Brown, *King's Works*, 1:36–7.

motte-and-bailey castle, but cost more in time and money to build. They also required a more skilled workforce for their construction. Stone needed less maintenance than timber, on the other hand.

All castles, whether of earth and timber or stone, shared certain characteristics and requirements in their construction. First, it seems unlikely to me that castles, in particular those built in England soon after the conquest, were sited according to some grand strategic plan, as J. Beeler has suggested.[214] Castle builders chose sites for tactical reasons, according either to the local physical geography or to the local political geography. The Conqueror advanced through England, and 'established castles at opportune sites.'[215] The siting of a castle could be offensive or defensive in this context. If it were placed at a key ford or bridge, or at a major road intersection, it aimed at offensive control of that feature and of the surrounding area. If it were on an inaccessible crag, it was intended as a safe refuge, immune to attack. The ideal site combined defensive strength and offensive control. Any appearance of strategic coordination is illusory, a result of the tactical siting of castles at successive points along lines of communication or around major cities, though the accumulation of castles in important areas could easily become strategically and politically significant.[216]

Second, all castles, whatever their site, needed certain features built in. Foremost was internal wells, to ensure a safe supply of water. Also necessary were safe provisions for grinding grain and baking bread: great slaughter took place at a siege of Courcy in 1091 around an oven which stood outside the walls of the fortress.[217]

There are numerous examples of castle building in the sources. A few cases will illustrate the various conditions under which castles could be built and the operations of the engineering system.

The speed with which motte-and-bailey castles could be built gained importance when they were thrown up in the course of a campaign. William's first action on landing in England in 1066 was to erect castles at Pevensey and Hastings, for instance.[218] The castles erected from Exeter to York in the course of 1068 and 1069 were likewise hastily thrown up

---

[214] Beeler, *Warfare in England*, p. 53. The concept seriously misinterprets the role of castles in medieval warfare: see below, Ch. 4; cf. the comments of Matthew Strickland, 'Securing the North: Invasion and the Strategy of Defence in Twelfth-Century Anglo-Scottish Warfare', *Battle* 12 (1989), 179–80.
[215] 'castella opportuna per loca stabilivit'; WJ, p. 134.
[216] Searle, 'The Abbey of the Conquerors', p. 159.
[217] OV, 4:234.
[218] WJ, p. 134.

in the face of a potentially hostile population, especially in the north.[219] Use of the *burgbot* service is evident in 1095, when Rufus compelled his generals, captains and other nobles and the population subject to them to help build a new castle to face Bamburgh.[220] In this case what they really built was a 'counter-castle', a common device for blockading and neutralizing a hostile fortress. Counter-castles were mostly little more than glorified siege works, and not full motte-and-bailey castles.

The greater cost of stone works resulted from the cost of skilled labor. When Rufus threatened Helias of Maine with a siege of Le Mans in 1096, he warned the count of these costs, saying 'send at once for masons and stone cutters greedy for pay' to repair the breaches in his neglected walls.[221] If the Angevin records are an accurate guide, labor made up the major expense – up to two thirds of total costs – as well as the major administrative challenge in castle building.[222]

Another engineering task associated with castles and requiring skilled labor was the construction of siege machinery for attacking and defending fortified positions. Making all types of machines required skilled carpenters under the direction of someone experienced in building and operating such engines. Robert of Bellême and Henry I himself often directed the building and use of siege machines.[223] I shall discuss the various types of machines in connection with siege tactics.[224]

Training

For many military systems, ancient and modern, the training of new recruits in the arts and rigors of warfare is one of the first tasks in preparing an army for warfare. It is the first topic discussed by Vegetius.[225] A complete examination of the Anglo-Norman military system, there-fore, should include a look at Anglo-Norman training procedures, if any. Two kinds of training are in question: how a man learned to use weapons (and horses, for some); and how men learned to fight in groups. The former lay almost exclusively beyond the scope of the military system. Men who were skilled in arms had been brought up using weapons and, in the continental tradition at least, riding horses

---

219 E.g. Florence, 2:2.
220 OV, 4:282.
221 OV, 5:230–2.
222 Brown, *English Castles*, p. 163; 'Royal Castle Building', p. 368.
223 OV, 4:288; 6:342; Symeon, *HR*, p. 274.
224 See below, p. 138.
225 Vegetius, Bk 1.

from their youth.[226] In the case of most infantry, including the fyrd, even this training needed be no more than minimal, for infantry weapons like the spear were simple to use and gained their effect from use *en masse*.

The only point of interest concerning this basic level of training has to do with tradition. In the continental style of warfare, a soldier learned to fight on foot or on horseback. In the Scandinavian style, a soldier learned to fight on foot or on shipboard. The conquest of England made the continental style dominant in the kingdom for the first time. Given the influence tradition has always had in military practices, this change in style or tradition may have played a role in the decline of the English combat navy after 1066.[227] The difference may also reflect differences in strategic conceptions for meeting sea-borne invaders: no navy, numerous castles, cavalry and avoidance of battles on the continent; a navy, a few fortified towns, infantry, and seeking battles in England.[228]

If the military system had had anything to do with training, however, it would have been on the group level rather than on the individual. But the Anglo-Norman system does not seem to have provided much unit training. The fyrd owed no annual training period; the feudal host in England may have owed 40 days service a year in peace, but it is not clear how this time was used.[229] Selection of the better soldiers in a group may have replaced special training to some extent in a force like the *familia*, but in general soldiers of the twelfth century learned to fight in groups by experience.[230] The importance of experience to troops and commanders may be noted in Henry of Huntingdon's account of Tinchebrai; Henry's victory was the more laudable in that his opponent, Duke Robert, was 'trained in the wars for Jerusalem.'[231] But as for peacetime training, even a government as

---

[226] Thus the Carolingian proverb, 'You can make a horseman of a lad at puberty; later than that, never.' Cited in Bloch, *Feudal Society*, 1:152.

[227] The argument that English control of the northwest coast of France reduced the need for a combat navy (Murray, 'Shipping', p. 176) seems questionable in that by the time the threat of Scandinavian invasion receded, England had lost control of the French coast until 1105, due to the division of the realm. After 1106 there was less need for a combat navy, but traditions of individual training still had their influence. And see Hooper, 'Some Observations on the Navy', pp. 205–6, on the disbanding of much of the professional Danish-Saxon fleet as early as 1051.

[228] This suggested difference in strategy is very impressionistic; it would have to be worked out in far more detail than is possible here.

[229] Hollister, *A-S Mil. Inst.*, p. 88; *Mil. Org. Norman Eng.*, pp. 94–5.

[230] Experience gained in the *familiae* of the warrior's lord, the basis of the tactical divisions and capabilities of medieval armies at this level. Cf. Brown, 'The Battle of Hastings', *Battle* 3 (1980), 1–21.

[231] HH, p. 235.

rich as that of the Norman kings simply did not have the resources to bring masses of troops together regularly for tactical and marching drills.

The tastes of the warrior aristocracy did fill this breach in one way: by creating the tournament.[232] But once again, the sort of training and experience a tournament provided was more valuable for the small groups of horsemen that dominated these events than for non-aristocratic infantry formations, though infantry did play a role in early tourneying. The military value of such exercises in the eyes of the Norman kings is very much open to question, however, given that they regularly prohibited tourneying in their realm.[233]

As a result of the lack of large scale group training, Anglo-Norman armies, especially the infantry, were not capable of the sort of close order formation changes and unit movements that Alexander the Great's army or the Roman legions had been. Such capabilities were not reintroduced into European warfare until the fifteenth century at the earliest, in general. This should be borne in mind when we evaluate Anglo-Norman tactics on the battlefield.[234]

We do have one remarkable piece of evidence that tactical training was not completely beyond the capacities of the Norman kings, however. Henry I faced Duke Robert's invasion of 1101 with the support of the English people – presumably the fyrd – according to William of Malmesbury. Grateful for their fealty and concerned for their safety (as well as his own, we might add), he went around the ranks and 'taught them how, in meeting the attack of the knights, to defend with their shields and return blows,' and thereby defeat the invading Normans.[235] This bit of instruction by Henry in the methods of meeting a cavalry charge was probably a product of unusual circumstances. He was relying more than usual on less well trained troops, who happened to be gathered in advance in a convenient spot. But we cannot be sure that instruction of this or a similar type did not go on at least occasionally.

Finally, the imposition of uniform discipline on an army, such as was imposed on the core of the Anglo-Norman army through the regulations of the *familia*, in effect formed a type of training. Beyond tactical

232 On tournaments, see Juliet R.V. Barker, *The Tournament in England, 1100–1400* (Woodbridge, 1986).

233 Barker, *The Tournament*, pp. 17–44, for infantry in early tournaments and for a very unconvincing discussion of the importance of tourneying as training for war.

234 See below, pp. 146–47.

235 . . . *docebat quomodo, militum ferociam eludentes, clypeos objectarent et ictus remitterent; quo effecit ut ultroneis votis pugnam deposcerent, in nullo Normannos metuentes.* Malmesbury, *GRA*, p. 472.

manoeuverability and specific methods of attack and defense, much of the point of military training is to instill a group cohesion and enable a unit to act together without breaking apart under pressure.[236] The uniform discipline of the *familia* probably went a long way in replacing this effect of group training. This too should be borne in mind when we examine the tactical capabilities of Anglo-Norman royal armies.

The Anglo-Norman military system thus performed its tasks – raising men, turning them into an army, and then supporting them – efficiently and effectively. The Norman kings could raise armies quickly to meet threats in any part of the realm. The *familia* gave these armies an organizational strength and operational flexibility vital to the success of the kings' rule.

DEMOBILIZATION

The permanent, year-round soldiers of the *familia* formed the core of Anglo-Norman royal armies. But as we have seen, temporary soldiers, either mercenaries or territorial troops, often augmented the *familia*. How were such temporary soldiers dismissed when they were no longer needed?

Demobilization differed depending on whether the soldiers to be sent home were mercenaries or territorial troops. Territorials could simply be released to return home: the king owed them no transport, and barring cross-Channel transport they usually needed none. It is probably safe to assume that when large numbers of territorial troops needed naval transport, as for instance the English troops who helped William I conquer Maine in 1073 and 'afterwards went home to England',[237] the king did provide it. It is unlikely that territorial troops needed much persuasion to leave if the king or his subordinates ordered them to return home, as Ranulf Flambard did in 1094 with the fyrd.[238] Warfare was not their livelihood, so they had no incentive to serve beyond their term of service.

Mercenaries, on the other hand, made money on campaign and may well have been reluctant to terminate their service. The Norman kings therefore had to handle the demobilization of mercenaries in such a way as to persuade the troops to go home (or at least, if they served in

---

[236] This is one of Vegetius' constant themes: Vegetius, *passim.*
[237] ASC (E) 1073.
[238] Florence, 2:35.

England, to leave the country) without alienating them. Disgruntled mercenaries could become brigands, in the first place; in the second, the king would wish to maintain the goodwill of demobilized mercenaries in case he wished to remobilize them at a later date. Commonly, the king dismissed the troops with a generous final payment that was part severance pay, part gratuity, and provided transport where required. Thus after the 1066 campaign William prepared to return to Normandy from Pevensey; there he paid the *milites* a large bonus as they prepared to return home.[239] The Flemish money fief of 1101 includes provisions for demobilizing the knights in Henry's service that follow these general lines. Transport is provided for, and the settling of accounts is left to Count Robert, to whom the fief payment was made.[240]

Even members of the *familia* at times demobilized, or went off active service, along with other mercenaries, and their rewards could be even more substantial than standard severance pay. After settling the wars and rebellions of 1116–19, Henry felt secure enough to put much of his military establishment on a peacetime footing. He paid generous wages to the *milites* who had fought long and faithfully for him, and decided to raise up some by 'giving them extensive honors in England.'[241]

A final act of demobilization shows that expectation of future service was not necessarily the prime reason why the Norman kings granted their troops generous bonuses at the end of their service. One of Henry's deathbed wishes concerned his loyal and long-serving soldiers: he ordered his son Robert to take 'sixty thousand pounds' from his treasury at Falaise, and pay out wages and bonuses to his *familia* and stipendiary *milites*.[242]

Henry's deathbed orders are a fitting conclusion to this examination of the military system of 1066–1135. The king showed concern for the welfare of his troops after his death, and expressed gratitude for their service as one of his final acts. No other incident better sums up the peculiar combination of personal and professional ties at the heart of the Anglo-Norman military system. Friendship and money formed the twin foundations of the *familia*; the *familia* formed the foundation of the military system. The bonds of loyalty and the permanent structure created by friendship and money created the operational capabilities of Anglo-Norman royal armies on campaign and in battle.

A full appreciation for the abilities of the Anglo-Norman military

239 OV, 2:196.
240 Chaplais, no. 1.
241 OV, 6:294.
242 OV, 6:448.

system, however, requires a thorough analysis of how Anglo-Norman military forces performed in warfare. And placing warfare against its institutional background will illuminate patterns that otherwise might be missed. Warfare – patterns, campaigns and tactical action – are the subject of the next two chapters.

Chapter Four

WARFARE I:
PATTERNS AND CAMPAIGNS

THE ROLE OF CASTLES

Some confusion has at times arisen from a failure to distinguish between the role of castles and the role of castle garrisons. We are concerned here with the role of the actual buildings – motte-and-bailey or stone donjon – in Anglo-Norman warfare. It will be seen that castle garrisons had, naturally, a part in the effect of castles, but that this effect may be explained in terms of the garrison acting as a field force. Thus we may divide the roles of Anglo-Norman warfare between buildings and men, castles and field forces.

The central role of castles was to act as a base for the operations of field forces. This involved two things: the establishment in the castle of stores of supplies, so that the castle could act as a depot; and use of the castle as safe housing for troops not on campaign, safe meaning unable to be easily attacked or overrun, as a simple campsite could be. It was, of course, the intrinsic defensive strength of the castle that allowed it to act as a base of operations, for barring an act of treachery it took a major siege or assault to break into a castle.

The administrative system for supplying castles, as well as the regular items which made up a castle's store of supplies, were discussed in the previous chapter. Stocking castles was virtually the first step in going to war, for the supplies that castles protected supported any friendly troops in the area, especially if forage were for some reason not available. For instance, when a Danish fleet threatened to invade in 1075 in support of the earls' rebellion, William I ordered castles along the east coast to be stocked with provisions and arms, and had the coastal areas stripped of supplies to prevent the enemy foraging.[1] Though castle supplies were vital to the actual defense of the castle – the introduction of fresh

[1] *RRAN*, 2:no. 83.

supplies during a siege could induce an attacker to give up[2] – the inclusion of fodder for horses in a castle's stocks indicates that the possibility of offensive action on the part of the garrison or other friendly forces was just as important as defense to the castle's role as a depot.[3]

The castle's role as safe housing for troops, the second aspect of its use as a base of operations, was just as double edged. Troops housed in a castle were protected by the castle from easy assault. The castles built in England just after the conquest certainly protected Norman troops from attack by the native population while they pacified the country: the fate of Robert of Comines and his troops at Durham in 1069 – surprised at night by the townsmen and slaughtered – shows what could happen to soldiers caught outside a castle and unprepared for campaigning.[4] Armies almost always spent winter, when campaigning was rare and housing for full-time troops particularly necessary, in castles. The troops inside the castle in turn defended it when a major assault took place. But this defensive task of a castle's garrison was obviously an emergency measure. The more important role of the troops based in the safety of a castle was offensive. The troops had to be free to leave the castle and act as a field force, either alone or in concert with other garrisons or with a large field army raised for the campaign. I shall discuss the role and activities of field forces in detail in the next section, but a few examples will illustrate the importance of castles as bases for operations beyond their walls.

In the first place, unless the garrison were to hold only the castle and allow enemy forces to roam freely about the countryside – an expensive and pointless proposition – it had to sally forth to oppose enemy incursions into friendly territory. Thus in his preparations before the siege of Gerberoy in early 1079, William I assembled a strong army in border castles near the enemy, 'to prevent any of his lands from being plundered with impunity'.[5] The king's army then advanced to the siege from these base castles. Such a strategically defensive but tactically offensive sally by *familia* detachments defeated Norman rebels at Bourgthérolde in 1124; in the same way, the royal garrison of Lincoln destroyed a rebel raiding party in 1069.[6] The garrison of a castle could also sally forth to conduct its own raids and attacks, instead of meeting an enemy offensive. When Rufus bought control of several castles in 1090 as the first step in the struggle with his brother for the duchy, he stationed *milites* in them 'in

2 OV, 4:201.
3 OV, 4:124.
4 OV, 2:222; Matthew, *Norman Conquest*, p. 139.
5 OV, 3:108–10.
6 OV, 6:348–50, 2:226.

order to devastate Normandy'.[7] The garrisons of border castles regularly conducted raids into enemy territory, often in revenge for raids they had just defended against, as, for example, Rufus' *familia* did in the Vexin in 1097.[8]

The effectiveness of a castle as a base of operations depended, therefore, on the freedom of its garrison to leave the castle and act as a field force. A castle whose garrison was restricted to within its walls was basically neutralized as a force in war. William I recognized this: having built a castle at Hastings as a base of operations for the invasion of 1066, he was warned by Robert fitz Wimarc of Harold's victory at Stamford Bridge and urged to stay within the walls and refuse to engage in battle. William refused this advice, according to William of Poitiers, saying 'I will not trust myself to the strength of walls or ramparts, but engage in battle as soon as possible with Harold.'[9] As the story is told, it has a tone of boasting fearlessness. But it reveals the sensible recognition by Duke William that he could accomplish nothing behind his walls but starving his own army into defeat. Baronial rebels, on the other hand, tended not to recognize this fact. Such rebels, particularly in England, usually shut themselves in their castles and waited to be attacked one-by-one by royal forces. When a rebel castle could not be taken immediately, or proved difficult to assault, the counter-castle was an effective device. The royal troops in a counter-castle contained the raids of the rebel garrison, preventing them from doing damage or gathering supplies. Such restrictions neutralized the castle and it could then be dealt with later.[10] When rebels did recognize this limitation on the effectiveness of castles and left a subordinate – constable or wife[11] – in charge of their forts while they stayed free to move, the rebellion was the more dangerous.

As a defensive and especially as an offensive base of operations for field forces, castles were the points from which the control of the surrounding countryside or adjacent cities emanated. The castles built after the conquest may have sheltered Norman troops unprepared for campaigning,

---

7 Florence, 2:26.
8 OV, 5:216.
9 WP, p. 170.
10 E.g. OV, 4:46–8.
11 Wives were not uncommon as the leaders of defence of castles. While this would have been essentially a political role involving representing the bonds of lordship that held the garrison together and negotiating with the besiegers, the ability of the women of the warrior class to defend themselves in time of need should not be underestimated. See Chibnall, 'Women in Orderic Vitalis', pp. 114–16; she cites the story from Orderic (OV, 4:215) about Isabel, wife of Ralph of Conches, who 'in war rode armed as a knight among the knights; and she showed no less courage among the knights in hauberks and sergeants-at-arms than did the maid Camilla among the troops of Taurus'.

but when they were prepared, their sorties helped prevent rebellion or met it when it arose.[12] Mounted soldiers based in a castle could easily cover a wide area around the castle: Suger claimed of a motte-and-bailey castle at Le Puiset that 'when it was in hostile hands one dared not approach within eight or ten miles of it.'[13] The control a castle exercised over the surrounding countryside could become psychological as much as physical. That is, a strong castle, looming as a visible center of authority in the midst of a district or city, could discourage a popular rising without a soldier riding out. Control of the countryside was important on a local level because the district surrounding a castle usually contributed significantly to the castle's maintenance both in labor for repairs and, more importantly, in food. Strategically, the military control of the country emanating from royal castles kept the king's peace and enforced the authority of royal government.

Because castles were so central to the operations of field forces and to control of the countryside, they almost always formed the focus of military campaigns. Castles secured or blocked lines of communication – the rebels of 1088 depended on the castles at Rochester, Tonbridge and Pevensey for communications with Normandy, for example.[14] Thus offensive campaigns aimed at capturing enemy castles, defensive campaigns aimed at preventing the capture of friendly castles. Field armies had other aims, as the following section will discuss, but whatever their activities, armies were based on castles, and taking or defending them was central to the conquest and control of an area.

THE ROLE OF FIELD FORCES

Though the castle was central to Anglo-Norman warfare as a base of operations and thus as the focal point of campaigns and control of territory, warfare was conducted by men, not buildings. Therefore the activities of field forces – including, it is to be emphasized, castle garrisons on forays outside their forts – were what constituted warfare in the eleventh and twelfth centuries. The first step in understanding the activities of field forces is to examine what a field army was expected to accomplish and why the intended goals were important. Basically, the role of field forces was to accomplish one (or more) of four goals: to ravage and plunder; to take enemy castles and cities; to intimidate a

---

[12] OV, 2:218; WP, p. 236.
[13] Cited in Brown, *English Castles*, p. 173.
[14] OV, 4:126.

hostile nation into peace by a show of force; and to defend against enemy armies, i.e. prevent a hostile force from accomplishing any of the first three goals. Field forces accomplished each of these goals in a variety of ways and for a variety of reasons.

I

The phrase 'ravage and plunder' has an immediate emotional impact, but the activities included in this phrase should be more precisely defined before the effects of and reasons for this activity are examined.

Crops were often a target of destructive action. Whatever troops could not cart off they burnt or trampled; they uprooted vineyards and chopped down hedges. They often looted villages and cities, or simply smashed up the buildings and their contents. Fire was deadly in medieval towns, with their closely packed wooden houses: a fire started in one quarter of a city could easily spread throughout the town in a short time, and armies burnt whole cities, as well as numerous villages, to the ground in this period. Troops either drove off cattle and other livestock – on the Welsh and Scots borders many 'military raids' were little more than cattle rustling expeditions – or slaughtered them on the spot, either for food or simply to destroy the herds. Finally, the human population of a ravaged area suffered badly. Those villagers or city dwellers not killed outright were likely to be left homeless, with many of their possessions destroyed. In some areas, the Scottish marches in particular, members of the local population, especially young females, were liable to be taken off into slavery. And where crops and livestock had been seriously damaged, famine and pestilence usually followed.

Ravaging and plundering was undoubtedly the most common activity of field forces in Anglo-Norman warfare. The brutalities of warfare caused widespread suffering and the misery of the population affected by warfare was compounded by the fact that supposedly friendly armies often caused as much damage as enemy forces. The charters of William I, Rufus and Henry include grants of land and liberties to churches in compensation for damage the kings had 'unwillingly' done in the course of campaigns; and there are private charters of a similar nature, showing soldiers suffering pangs of conscience for their deeds.[15]

---

[15] CDF, nos. 1016, 625; RRAN, 1:no. 302; 2:no. 905. C. Harper-Bill, 'Piety of the Anglo-Norman Knightly Class', p. 65, discusses the close ties between warriors and monastic institutions, and the latter's spiritual duty to knights 'providing that they made some tangible gesture of repentance'. See also Chibnall, 'Feudal Society in Orderic Vitalis', p. 37.

Yet the effects of ravage and plunder should not be exaggerated. Most of the destruction took place in a limited area around the borders of the realm; when wider areas were affected, it was likely to be a one-time catastrophe, unrepeated for many years. There seems to have been some standard of brutality, moreover, for William I's infamous 'harrying of the north' in 1070 was widely regarded at the time as exceptional and unforgivably cruel.[16] Finally, there were long periods of peace, more in England than Normandy, during which war did not touch the population. Concerning these periods, it should be remembered that there was much less contrast between the conditions of war and peace in the twelfth century than in the twentieth. Crop failure, pestilence and famine could strike without the aid of war, as the ceaseless lamentations of the Anglo-Saxon Chronicle show, though the fact that they did must have made the human instigation of such disasters even harder to bear at times. But man-made misery was not the sole province of war, either. It was a violent age at all levels of society, not to mention the burdensome visitations on peasants of royal tax collectors and justices. As the *Leges Henrici Primi* claims, the people may be 'more severly harmed by corrupt judges than by bloodthirsty enemies'.[17]

The ravaging and plundering carried out by Anglo-Norman armies was rarely simply senseless destruction. Armies plundered as a means towards a variety of other ends. The following examples of ravage and plunder as a tool of warfare will also illustrate the different types of destruction discussed above. The reasons for ravaging may be divided roughly into six categories, though there is naturally some overlap.

First, ravage and plunder was used to intimidate enemy strongholds into surrender. This could be done in several ways. Ravaging the surrounding countryside could induce capitulation if the defenders had no other way to stop the destruction, or if it threatened isolation and starvation for the stronghold. The Anglo-Saxon Chronicle describes this method at work in William I's Maine campaign in 1073:[18]

In this year king William led an English and French force overseas and conquered the country of Maine; and the English damaged it severely: they destroyed vineyards and burned down cities, and damaged the country severely, and made all the country surrender to the king. And afterwards they went home to England.

[16] OV, 2:234; William Kapelle, *The Norman Conquest of the North. The Region and Its Transformation, 1000–1135* (Chapel Hill, 1979), pp. 117–19.
[17] LHP, c. 28, 2.
[18] ASC (D) 1074 (1073); cf. Florence, 2:10.

Likewise, William's march round London in 1066, the destructive effects of which are visible in Domesday, probably did much to persuade that city to open its gates to the Conqueror.

Enemy strongholds could also be intimidated into surrendering by the threat of damage to the stronghold itself. This was particularly effective against cities and towns – less so against castles, against which the threat usually had to be substantiated. Cities were especially vulnerable to the threat of firing and looting. The threat was even more effective when a leader made an example of one city early in a campaign. After Hastings, William advanced against Romney and savaged it; this brought quick surrenders from Dover and Canterbury.[19] When Henry I opened his campaign for the conquest of Normandy in 1105 he followed his father's example: he fired and looted Bayeux, the first city he stormed, inspiring other towns in his path to give in quickly.[20]

The second use of ravage and plunder was to reduce the enemy's capacity to make war. This could be done either offensively or defensively. Offensively, ravaging enemy territory disrupted the supply base and manpower pool upon which enemy forces depended. Thus when Waleran of Meulan rebelled in 1123, Henry burnt Waleran's towns of Brionne and Pont-Audemer and the surrounding district, 'so that his enemies would find nothing to support their crimes'.[21] Disrupting the supply base was to some extent the effect of devastating the area immediately surrounding a city or castle; if the stronghold were not intimidated into surrender, it was at least left with no local supplies to draw on. This could be useful if the stronghold could not be besieged immediately. In his first invasion of Maine in 1098, Rufus found himself unprepared to besiege Le Mans, but with a great mass of soldiers tore up their vines, trampled the corn and wasted the surrounding province in preparation for returning to besiege the city later.[22] In fact any damage done to enemy land for whatever reason had the secondary effect of reducing his supply base and thus his capacity to make war. Perhaps a more important effect of ravaging in terms of reducing an enemy's capacity to make war was political: by increasing disorder and discontent in an enemy's lands, the degree of control he was able to exercise in those areas was reduced. This affected his military machine directly. This was the intended (and

19 Douglas, *William the Conqueror*, p. 205.
20 OV, 6:78.
21 Symeon, *HR*, p. 274.
22 OV, 5:242.

achieved) result of the damage spread in Robert Curthose's Normandy by English royal troops in both 1090 and 1104.[23]

Defensive use of ravaging to reduce an enemy's capacity to make war involved stripping one's own land to deny its food to an invader: the 'scorched earth' defense. As mentioned above, William had some eastern coastal areas of England stripped in 1075 in anticipation of a Danish invasion. His 'harrying of the north' was in large part motivated by the same plan: he would deny Yorkshire and Northumberland to any enemy – Danish, Scottish or English – as a base of power.[24] And in effect, using ravaging against a rebel as Henry did in 1123 was as much defensive as offensive; in any case it was land in the king's realm which was affected.

Third, ravaging enemy territory was used to provoke a response from enemy forces, either to draw them into battle or to draw them away from a threatened friendly stronghold. Duke William used this method in 1066, devastating areas of Harold's own earldom, Sussex, to draw the king into an early battle. Harold, when he heard that the Normans had ravaged the vicinity of the castles, was furious and readily complied.[25] Ravaging the area around a stronghold might also draw the garrison out into a battle,[26] though this did not always turn out to the attacker's advantage, as William's defeat at Gerberoy shows.[27]

Fourth, plundering enemy territory (but not necessarily devastating it) was the most important, indeed virtually the only means of supplying the material needs of an army in enemy territory. In the right season, an army could meet almost all of its food needs by foraging.[28] Such practices were not, in fact, limited to enemy territory or even war time: the rapacity of Rufus' *familia* on royal progresses in England was, as has been noted, infamous.[29] Armies often plundered for profit as well as for immediate supplies. Seaborne attacks by the sons of Harold Godwinson in 1069 turned into little more than piratical plundering raids,[30] and the cattle rustling expeditions that characterized much of the warfare on the Welsh and Scots borders conforms to this pattern. The Worcester Chronicle offers a good description of the use of ravage and plunder as a means of gathering supplies and profit. To prepare for his rebellion against king Henry in 1102, Robert of Bellême and his allies plundered part of Staffordshire, and carried off oxen and other livestock as well as men into Wales.[31]

Leaders also used ravage and plunder to punish a rebel or invader, and

---

[23] HH, pp. 215, 234.
[24] Kapelle, *Norman Conquest of the North*, p. 119.
[25] WP, p. 180.
[26] OV, 6:204.

[27] See below, p. 168 for this battle.
[28] See below, p. 124.
[29] HH, p. 230.
[30] WJ, p. 141.
[31] Florence, 2:50.

finally simply to avenge enemy devastation of friendly territory. It was on this level that ravage and plunder became little more than senseless destruction, carried on not to further some other aim of warfare, but simply because it was the standard way of opening hostilities along a border or of carrying warfare to an opponent. As Vegetius says, 'The main and principle point in war is to secure plenty of provisions and to destroy the enemy by famine.'[32] Thus Henry of Huntingdon speaks of Henry I's attack on Fulk of Anjou in Maine in 1111 as in accordance with the laws of war, the *werrae leges*.[33] Ravage and plunder were recognized consequences of warfare, expected though not condoned. Exceptional destruction such as the 'harrying of the north' may have violated the *werrae leges*, but the usual level of damage fell within the limits of tolerance. The same chronicler who expresses such outrage at the events of 1070 reports the hostilities of 1116 between Henry I and Louis of France sadly, perhaps, but matter-of-factly: the hostility of the two kings led to 'continual attacks that devastated the lands of both'.[34]

In sum then, ravaging and plundering, one of the goals of field forces in Anglo-Norman warfare, served several purposes: to intimidate enemy strongholds into surrender; to reduce the enemy's capacity to make war; to provoke an enemy response; for supply and profit; to punish an enemy for going to war; or in revenge. It could degenerate to senseless destruction, but formed an important part of the role of field forces, and was certainly the most frequently performed act of war during this period.

II

The second goal of field armies in Anglo-Norman warfare was to take hostile castles and cities. The reasons for the importance of this goal are straightforward. If a hostile district were to be conquered, the castles and cities had to be taken, for from these strongholds control of the countryside emanated, as discussed above. When baronial rebellions arose, they were based on castles. If the rebellions were to be crushed, the castles had to be returned to royal control. Field forces could take hostile castles and cities in several ways.

First, enemy strongholds could be intimidated by the threat of damage, as discussed in the previous section. Failing this, strongholds could be blockaded into eventual starvation. This usually involved placing a small

[32] Vegetius, p. 69; translation from T.R. Phillips, *Roots of Strategy* (Philadelphia, 1940), p. 128.
[33] HH, p. 238.
[34] OV, 6:184.

force in a counter-castle blocking the main points of access to the stronghold. It was a small step up from blockade to full scale siege and assault, the most direct way of taking enemy forts. The details of methods of siege and assault, blockade, and defense of strongholds under attack will be discussed in a later section.[35] Finally, perhaps the most effective way of taking enemy strongholds was to come into the field unopposed by enemy field forces. This carried the threat to the strongholds of a siege without hope of relief or distraction of the attacker, a situation properly construed as hopeless in most cases. How did armies achieve unopposed occupation of the field of war?

With surprise and a bit of luck, a campaign could be conducted before the enemy had time to bring his field forces into action. William I achieved this in Maine in 1073, rushing into the county when Angevin forces were unprepared to oppose him. As a result, each town he approached to besiege quickly surrendered: there was nothing to counter his large army and his personal leadership.[36] More often, if the field of war were to be possessed alone, enemy armies had to be defeated in battle. It helped even more if the enemy leaders could be killed or captured in the process. This proposition carried risk due to the uncertainty of battle,[37] and the fact that defeat left the enemy in control. But if a battle were successfully waged, or the enemy forces could be driven off without a battle by vastly superior force, the strongholds were at the victor's mercy. William's conquest of England depended ultimately on his victory at Hastings, which succeeded beyond expectation in clearing the country of enemy forces. Normandy submitted to Henry after Tinchebrai, and Maine fell to Rufus in 1098 after Helias and Fulk had been defeated in the field.

The position of rebels in England illustrates well the importance of sole control of the field in taking enemy strongholds. It has already been noted that baronial rebels always shut themselves inside their castles, surrendering the countryside to royal forces. But they almost always did this in the expectation that field armies would soon arrive in England from either Normandy or Scandinavia in their support. When such support did appear, as in 1069 and 1101, it could be dealt with directly, in battle or diplomatically. Once the field support was eliminated, the rebellion collapsed. But when, as in 1075 and 1088, the support remained potential but did not arrive immediately, royal forces were in a difficult

35 See below, p. 136.
36 OV, 2:306–8.
37 See below, p. 149.

position. In effect, they could not clear the field of enemy forces. The rebel strongholds had to be dealt with as if they were supported by field forces – meaning full scale siege and assault tactics – yet no field forces could be driven off or attacked to further the siege. After Robert of Bellême's rebellion collapsed in 1102, his Welsh allies having been bribed to go home, no quarter remained from which would-be rebels could realistically expect field support. This was one reason why the 1102 revolt was the last in England in this period.

So the threat of damage, blockade, siege and assault, or winning sole possession of the field of war were the means by which field forces could take enemy castles and cities. Capturing enemy strongholds was at the heart of the offensive role of field forces in Anglo-Norman warfare, for ravage and plunder was mostly conducted, directly or indirectly, in support of this goal.

III

Anglo-Norman field armies did have one other offensive goal, however. This was to intimidate a hostile nation into peace by a show of force. In fact, the mere existence of an army, rather than any specific action it might undertake, was enough to act as a deterrent when the enemy was vulnerable to such a threat. The trouble was that only certain foes at certain times would submit to a mere show of force. The Welsh were the main target of such displays; and only in the reign of Henry, when the Anglo-Norman realm was at the height of its power and reputation, did the deterrent prove effective. We may attribute the freedom of England from rebellion in part to the deterrent effect of the royal army; but the two main episodes which illustrate this use of the royal army are Henry's Welsh expeditions of 1114 and 1121. In the former year, the king led an army into Wales; the Welsh sumitted to him following the appearance of the royal force.[38] In the latter, the Welsh burnt some castles in a rising so Henry raised a vast army from all of England, intending to ravage Wales.[39] This brought the Welsh to terms: Henry, taking hostages from them, subjected all of Wales to his terms.[40] No fighting was necessary; the mere presence of the royal army was sufficient to bring peace.

One other example of this use of the royal army shows Henry's power in the latter years of his reign. Untroubled by rebellion since 1124, despite an unpopular succession settlement, and free of foreign conflict

[38] HH, p. 239.
[39] Symeon, HR, pp. 268–9.
[40] Florence, 2:76.

since 1119, in 1128 Henry faced one of the last of his diplomatic problems. His nephew William Clito had just successfully claimed the county of Flanders, but was faced with rebellion and rival claimants supported by Henry. King Louis of France proposed to aid the new count, but Henry marched into France with his army. Staying at Epernon for eight days, 'as secure as if in his own kingdom', he compelled Louis not to aid the count.[41] Once again Henry had not had to do any actual fighting. The existence of his army in the field had been enough to enforce his will.

IV

The above three goals constitute the offensive role of Anglo-Norman field forces. The defensive half of their role was, simply, to prevent enemy field forces from accomplishing their own offensive tasks. As was pointed out above, defense (as well as offense) was based on castles. But castles were not a sufficient defense in themselves against enemy field forces.[42] Castles were tactically defensive, and their garrisons had to leave the castles or be supported by other field forces to defend the countryside from ravage and plunder. Even in defense of the castles themselves, the garrisons had to be supported by forces operating in the field, or their defensive efforts, confined to within the walls, were usually futile. When Helias of Maine invaded that county in 1099 to wrest it from Rufus' control, the unsupported defenders holding the castles in their charge sent messages to the king, urgently looking for 'relief by the royal army against the enemy force surrounding and assaulting them'.[43]

If relief were not forthcoming, the defenders of a stronghold were left with little choice. Fulk of Anjou besieged a Norman castle while Henry was occupied elsewhere in 1118; as a result the defenders, 'seeing their food gone and that no help came from any region', surrendered the tower.[44] Defense thus fell in the province of field forces, whether the task was preventing ravage and plunder of the countryside or keeping friendly castles and cities from being captured. Field forces carried out their defensive goals in several ways.

First, an enemy army could be drawn away from a friendly district or stronghold by a counter-threat to one of his districts or strongholds. If the king of France threatened a Norman castle, for instance, the Norman

41 HH, pp. 247–8.
42 Cf. Strickland, 'Securing the North', p. 187.
43 OV, 5:256.
44 OV, 6:208.

ruler could threaten a French castle rather than defend the Norman castle directly. Ravage and plunder sometimes served this purpose, as discussed earlier. Clearly this method could only work if the enemy targets threatened were more important than the friendly areas in danger; only then would the enemy prefer to defend his own possessions directly rather than carry on with his offensive. If he did not respond to the counter-threat, the campaign could result in an exchange of castles, as happened in 1094, when Rufus took Bures while Robert Curthose and Philip of France took Argentan and Hôlme.[45] Furthermore, the Anglo-Norman kings did not always have the freedom of action to use this indirect method of defense. Ringed by enemies for most of their reigns, they preferred, of necessity, more direct means of meeting enemy attacks, of which there were several.

The first possibility was to block access to the enemy's targets, using the army in conjunction with the terrain. This was Henry's intention in 1101 when he placed his army near Hastings, Robert's expected landing point, so as to be between his brother and the rest of the kingdom.[46] Harold had done the same against Henry's father in 1066, forcing William into a battle on unfavorable terrain. In the event, Robert out-flanked Henry's initial position, and the king had to do some fast marching to block his brother from London and Winchester. Rufus had this method used against him in 1098, when Helias' army blocked his first attempt at invading Maine, in February, in the middle of difficult and narrow terrain, where the blocking force could not even be brought to battle.[47]

But an enemy invasion could not always be blocked before it reached friendly territory. If an enemy army were in the process of attacking the realm, and in particular if it were threatening or actually besieging a friendly stronghold, the field forces moving to oppose it had three courses of action available to them to lift the siege: threaten or disrupt the besieger's supplies; threaten the besieger with battle; or bring him to battle. These tended to merge with each other, for they represent stages in a process of bringing increasingly direct pressure on the enemy force. At what point the besieger broke under the pressure and abandoned the siege or invasion determined how far the defending force had to push its defensive measures.

The besieger's supplies could be attacked in two ways, depending on

45 HH, p. 217.
46 Florence, 2:55.
47 OV, 5:234.

what source of supply he was using. If he were dependent on supplies carted from one of his own depots, these could be intercepted en route.[48] If he were dependent on forage, as he almost always would be in an invasion, his attack could be thwarted before it even started by use of a scorched-earth defense: again, a use of ravage and plunder as discussed above. If this were not possible or desirable, his foraging parties could be attacked and harassed. The besieger's supplies were usually drawn from a combination of cartage and forage, the latter for food, so that bringing a field army close to the besiegers along the main line of communications restricted both methods of supply. This often succeeded in driving a besieger away, especially as making attacks on foraging parties implicitly threatened the entire besieging army with battle. Thus in 1091 the arrival of Rufus in Normandy was enough to drive Robert Curthose and Robert of Bellême from their siege of Courcy; and the arrival of Henry with a strong force of English, Normans and Bretons drove Louis of France from a threatened siege in 1117.[49] To guard against relief forces, the besieger had to maintain part of his army ready for battle: at Bamburgh in 1095 Rufus compelled the local population to construct his siege works while he kept his field army mobilized and ready for battle.[50]

Full scale battle was a risky operation, and the threat of battle often sufficed to drive a besieger away. But skirmishing was not uncommon, either when the besieger's foraging parties were attacked, or when the relief forces attempted to get a party into the besieged castle in order to introduce fresh supplies and defenders into the stronghold. An attempt of the latter type, led by Theobald and Stephen of Blois, actually escalated into full scale fighting between Fulk of Anjou and Henry's relief army at Alençon in December of 1118,[51] for if a strong relief army came up against a determined besieger, a battle could result. Perhaps because they were more determined besiegers than their opponents, the Anglo-Norman kings resisted relief attempts when they besieged enemy castles. This led to two of the major battles of the period: William I's defeat at Dol in 1076 by a relief force under Philip of France; and Henry I's victory at Tinchebrai in 1106 when his brother Robert came upon him with his army to drive Henry away.[52]

In sum, then, general defensive measures undertaken by Anglo-

---

[48] This would be rare, and largely limited to supplies other than food, such as siege materials. See below, pp. 127–28 on the limits of cartage.

[49] OV, 4:236; HH, p. 240.

[50] OV, 4:282.

[51] OV, 6:208.

[52] Florence, 2:55.

Norman field forces included counter-threats and blocking access to enemy targets; measures usually used to prevent the capture of friendly strongholds included supply threats, threat of battle, and bringing the besiegers to battle. Battle could also result from blocking actions, as at Hastings. Numerous small skirmishes resulted from defenders blocking the path of an invading army or raiding fleet: contingents of Swein's fleet were repulsed at Dover, Sandwich and Ipswich in 1069 before landing in Yorkshire; rebel forces under Ralph of Norwich were blocked and defeated in battle by royal forces in 1075 when they tried to meet with rebel forces from the west.[53]

The last type of defensive action undertaken by Anglo-Norman field forces was to fall on enemy raiding parties after they had ravaged and plundered, blocking their path home and catching them loaded with plunder. This type of action was a bit after-the-fact as a defensive measure, but tended in fact to be quite effective in preventing repeat raids. The destruction of a foraging party under Edgar Atheling by the royal garrison of Lincoln has already been mentioned; in 1090 Ralph of Tosny, commanding a contingent of Rufus' *familia*, defeated a force led by Count William of Evreux as it was marching away laden with loot.[54] And of course, Bourgthérolde was just such an operation, as Henry's *familia* blocked Waleran's plundering party on its return to his castles.

V

Before examining the details of how Anglo-Norman field forces accomplished the various offensive and defensive tasks that made up their role in warfare – details of movement, maintenance and tactical action – some general comments are necessary concerning the role of field forces.

In the first place, logistics governed the operations of field forces in important and pervasive ways.[55] The strategic patterns of attack and defence, as we have seen, were shaped by supply considerations. Armies could only move where supplies were available, and could not stay in one place for too long without eating the area bare. These logistical limits

---

[53] OV, 2:226, 316.
[54] OV, 2:226; 4:216.
[55] Cf. Gillingham, 'William the Bastard at War', p. 148. The general principles of logistics and resulting patterns of warfare are discussed in two excellent works: Donald Engels, *Alexander the Great and the Logistics of the Macedonian Army* (Berkeley, 1978); and Martin van Creveld, *Supplying War. Logistics from Wallenstein to Patton* (Cambridge, 1977). Although the former looks at the ancient world and the latter starts with the seventeenth century, the basic limitations of logistics before mass mechanical transport clearly apply to the middle ages.

combined with the roles of field forces and castles made mobility the key to a field force successfully prosecuting its offensive and its defensive tasks. An army held in place was an army neutralized and perhaps incapacitated by supply problems. The importance of mobility for the garrisons of strongholds was discussed above; the same applies to field forces. If an enemy force could be trapped in a castle and blockaded there, it became useless for any role except internal defense of that particular castle. Besieging enemy strongholds had its own dangers in this respect, however, for the longer a siege went on, the longer the besieger was immobilized along with the defender. Thus in 1117, surrounded by enemies and unsure where the next rebellion would break out, Henry was unwilling to conduct a long siege which would have tied up his forces.[56]

The importance of strategic mobility to Anglo-Norman royal armies was one of the major reasons that the core of the Anglo-Norman military, the *familia*, consisted of mounted troops. The horse was the only form of strategic transport available for increasing marching speed. This had nothing to do with tactical use of the horse in battle: the Anglo-Saxon housecarls had been mounted for reasons of strategic transport; they usually fought on foot, as their successors, the *milites* of the *familia*, often did.[57] But for long distance marching housecarls and *familia* were mounted, for it was essential that the elite core of the army be able to keep pace with the king on his rapid movements from one end of the realm to the other.

The importance of mobility also accounts for two other features of Anglo-Norman warfare. The first was the extraordinary difficulty posed by Scandinavian invaders as against any other type of attacker. This difficulty arose from the invaders being based on a fleet rather than on castles. If a continental invader or a baronial rebel were driven back on his bases, he was immobilized there; even if he reemerged to attack again, it was in the same area. Measures could therefore be taken to meet and contain the attacks in advance: contingents of the royal army could be based in nearby friendly castles; the stronghold could even be assaulted and the enemy force captured or driven off. But if a Norse army were driven back on its base, the fleet, it was still mobile. It could sail off and return to attack hundreds of miles away. The danger this posed to the Anglo-Norman realm is reflected in the extraordinary measures taken under William I to counter the Scandinavian threat: the 'harrying of the

---

[56] OV, 6:200.
[57] See below, p. 156.

north' and the mass of mercenaries hired in 1085, the housing of whom led to Domesday, are the prime examples.

The second feature of Anglo-Norman warfare explained by the importance of mobility was the tendency for campaigning to cease for the winter, though this was by no means always true. To the extent that it was true – and warfare waged between mid-December and early March was rarer than at other times of the year – this was because the winter weather restricted army mobility in several ways. Bad weather made roads impassable, or at least slow. More importantly, forage was unavailable and cartage of supplies was at the same time more difficult. This meant armies had to operate in a smaller radius around their depots. The shortage of forage was most critical for horses: the winter season robbed the main form of Anglo-Norman strategic transport of its fuel and armies thus ground to a halt. It is significant that in his winter march over the Pennines to Chester in early 1070, William's men suffered from lack of food, but survived by eating the horses which died from insufficient fodder.[58] It is also significant that most of the operations conducted in the winter months were sieges, for which horses and long-range mobility were largely unnecessary.

The other important point to be made about the role of field armies in Anglo-Norman warfare is that fighting battles was not a primary goal nor even a frequent necessity. The place of battle as a tool of warfare paralleled the place of warfare as a tool of policy: it was a risky last resort, to be used only when no other tool would serve, or at best a course of action to be forced on an inferior enemy army by surprise. Military historians have often criticized medieval generalship for avoiding battles – for not being 'Clausewitzian' – but this criticism misunderstands the nature of medieval warfare and in particular the role of field armies in warfare.

---

[58] OV, 2:236. Cf. Davis, 'Warhorses of the Normans', p. 75, on the difficulty of sustaining horses in winter weather.

FIELD FORCES ON CAMPAIGN

Movement

Mobility was the key to field forces performing their role: how armies were mobile determined how they performed their roles. There were four aspects of movement: gathering an army; marching; camping; and naval transport.

I

Gathering an army worked differently depending on the amount of time available to gather the force together and how large a force had to be gathered. Clearly, if the contingents being gathered came from widely separated places, this could be a time consuming process: it would take at least two weeks to call together all the troops within one week's ride (or march) of a central rendezvous, for instance, due to the time necessary to spread the call. In addition to being slow, gathering a large force had to be arranged well in advance or it became disproportionately expensive, as early arrivals had to be housed and fed while they waited for more distant forces to arrive. Even setting a specific rendezvous date was no guarantee that a large force could be gathered conveniently. The time and expense necessary to gather a large army account in part for the generally small size of armies in Anglo-Norman warfare, as well as for the importance of the *familia regis*. Part of the *familia* always stayed with the king ready for action, and the contingents of the *familia* stationed through the kingdom would have been somewhat more easily called together than bodies of mercenaries or territorial troops who might not be prepared instantly to meet a summons.

For short notice summons, the king or his lieutenant sent out riders on the spot; these riders quickly spread the call to troops in the immediate area. We get a good example of this process at work in 1097, when a Norse fleet off north-west Mercia was mistaken for an invasion force, and the royal and territorial troops in the region hurriedly assembled from the counties of Chester and Shrewsbury, despite hostilities with the Welsh that were quickly suspended. 'The two earls who commanded in Mercia . . . quickly sent out riders through all their lands, and ordered both French and English soldiers to rush to the aid of their country against the invaders.'[59]

We have no way of knowing if a regular system or hierarchy of regional

[59] OV, 5:222.

command existed for use in such situations, with the king's riders simply contacting certain men and leaving them to send out secondary messengers. But it seems likely that some such system existed, based on the organization of the various forces called out: the command connections of the *familia*, the feudal, familial, and shrieval hierarchies of the territorial troops.[60] Certainly such organization would have been necessary for large scale use of the emergency system, as when Rufus rushed through Normandy in 1099 to meet Helias' attack in Maine – sending out messengers, he rapidly gathered a large army on the march – or when Henry moved against an invasion by Fulk of Anjou in 1117: 'dispatching riders he collected the forces of all of Normandy for the fight.'[61] Riders were also used by Swein of Denmark to raise English troops against William I in 1069 and by Fulk in the campaign of 1118 leading to Alençon.[62] Yet even using swift riders and taking advantage of the organizational structure of the armies to be raised, gathering troops took some time: Harold stopped in London for almost two weeks between Stamford and Hastings to gather fresh troops, yet still left for battle with a substantial part of his army not yet gathered.[63]

The procedure for summoning an army when more time was available differed in some respects from the procedure for short-notice summons. Messengers were sent out, but rather than carrying orders for immediate marching, they set a date and place for meeting the king, often many weeks in advance. If contingents of the *familia* were summoned, the orders may simply have been delivered verbally, but the feudal host, and perhaps the fyrd as well, probably received writs of summons, reflecting the legal, contractual nature of their military obligations. The writ issued by William I to Aethelwig, Abbot of Evesham, in 1072, illustrates this process, though the problems of feudal organization and authenticity it raises should be borne in mind.[64]

The king issued this summons almost eight weeks in advance for a campaign against Scotland which did not begin until September, and it reveals the hierarchy of authority which was probably used in short notice summons as well, though without the written orders. The time it took to gather an army was not always so extended. In 1113, Henry was winding down his first continental war. Louis of France, his last external

---

[60] If a lord's *familia* were with him, it made gathering that much easier: CDF, nos. 1325, 1326.
[61] OV, 5:256; 6:194.
[62] WJ, p. 140; *Chroniques des Comtes D'Anjou*, p. 156.
[63] Florence, 1:227.
[64] Stubbs, *Select Charters*, p. 97; see above, p. 71.

enemy, made peace in the vicinity of Gisors, near the end of March. Henry then gathered the army of all of Normandy and moved against Bellême, the last rebel stronghold in the duchy, which he besieged from 1 to 3 May.[65] Bellême was only about a week's march from Gisors,[66] so about three weeks were necessary for Henry to gather soldiers from all of Normandy.

The gathering of an army took longest when large numbers of foreign mercenaries were involved, especially when finding and hiring the soldiers formed part of the process. When William I brought horsemen, foot-soldiers and archers from 'all of France' in 1085,[67] the operation must have taken months, just as it had when William gathered his invasion force in 1066. Soldiers serving under an agreement such as the Flemish money fief could be gathered more quickly, as their terms were set in advance and they could be summoned in the same way that other royal troops were.

The 1101 money fief offers some useful details concerning the mechanics of gathering armies.[68] If Count Robert and his 1000 *milites* were to serve in England, Robert was to have the soldiers in port ready to sail 'within forty days after Count Robert shall have been summoned by the directions of a royal legate or by dispatch'. This shows the equivalence of verbal and written summons; the time allowed for Robert to gather the troops, 40 days, is in the same range as the time Henry took to gather the Norman army in 1113. Of course the total gathering time for the Flemish troops from Henry's point of view was more than 40 days, as the troops still had to be transported cross-channel and marched to join the royal army. This extra time would have been less when the Flemish soldiers were used in Normandy or Maine: the treaty allowed the soldiers eight days *ad victum* of Count Robert prior to joining Henry's army.

II

Once the army was gathered together, its rate of travel as a whole depended on several factors. Clearly these same factors also affected how quickly an army could be gathered. First, whether it was mounted or on foot. A mounted army could usually move faster than an unmounted one. Under some circumstances, though, infantry was nearly as fast as cavalry on campaign. Over good roads and with their arms and

[65] *RRAN*, 2:xxx; OV, 6:182.
[66] See below, p. 114 for a discussion of rates of march.
[67] Florence, 2:18.
[68] Chaplais, no. 1.

equipment carried on packhorses with them, infantry could make remarkably good time. And in rough terrain – heavily forested, hilly or broken ground, poor roads – travel on foot was sometimes the only way to go. The mode of travel, the road system, and the terrain were thus the factors which affected Anglo-Norman armies' rates of travel.

There is little detailed evidence for standard rates of march in Anglo-Norman warfare, that is for average daily mileage over adequate roads in open terrain. Sir Frank Stenton has calculated the following rates of travel for individual travellers and non-military groups: about 20 miles per day for mounted travellers, with up to 30 or 40 miles possible in emergencies; 8 to 15 miles per day for herds and travellers on foot; 5 to 10 miles per day for wheeled traffic, depending on the quality of the roads used.[69] This provides some guidance for military rates, as do the *Leges Henrici* on the time allowed a person summoned to court: basically, one week per county travelled up to four weeks, or six weeks and one day for an overseas summons.[70] But these are only rough guides.

One of the difficulties in determining rates of march is that the sources rarely offer detailed itineraries of an army's route. One exception to this is the itinerary of Rufus' invasion of Maine in June of 1098 given by Orderic.[71] Starting from Alençon, the king spent the first night at Rouessé-Fontaine, the second at Montbizot, and the third at Coulaines on the Sarthe, in the vicinity of Le Mans. Detachments of his army took detours along the way to take the surrenders of Fresnay, on the first day, and Ballon, on the second, both of which received royal garrisons. This works out to daily stages of approximately fifteen, ten, and ten miles for an advance into hostile territory. The advance was not, apparently, made at top speed, for William returned to Normandy shortly after arriving near Le Mans, and the return trip was made in fewer days, it seems, than the advance,[72] though we do not have the details of that march. William's was a mixed force of mounted and unmounted troops, so this gives us a fair idea of the minimum capabilities of Anglo-Norman armies on the march. Mixed forces were able to march ten to fifteen miles a day regularly, perhaps as much as twenty to twenty-five at times, estimating from the return journey. This is in fact the usual range for infantry forces of comparable equipment and methods of supply throughout military history.[73]

---

[69] Stenton, 'Road System', pp. 16–17; I believe the last figure may be low.
[70] LHP, c. 41, 2a, 2b.
[71] OV, 5:243.
[72] R. Latouche, *Histoire du Comté du Maine Pendant le Xe et le XIe Siècle* (Paris, 1910), p. 47.
[73] Cf. Alexander's rates of march: Engels, *Alexander the Great*, p. 153.

The capabilities of a smaller, all mounted force were undoubtedly higher. The mounted core of Harold Godwinson's army left many of the foot soldiers behind on the forced march from York to London. Such a force could probably make thirty to forty miles per day, though neither the horses nor the men would be very fit for fighting at the end of such a day or even on the day after a series of such marches.

The upper limits of marching capabilities are more important than trying to calculate average rates of march, for the pattern of Anglo-Norman warfare meant that armies rarely had to make 'average' marches. Rather, operations in restricted areas, in which marches of five miles a day might be the longest necessary, were connected to each other by long-range movements at high speed. William I's reign is particularly notable for such a pattern, as he often faced widely separated enemies who had to be met in a short space of time.[74]

The Anglo-Norman kings virtually never used marching at night to extend the range of an army. It was likely to do more harm in terms of fatigue and disorganization than good in terms of coming upon the enemy sooner. The only sure evidence we have of night marching is William of Jumièges' account of Harold riding all night from London to get to Hastings,[75] and the reliability of this report is not certain.

As was noted, the rates of march discussed above are for troops using adequate roads in open terrain. Surviving Roman roads were the most important militarily of the types of roads in use, but ridgeways, cartways and trackways, in use since ancient times, also bore heavy traffic.[76] Roads were vital to wheeled transport, which could not even traverse tracks, paths, or open fields. Roads were also especially important in rough terrain: cavalry in particular could not negotiate woods or broken ground without roads. Duke William went on patrol around Hastings after the invasion, but he and the 25 milites with him had to return on foot due to the roughness of the terrain; William had to carry both his and William fitz Osbern's hauberks on this return march.[77] Armies depended on roads through passes and into hilly or mountainous areas. Bridges and fords formed part of the road system and were equally vital in opening a passage over rivers that could block an army's path. In populated areas of the realm where roads were numerous and alternate paths easily available, the military historian, like the armies of the time, may almost take

[74] Cf. Gillingham, 'William the Bastard at War', p. 151.
[75] WJ, p. 134.
[76] Stenton, 'Road System', p. 6.
[77] WP, p. 168.

roads for granted. But when a single road in rough terrain or over a river was the only route available in a campaign, its importance increased, for it became a potential bottleneck, as the following examples show.

An unbridged, unfordable river held up William I for three weeks at Pontefract when he advanced against rebel forces at York in 1069. It was only after three weeks that his scouts found a deep, dangerous ford miles away which they forced in spite of enemy opposition.[78] In February of 1098 Rufus invaded Maine for the first time, but Helias and his army blocked the king at river crossings, barriers, and difficult paths through woods.[79] And Henry I's *familia* troops forced battle on Waleran's rebel forces at Bourgthérolde by blocking their return route on a road where it emerged from a wood.[80]

Thus roads were important in the movement of Anglo-Norman armies, but their importance could backfire if there were a bottleneck on an army's route. Even worse for the movement of armies were inadequate roads in rough terrain, such as confronted the English kings when they invaded Wales.[81] The terrain in this case could be a greater enemy than hostile troops. Rufus' two invasions of Wales are typical of the disastrous effect on the movement of armies of harsh terrain. In 1095 he entered the country, but unable to follow the Welsh into their mountain and forest refuges, accomplished little or nothing while losing many men and horses.[82] He tried again in 1097; when he could bring the Welsh to battle he had some success, but more often lost men in the difficult terrain. Seeing that his enemies were 'more unconquerable because of the land than their arms and men', he returned to England. He built border castles to guard against further Welsh raids, but had once again lost many men and horses on the campaign.[83]

A final aspect of the movement of Anglo-Norman armies by marching is the 'order of march', or rather the lack of one. Roman armies had a standard march formation, with the baggage train preceded and followed

---

78 OV, 2:231.
79 OV, 5:234.
80 OV, 6:348.
81 'Rough terrain' here means hilly and wooded. Such terrain posed two problems for Anglo-Norman armies. First, it was unsuited to the usual tactics of massed blocks of infantry and charges by heavy cavalry. Second, and even more important, it was non-agricultural land, which therefore posed major logistical problems. It would have been impossible to cart more than a few days supplies into areas without extensive cultivation, and small disruptions of cartage could have serious results: see the calculations in Engels, *Alexander the Great*, pp. 18–22.
82 HH, p. 218; Florence, 2:35, 39.
83 HH, p. 230; Florence, 2:41.

by the infantry; cavalry made up the van and rear, and small mounted units scouted ahead and laterally.[84] There is no evidence that Anglo-Norman royal armies had any such standard order, in large part because the components of Anglo-Norman armies were not standardized. It also reflects the fact that marching Anglo-Norman royal armies did not consistently face danger from enemy activity, though royal forces did occasionally surprise their enemies on the march, as has been noted. The crusading armies, by contrast, quickly developed a standard march formation – a hollow square of crossbowmen around the cavalry and baggage – in the face of Turkish pressure on the march.[85] It is probable that Anglo-Norman armies used some sort of pragmatic order of march when infantry and baggage carts joined mounted troops on the march: the cavalry probably made up the van and possibly the rear guard. But this is only speculative. I shall discuss scouting at greater length in a later section, and consider there the question of how enemy threats to royal forces on the march were countered.[86]

III

An aspect of the movement of Anglo-Norman armies closely connected with marching is camping, or more generally the housing of an army on the march or on campaign. The evidence for how armies were housed is not extensive, but the basic outline may be discovered from various sources. We are concerned here not with the housing of troops in friendly castles, but housing arrangements when friendly castles were not available. Such arrangements were temporary; if an army had to stay in one location for any length of time in the vicinity of enemy forces, as for instance to blockade an enemy fortress, a motte-and-bailey castle could be thrown up in a very short time, providing a base of operations more secure than a temporary campsite.

Temporary housing consisted of a combination of billeting and camping. It is rarely possible to determine exactly how the combination worked in individual cases – billeting was not always possible, camping was not always necessary. Generally camping was probably the more important element, the more so the larger the army. In friendly territory, the potential damage of billeting restricted its use somewhat. Thus Henry ordered 'all his barons and his household and marshals to take no lodging in the houses and hospice of the canons of St. Peters of York

---

[84] Vegetius, pp. 75–80.
[85] Smail, *Crusading Warfare*. pp. 156–64.
[86] See below, p. 131.

within the city, nor in their manors (*villis*) outside the city', and similarly ordered his household not to lodge in Wheatley [Oxon.] of St Mary of Abingdon.[87] However, as such orders were similar to charters of liberty, they show that billeting occurred regularly, especially for members of the king's *familia*. In enemy territory, camping could be made more secure than billeting because the troops could be housed more closely together and guards more easily posted. And a large army might not fit in the available space of a village, manor or monastery; part of the force, at least, would have had to camp in such cases.

When pitching camp an army pitched tents,[88] but we have no evidence of a standard camp layout or routine.[89] An Anglo-Norman army made camp in a suitable location,[90] pitching their tents probably without further preparation of the site. The equipment necessary for making camp in the field must have formed a large part of an army's baggage. Tents, bedding, containers for storing and preparing food, and the

---

87 *RRAN*, 2:nos. 713, 961.
88 OV, 6:198.
89 Bernard Bachrach, 'Some Observations on the Military Administration of the Norman Conquest', *Battle* 8 (1985), 5–11, argues that William the Conqueror used Roman and Byzantine models for construction of his base camp at Dives in 1066. This argument, like others based on the use of classical authors for practical matters (especially the use of Vegetius by medieval generals) is hard to prove or disprove. There is no direct evidence for such use, and the indirect arguments are almost exclusively of the form 'the Romans worked out such and such logical principle; medieval generals appear to follow the same principle; therefore they read the Roman source'. The trouble with this argument is that the principles worked out (e.g. in the case of camping, centralised distribution of supplies, maintenance of discipline, providing an exercise area for men and horses) are such basic, common sense measures that any intelligent general (or military culture as a whole) should have been able to work them out independently. The assumption that medieval generals depended widely on classical sources, especially Vegetius, seems to denigrate their intelligence. While the point is certainly arguable, I have made the assumption throughout this work that Anglo-Norman military leaders were competent enough to work out their own principles of camping, strategy, tactics, and so forth. Cf. Gillingham, 'William the Bastard at War', p. 148 n. 43, who thinks Vegetius could well have been used because 'common sense principles . . . do not date'. It is precisely the common sense parts of Vegetius – Gillingham is referring to the general strategies in Book III – that could most easily be worked out independently (indeed, the optimal course of action was virtually dictated by logistical considerations in many cases). The parts of Vegetius that clearly were not used in the middle ages (on mass conscription and training of infantry, above all – that is, almost all of Book I) were the parts that are not as immediately obvious or so closely confined by logistical considerations. See also Bachrach, 'The Practical Use of Vegetius' *De Re Militari* During the Middle Ages', *The Historian* 47 (1985), 239–55 (did Fulk have to use Vegetius to place his castles close enough to each other that his horses wouldn't wear out getting from one to another? pp. 248–9. It seems unlikely to me.)
90 Florence, 2:48–9.

saddlebags and backpacks in which some equipment was carried, all were necessary items in an army's baggage. When William I's army was defeated at Dol, it retreated in confusion and abandoned 'tents and baggage, with vessels and arms and furnishings of all kinds'.[91]

Though Anglo-Norman armies did not lay out and fortify their campsites unless a long stay were planned, elementary security precautions were not neglected when enemy forces were known to be near. When Rufus arrived at Coulaines in the vicinity of Le Mans in his invasion of Maine in June 1098, he established a secure campground: 'there were crossbowmen and archers in the vineyards by the wayside, who carefully explored the paths to prevent the enemy passing through in safety and harassed all comers with showers of missiles.'[92] But whether such provisions for camp guard formed a regular feature of Anglo-Norman camping is impossible to say. Probably they did, especially when enemy forces were nearby. Lack of campguard and a regular camp layout and discipline could have disastrous results, as Robert Curthose discovered in 1102. His army camped at Vignats while besieging the castle there when dissidents in his own party burned their own tents and disrupted the entire army. The trouble-makers fled, and in the confusion Robert's whole force broke up and retreated.[93] Campguard and order might not have prevented the initial damage, but would at least have held the army together afterwards.

IV

The last aspect of the movement of Anglo-Norman armies is naval transport. The main use of naval transport was in crossing the Channel and in moving supplies. The naval expeditions to Scotland along the coast in 1072 and 1091 in conjunction with land expeditions did not involve carrying troops. As for the use of inland waterways for moving troops, there is no example of this in the sources. Waterways supplemented roads in the civilian economy,[94] and while they seem never to have seen military use for troops, they must have been crucial for moving supplies and stocking castles. The only case of naval transport on inland waterways in the warfare of 1066 to 1135 shows the water less as a highway than as an obstacle to be crossed. In 1071, the English rebels who remained from the Scandinavian supported rebellions of 1069–70,

91 OV, 2:352.
92 OV, 5:242.
93 OV, 6:24.
94 Stenton, 'Road System', p. 20.

including Earl Morcar, Bishop Aethelwine, and the renegade Hereward, were entrenched on the isle of Ely. 'But when King William found out about this, he called out a naval force and a land force.'[95] The small boats gathered by the king ferried his troops onto the isle across a narrow part of the Fens, and routed the rebels. This was a unique operation of naval transport. The only other example of naval transport beyond the range of the Channel never got past the planning stage. In 1100 Rufus had the chance to buy Poitou from William VII of Aquitaine, so he ordered a great fleet prepared and a large expedition gathered from England.[96] His death cut the project short.

Crossing the Channel was the only regular form of naval troop transport. The problems associated with such operations were the gathering and loading of fleets; the size of fleets and ships; and the time required to make the preparations and the crossing itself.

The gathering and preparation of a fleet could take days to months, depending on the size of the fleet and the method used to raise it. Building even part of a large fleet, as Duke William had to do in 1066, was a difficult and time-consuming process: the Duke's supporters wondered whether the ships could possibly be finished in the space of a year.[97] On the other hand, the fifty-seven ships maintained for the king's service by the Cinque Ports were available on short notice. Regular royal crossings in the course of the king's itinerations probably became subject to routine organization. John Le Patourel has pointed out that a *transfretatio* was a stage in the royal progress extending well beyond the actual time spent on board ships.[98] Thus the gathering and fitting out of ships could be planned and carried out carefully in advance by officials experienced in the process.

When larger fleets needed to be gathered, the arrangements were similar to those used in gathering a large army. The date and place of meeting were set in advance, and the orders, written or verbal, sent to the appropriate authorities. The Flemish money fief of 1101 illustrates this. When Count Robert was summoned to his ports with the 1000 *milites* he owed for service in England, Henry was to find them ships and send them to one of two designated ports.[99] The most important difference between the gathering of a fleet and an army was the greater preparation a fleet needed between the time it assembled and the time it

---

95 ASC (D) 1072 (1071).
96 OV, 5:280.
97 WP, p. 156; C. Gillmor, 'Naval Logistics', pp. 115–17.
98 John Le Patourel, *The Norman Empire* (Oxford, 1976), pp. 170–1.
99 Chaplais, no. 1.

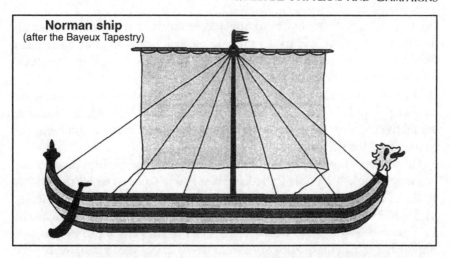

Norman ship
(after the Bayeux Tapestry)

sailed. The ships might have to be altered, depending on what they had to carry, and loading men, provisions, arms, and horses onto the ships took time. Therefore the ships had to be guarded during this time, and again during debarkation after the crossing. In the Flemish money fief, the responsibility for the safety of the king's ships fell to Count Robert: he was to ensure that the ships were safe 'going, staying and returning'.[100]

One of the most important alterations that might have to be made to ships preparing to transport a large force was to make them capable of carrying horses. Carrying horses in the relatively small ships of the time was no easy task. The special arrangements made in the Norman fleet of 1066 for the horses are shown in the Bayeux Tapestry.[101] William's ability to carry his horses with him to England was a crucial element in his subsequent success. But the transporting of horses seems to have been accomplished routinely. Count Robert's invasion fleet of 1101 carried

---

100 Chaplais, no. 1.
101 BT, pls 42, 43. It has been suggested that in these arrangements William took advantage of the knowledge gained of amphibious operations by his Norman cousins in Italy and Sicily in the decades just prior to 1066; some of these men were in his army. They in turn had probably learned the art of shipping cavalry from the Byzantines, who practiced it regularly: Douglas, *William the Conqueror*, pp. 204–5. The argument is worked out in detail in Bachrach, 'Some Observations on William the Conqueror's Horse Transports', *Technology and Culture* 25 (1985). This seems to me another case of devaluing the capabilities of non-'Roman' traditions (see note 89 above). For the alternate view that the northern tradition of shipping was sufficient to the task of transporting horses, see Gillmor, 'Naval Logistics', pp. 110–11; J. Neumann, 'Hydrographic and Ship-hydrodynamic Aspects of the Norman Invasion, A.D. 1066', *Battle* 11 (1988), 225–31.

cavalry, archers, and infantry to England.[102] And the terms of the Flemish money fief required Henry to provide enough ships so that each *miles* would have three horses, making for 3000 horses as well as the 1000 *milites* to be transported.[103]

On the numerous crossings of the Channel by small royal forces, on the other hand, horses probably did not need to be carried, for the king would have maintained horses on both sides of the Channel sufficient for himself and his personal troop.

The Bayeux Tapestry is the best source for the type of ships used by the Norman kings.[104] Double-ended, with a single square-rigged sail which could be supplemented by oars close to shore, the larger ships are clearly in the Norse style. But certainly a great variety of types and, particularly, sizes existed in the larger fleets. The variety of sizes among ships makes it impossible to calculate army sizes from fleet sizes or vice versa, even if we had a better idea of the usual capacity of medieval ships in terms of soldiers and horses. The sources do provide some figures of fleet sizes, however, and these give some idea of the problems of gathering and embarkation faced by William and his sons when they used naval transport on a large scale.

William's fleet in 1066 is said by William of Jumièges to have numbered 3000 ships.[105] This is probably an exaggeration, though not a radical one: a list of the ship obligations imposed by William on his barons totals about 777 and mentions a total for the fleet of 1100.[106] This fleet carried an army of 5000–6000 men, perhaps 3000–6000 horses (for 2000 cavalry), and equipment and some provisions for the entire army.[107] It is clear that this fleet included many small craft, for if the total fleet were 1000 ships, and only half of them were used to carry men, the average capacity of the fleet still only comes to ten or twelve men per ship exclusive of crews. By contrast, the invading army of Harald Hardraada, which was probably not very much smaller than William's own (but had no horses to be transported), arrived in England in a fleet

---

102 Florence, 2:48–9.
103 Chaplais, no. 1.
104 Naval archeology has also been providing much more data recently. See Sean McGrail, *Ancient Boats in Northwest Europe: The Archaeology of Water Transport to AD 1500* (London, 1987).
105 WJ, p. 134.
106 Douglas, *William the Conqueror*, p. 190; Van Houts, 'Ship List', p. 165.
107 Cf. the calculations in Bachrach, 'Military Administration', pp. 3–4, who places the figures for men a bit higher. Sailors and non-combatants would raise my numbers closer to Bachrach's, though I think his figures for combatants are too large.

of perhaps three hundred ships.[108] Swein Estrithson's invasion in 1069 is said to have comprised 240 ships.[109] The number of ships in fleets raised by the Norman kings is, curiously, almost never specified. Henry is said to have sailed to Normandy in 1104 'with a great fleet' and Rufus set out for Scotland in 1091 'with a fleet of no small size'[110] but no numbers are mentioned.

Given favorable winds, crossing the Channel took one day. But favorable winds were not always forthcoming. Duke William waited more than a month for a southerly wind in August and September 1066,[111] and in 1135 Henry was ready to sail with a contingent of soldiers but contrary winds delayed him.[112] Storms also posed a danger. The fleet Rufus prepared for Scotland in 1091 was sunk in a storm; despite this disaster, the king himself crossed to Normandy in the teeth of a storm in 1099, saying he had never heard of a king who had drowned.[113] But the danger of storms and the difficulties with the winds meant that crossings had to be accomplished in one shot: ferrying an army across in relays would have been extremely slow and difficult, and would have increased the danger both to the fleet from bad weather and to the army, which would have had to split into groups for days at a time. It has been suggested by J. Beeler that Duke William's army may have been shuttled across in 1066,[114] but if his fleet had to wait a month for southerly winds, how did any of his ships return to Normandy in the face of the now southerly wind to pick up a second load of soldiers? The time a shuttle might have been expected to take is indicated by the following provision of the Flemish money fief, in case Henry could not provide enough ships to take all 1000 *milites* at once: 'the remaining *milites* shall wait in port from the day that the ships leave for one whole month unless within the month they sail over.'[115]

---

[108] Douglas, *William the Conqueror*, p. 193. The White Ship went down with between 200 and 300 men (and women) on board: Symeon, HR, p. 259; OV, 6:296; but the ship was overloaded with passengers and carried nothing else but some casks of wine and the king's treasure (OV, 6:296), so this should not be taken to indicate the normal capacity of a large ship. Of course even estimating the size of the Scandinavian fleet and army is open to much controversy, as few of the figures we have are very reliable.

[109] ASC (E) 1069.

[110] OV, 6:62; Florence, 2:28.

[111] The story of William's delay by winds has recently come to be doubted by some scholars: Chibnall, *Anglo-Norman England, 1066–1166*, p. 11; Bachrach, 'Military Administration', pp. 8–9. But cf. Gillmor, 'Naval Logistics', p. 126.

[112] OV, 6:444.

[113] Florence, 2:28; HH, p. 231.

[114] Beeler, *Warfare in England*, pp. 9, n. 8; 14, n. 21.

[115] Chaplais, no. 1.

In sum, the larger the force to be carried, the more difficult and slow naval transport became. Carrying horses as well as men increased the difficulty. The regular use of cross-Channel transport was mostly by small, unmounted forces usually consisting of the king and his personal troop. This reduced to a minimum the problems of gathering a fleet and preparing it for sailing. The weather could cause problems to a small fleet, however. Naval transport was therefore clearly secondary to marching in the movement of Anglo-Norman armies.

Maintenance

Once an army was gathered and on campaign, it had to be maintained. This entailed three different sorts of actions. The army's material needs had to be met through a system of supply. Its security on campaign was guaranteed to a greater or lesser extent by scouts who would warn of enemy forces. And the army's morale and coherence had to be maintained by strong discipline, an often overlooked factor in the maintenance of armed-forces.

I

Supplies, primarily of food, could be obtained by an army on campaign in two ways: by foraging; and from central depots. Use of depots required cartage of supplies both to and from the depot. Once obtained, supplies had to be prepared and distributed. Finally, the effects of inadequate or tainted supplies could be as devastating to an army as enemy action.

Assuming that royal armies were fully equipped in terms of clothing, arms and armor when they went on campaign, food was then the major item of supply that needed constant replenishment. We have no way of knowing what standard daily rations were for Anglo-Norman soldiers, but we can get some idea of the most common foods, especially if we assume – as seems reasonable in this case – that the Pipe Roll records of Henry II's reign offer some guidance for earlier reigns. To take one example, about £550 were spent on food for Henry's Irish expedition of 1171.[116] More than three-fifths of this total, over £320, was spent on wheat. Bread was the staple of Anglo-Norman armies. Another £120 or so was spent on *bacones*; this proportion may be a bit high for the earlier period, but certainly cured pork was the primary source of protein for

---

[116] *PR 18 HII, passim,* for this and the following figures.

124

Anglo-Norman soldiers. The remainder but for £65 was spent on beans, salt and cheese; an unspecified amount was spent on wine.[117]

The men of an army were not the only consumers of food, however. Fodder for horses was a major part of the supply requirements of Anglo-Norman armies. Horses need at least ten pounds of hay each per day simply for maintenance, plus at least eight gallons of water per day. For doing heavy work – and carrying fully armed and armored men about the countryside certainly qualifies as heavy work – their diet must be supplemented to some extent by more nutritious foods, meaning at least another ten pounds of oats a day.[118] In Henry II's expedition, £65 of the total spent on food went to buy oats, presumably for the horses in the army.

It was noted above in connection with naval transport that the 1000 *milites* provided by the Flemish money fief expected to have three horses for each man. Spare chargers were no mere luxury. The supply requirements of horses made extra mounts a necessity. Even when a horse's diet is supplemented by oats, it can only eat enough to sustain about three hours of heavy work per day. If it is worked more than this day after day, it will lose weight; in five or six days it will break down and become unusable for any work.[119] A knight with three horses could use each horse every three days and so keep all in good health. But of course the necessity to keep three horses per cavalryman greatly increased the fodder requirements of an army. This supply restriction created perhaps the severest limit on the size of Anglo-Norman armies, at least when they were mounted. Clearly, keeping an army supplied with food was one of the heaviest burdens on the military system and a constant problem on campaign.

Foraging for supplies was easier than relying on depots, for there was no problem of transportation to deal with. Indeed, food supplies simply could not be carted more than a few days march. Trying to cart supplies further required more animals than would have been readily available, and beyond a certain range actually became impossible, as the pack animals would consume more than they could carry.[120] But forage, too, had several limitations. Its availability dependended on the time of year

---

117 Engels, *Alexander the Great*, pp. 18–19 and Appendix 1, works out the minimum daily rations for men and animals from a wide range of scientific and historical data.

118 Engels, *Alexander the Great*, p. 19 and Appendix 1.

119 For transport of supplies, horses and mules can do up to eight hours of lighter work per day, a significant advantage over oxen which can only do five: Engels, *Alexander the Great*, p. 15. See OV, 5:242 on the need for oats, 'without which it is almost impossible to keep up the strength of horses in western climates'.

120 Engels, *Alexander the Great*, pp. 19–22 for the calculations.

and the productivity of the land, and foraging could not continue for any length of time in the same place. Forage might be unavailable as a matter of policy, as well. It could cause considerable damage to the countryside – it was one of the uses of ravage and plunder discussed above – and the Norman kings therefore preferred when possible to keep their armies from foraging on friendly territory. A few examples will illustrate these problems.

The problems of winter campaigning were mentioned above: winter particularly limited forage, especially for horses. But at other times, too, forage was not readily available. In his invasion of Maine in the early summer of 1098, Rufus reached Le Mans in June, but could not immediately besiege the city for any length of time because of supply problems. His men and horses both suffered from food shortages, since it was the time between the old and new harvests. As a result he sent his forces home, ordered them to have their own harvests collected into their barns, and to be ready after the crops were gathered to besiege the enemies' castles.[121] The concern with the corn harvest once again emphasizes the primary place of bread in the military and civilian diets.

The difficulties of forage when an army stayed in a limited area are shown at several important stages of the 1066 campaign. Both Harold's army, quartered with his fleet along the south coast and on the Isle of Wight all summer and autumn, and William's army, quartered at the mouth of the Dives where the fleet was concentrated and waited for favorable winds, faced supply problems. William managed his better. He strictly forbade plunder and paid his troops regularly, and thereby succeeded in keeping the army supplied by regular markets, though in the end his supplies were running short and he only just kept his army together.[122] Harold's army, though, ate its district bare, and on 8 September, with provisions exhausted, both the fleet and the infantry forces returned home.[123] This was a critical turning point in the campaign. The second crisis of the campaign also resulted from supply problems. William had ravaged the areas around his beachhead to draw Harold into an early engagement. An early battle was vital to William, for his army was restricted to the Hastings peninsula and would quickly have run out of food if it could not have moved out safely. Indeed part of his army was already out foraging on the very morning of the battle, and had to be

121 OV, 5:242–4.
122 WP, pp. 150, 160.
123 Florence, 1:225.

called in quickly.[124] The Duke's success in provoking Harold to battle so soon probably saved his invasion.

Further examples of the importance of forage to the conduct of Anglo-Norman warfare could be cited; some of these, such as William's 'harrying of the north' to prevent enemy forces foraging in the area, were discussed in the relevant sections on ravage and plunder above. But its importance, as well as the major limitations on forage as a source of supply, should be clear.

When an army could not forage, it had to depend on supplies gathered in advance in central depots. For some items, such as arrows, replacement weapons and armor, and some food items (wine, salt pork), armies had to depend on depots or do without. But even for items such as hay for fodder, establishing depots ensured a regular and plentiful supply. There were five major sites in Normandy where 'le foin de roi' was gathered: Caen, Le Vaudreuil, Rouen, Avranches and Bonneville-sur-Touques.[125] As these were all important ducal residences, it is probable that the supplies were as useful in maintaining the ducal hunt as the ducal cavalry, though this does not detract from their military importance. For this same reason there were undoubtedly supply depots at royal residences in England, notably Woodstock under Henry. But both in England and the duchy, any royal castle could be and probably was a depot for royal forces – it had to be stocked with at least enough food and arms to withstand a siege.

The use of depots as a source of supply required efficient arrangements for transport. Materials had first to be carried to the fortress to establish the depot and then, if necessary, carried to an army in the field based on the depot. Thus when Rufus threatened Helias of Maine with a siege of Le Mans at the end of 1097, he warned him to rebuild his walls against the royal army, for he would have 'carts laden with bolts and arrows drawn there by oxen'; Rufus himself and his legions of soldiers would precede them to Helias' gates, 'even as the shouting oxherds hurry them along'.[126] In the event, as we saw above, when Rufus did arrive at Le Mans in June of 1098, his ox-drawn carts may have given him a plentiful supply of spears and arrows, but neither they nor the land of the district

---

124 WP, p. 180.

125 Musset, 'Le foin du seigneur roi', p. 375.

126 OV, 5:232. The implication that the ox drawn carts would arrive more slowly than the rest of the army is to be believed. Oxen can not only work less than horses, they are much slower, being capable of sustained travel at only 2–3 miles per hour: Engels, *Alexander the Great*, p. 15. In addition, the poor quality of the road system meant that wheeled transport would be slower than using pack animals.

could provide him with food, and he had to retire until they could. By contrast, the transport of supplies worked admirably for royal forces besieging Norwich for three months in 1075. The army received daily reinforcements, and ample supplies of food and other necessities arrived for the prosecution of the siege.[127]

The use of cartage to supply an army dependended on good roads to an even greater extent than the movement of armies. Packhorses reduced this problem; one of a knight's horses was certainly a packhorse. Shipping on suitable waterways could also supplement cartage: William I's invasion of Scotland in 1072 combined land and sea operations in part so that the fleet could carry supplies for the army as it advanced far into hostile territory along less than perfect roads. Similarly, successful Norman advances into Wales tended to take place along the coast. Rufus' expeditions into the interior of the country foundered mostly because the land provided no forage and the country's roads did not allow adequate cartage of supplies to the royal army. Naval transport was the only way to supply large stationary forces, so the gathering of armies in advance had to take place on a coast or navigable river.[128]

It was one thing to get supplies to an army, it was another to prepare them and distribute them to the individual soldiers of an army. On this subject there is much less information available than for forage and cartage. Preparation of food required that a certain number of cooks and bakers accompany an army in the field;[129] some provision for grinding grain foraged on the spot must also have been made, though we do not know how this took place. As mentioned above, we have no idea what the standard daily rations were in Anglo-Norman royal armies, but we do know that standard daily rations existed. The allowances given for officers of the *familia* in the *Constitutio Domus Regis*[130] are little guide for rank and file soldiers, but do show that daily allowances were established; they were what soldiers who were *ad victum regis* received *sicut mos est reddere familie sue*.[131] Daily distribution (as opposed to periodic distribution calculated on daily rates) is indicated in the 1066 campaign. In the

---

127 OV, 2:316. Both for supplying castles and for supplying a long siege, particularly one such as this in friendly territory, transport of supplies by water – sea, river and canal – would have been vital, as the limits on animal's food carrying capacity would soon make land transport inadequate.

128 See Bachrach, 'Military Administration', p. 8 and *passim*, on William's camp at Dives and the logistical problems associated with maintaining it.

129 OV, 6:472.

130 See above, p. 61.

131 Chaplais, no. 1.

last stages of his sojourn at St Valery waiting for favorable winds, William saw his supplies running short. To keep his army together, he increased the daily rations to disguise the shortage.[132] But this still gives us no idea how distribution was actually handled.

The most we can conclude is that soldiers received their rations, as well as their wages and more periodic reimbursements (about which more below), from their officers. Orderic assumes this as common knowledge when he explains the promotion of churchmen at court to higher posts in the church by comparison with the military practice: clerks accept posts for service at court, he says unfavorably, 'like recruits who receive wages from their officers for their service in war'.[133]

Two other problems connected with the distribution of supplies also present questions which are interesting but virtually unanswerable. First, some supplies – arms, armor, replacement horses – could not be distributed daily. Losses must have been made up when necessary, but was immediate replacement always possible? If, as seems probable, the government made losses good by paying the soldier the replacement value of the armor or horse and leaving procurement to him, when was the payment made? As soon as possible, or through a periodic reckoning of accounts? Probably payments for replacement of losses were included in the 'gifts and allowances which are made from the Treasury of the king and from his chamber' and for which the master-marshal kept tallies.[134]

Second, and more difficult, is how the professional soldiers of the *familia* and its mercenary extensions, who were *ad victum regis*, and the territorial soldiers of the fyrd and feudal host, who were not, were supplied at the same time but by different systems. Once again we can only speculate as to what seems most probable. Soldiers not *ad victum regis* must have had to buy their rations from the *familia* or from local markets when possible; it will be remembered that half of the fyrd's 20s. was *ad victum*. Such purchasing may have been done by the officers of the soldiers – by a baron for his *familia*, for example – as this would have made keeping track of the distribution of rations substantially easier. Or perhaps in practice, all the king's soldiers, mercenary and territorial, served *ad victum regis* for the sake of efficiency and convenience, as they certainly did in later periods.[135]

Supply problems could be deadly for armies in the field, for insufficient

132 WP, p. 160.
133 OV, 2:268.
134 *Const. Domus Regis*, in *EHD*, 2:426.
135 Stubbs, *Select Charters*, p. 174, for Henry II. Service by 'feudal' troops at the king's expense under Edward I is well known.

or tainted supplies of food resulted in famine and disease. Until World War I, these two horsemen of the apocalypse always caused more casualties than combat in the conduct of warfare, so this was a serious problem: as Vegetius says, 'famine makes greater havoc in an army than the enemy, and is more terrible than the sword'.[136] The sites most vulnerable to an outbreak of pestilence were besieged cities. If a siege went on for any length of time, it was likely to produce a combination of conditions highly conducive to diseases: overcrowding, especially if the defensive garrison were large; food shortages; and a dearth of fresh food in the later stages of the siege. For example, plague broke out in Rochester while Rufus besieged the city in 1088.[137] But of more concern to the Anglo-Norman kings when they led an army into the field was tainted or improperly prepared supplies, for none of the Norman kings was ever besieged. William I, for example, ran into the disease problem during the 1066 campaign. In Dover, he and a large part of his army, having eaten freshly butchered meat and drunk local water, came down with dysentery.[138] This stopped the Conqueror's progress for several weeks and was the greatest threat to his adventure's success – and to his own life – outside of the battle of Hastings. The fact that we know of very few such outbreaks of dysentery in Anglo-Norman royal armies between 1066 and 1135 attests to the effectiveness of the royal supply system. Thus the best description of the causes and effects of dysentery in a medieval army comes from just after 1135 and concerns an Angevin rather than an Anglo-Norman army. In 1137 the Angevins invaded Normandy; as they marched through the duchy, they plundered for food:[139]

> They slaughtered many flocks and herds, and ate the meat raw or half-cooked without salt or bread . . . [and] there were not enough cooks and bakers to serve such a multitude. . . . As a result of foolishly eating uncooked food, . . . almost all suffered from dysentery, and plagued by diarrhea left behind them a trail of filth.

This is an excellent example of the importance of a good supply system, including provisions not just for obtaining food but for preparing it as well, to the maintenance of an army in the field. The success of the

---

[136] Vegetius, p. 69; trans from Phillips, *Roots of Strategy*, p. 128; van Creveld, *Supplying War*, p. 37.
[137] OV, 4:128.
[138] WP, p. 212.
[139] OV, 6:472.

Anglo-Norman kings in keeping their armies generally well supplied and healthy again deserves emphasis.

II

Unlike supply, scouting was not an activity always or strictly necessary for the maintenance of an army in the field. But when it did occur, its role was to protect an army from destruction by surprise attack, or more generally to warn of enemy strengths and actions, so it may be included as an action of maintenance.

From earliest times to the motorizing of warfare in the twentieth century, scouting has been the province of mounted troops because of their mobility. It has been claimed by J.E. Morris, among others, that in the twelfth century 'practically all cavalry action was shock action, and the only duty of cavalry was to charge, not to scout'.[140] This does not, however, seem to be true. Scouting by mounted troops was perhaps not always the automatic action, performed at all times and in an organized way, that it was in later centuries, when cavalry acted as the 'eyes' of an army. Anglo-Norman scouting was sometimes haphazard, often ineffective even when attempted, and at times supplemented by the reports of non-military envoys. But when it did take place, mounted troops participated whenever possible. A few examples will demonstrate this, and show both the successes and shortcomings of Anglo-Norman scouting.

After he had landed in England in 1066, William's first news of Harold's army came from one Robert fitz Wimarc, a Norman living in England, who warned William of Harold's victory at Stamford Bridge and his advance south at the head of a 'most numerous and powerful' army.[141] But when Harold's army got nearer, William took matters into his own hands: he sent out selected cavalrymen as scouts to warn of the enemy advance.[142] Unlike Harald Hardraada's army, William's had plenty of warning of Godwinson's advance and averted an overwhelming surprise attack.

A classic example of cavalry scouting action occurred early in 1068, as William moved to besiege the rebel city of Exeter. 'The king first rode closer with five hundred *equites* to scout out the field and fortifications, and find out what the enemy were doing.'[143] It was only after he and his

---

[140] J.E. Morris, 'Mounted Infantry in Medieval Warfare', *TRHS* 8 (1914), 78.
[141] WP, p. 170.
[142] WP, p. 180.
[143] OV, 2:212.

cavalry had scouted the situation that the rest of his army, including a number of English infantry, was brought up to prosecute the siege.

Scouts were also in action before the battle of Brémule, as well, but on the French side. Four *milites*, posted by Louis as lookouts while his army foraged, spotted Henry's army a good ways away, and reported this to the king. As the two forces approached each other, they were informed of each other's presence, though with no great precision, by messengers and 'rumor-mongers' spreading reports every which way; soon, it seems, everyone in the vicinity knew that the two kings had advanced with their armies and could join battle immediately if they wanted to.[144] Yet the events also demonstrate the shortcomings of both sides' scouting. Neither king seems to have known exactly how close or where his opponent's army was; the English finally took their bearings from the smoke rising from a barn burnt by the French troops.

Having cited these examples, however, it must be admitted that there are few cases of scouting to be found in the sources. This is partly because armies scouted automatically and authors could take it for granted. It was important enough that William I, for example, regularly did his own scouting.[145] But at times, even when regularly performed, Anglo-Norman scouting miscarried. William in fact suffered from lack of scouting at Dol in 1076, for Philip's relief army seems to have caught him by surprise.[146] Yet in general, Anglo-Norman royal armies seem to have been secure on the march and in camp, despite the difficulties of scouting. In considering why, it is interesting to bear in mind at the same time the related question of the lack of a standard order of march for English royal armies. Probably several factors contributed to the security of royal armies.

First, their enemies resembled them very closely in weaponry, tactics and the social conventions of warfare, so that their attacks presented no unusual problems requiring extra time or organization to prepare for. The contrast with the problems presented to crusading armies by the Turks is again instructive.

Second, and perhaps more important, was the small size of armies. An army of several hundred mounted troops was its own scouting column, and was not much more vulnerable to attack when on the march than when drawn up for battle. Even when royal armies included substantial numbers of infantry, their overall numbers were not large, as has been

---

[144] OV, 6:234.

[145] Gillingham, 'William the Bastard at War', p. 151.

[146] OV, 6:236. William was by this time getting corpulent and probably no longer led scouting expeditions himself.

noted. The effectiveness of attacks on an army in motion is largely based on forcing the army to fight before it is in battle formation. The smaller an army is, the less time it takes to form up for battle. It seems likely that the mounted element in royal armies could have delayed any surprise attack long enough to allow the few thousand infantry in the column to form up. Surprise attacks against an army on the march therefore offered little extra advantage to the attacker, leaving the risk of battle relatively high. The attacks by royal forces against enemy forces on the march were, it should be remembered, against troops heavily laden with plunder and feeling secure at the end of a raid. In fact foraging and plundering, not marching, was most likely to disperse an army and make it vulnerable to surprise.

The small size of armies, then, would account for the lack of a standard order of march and camp layout and for the infrequency of independent scouting activity. Ensuring security on the march and in camp was thus the aspect of maintenance most easily seen to by the Anglo-Norman military system.

III

No matter what the size or composition of an army, on the other hand, discipline was as necessary as supplies in keeping it together and functioning. It prevented desertion, kept morale up, and laid the foundation for success in battle.[147] The regulations established by the Anglo-Norman kings concerning discipline, particulary those relating to relations between the *familia* and the outside world, were discussed earlier. What we are concerned with here is the evidence for enforcement of discipline within royal forces on campaign.

Discipline was in the first instance dependent on strong, successful leadership. As has been noted of the Conqueror, 'William's control over his men was the discipline of a successful general.'[148] Success was a key ingredient in the formula for discipline because obedience resulted from a combination of promised rewards and threatened punishments. Only a general with a record of success – or at least able convincingly to promise success – could hold forth to the common troops the prospect of suitable rewards in the course of a campaign, including plunder and loot at opportune moments. Controlling plunder was in fact one of the main

---

147 Discipline is the constant theme of Vegetius.
148 Matthew, *Norman Conquest*, p. 72.

disciplinary tasks of the leaders of royal forces. The opportune moments had to be chosen by the leader, not the soldiers, and if plundering got out of control, the army could become highly disorganized and even damage itself: William I's army became disordered when the burning of Mantes in 1087 got out of hand, and the Conqueror himself was mortally injured in the city.[149] Troops could only be prevented from plundering if they could reasonably expect greater rewards at some point in the future. The promise of plunder in England undoubtedly played a large part in William's successfully preventing plunder while his army waited for favorable winds at Dives; he backed up the promise with immediate incentives, regularly paying the *milites* their wages.[150]

Positive incentives alone, however, could not have kept soldiers in line. Individuals who violated orders or regulations could expect harsh punishments backed up by the full force of the Anglo-Norman legal system. William I set the pattern for royal forces immediately after his coronation: 'as he restrained the people with arms, so he restrained the army with laws'. He prohibited rape, murder, drunkenness, and plundering; and set up the machinery of enforcement: he appointed judges, 'whom the common soldiers fear', and decreed severe penalties for those who committed crimes.[151] Similarly, Rufus established laws and promoted order in his army before the siege of Rochester in 1088;[152] Henry's extensive reforms at the outset of the 1105 campaign were discussed earlier.[153] The *Leges Henrici* reflect these measures, specifying murder or breach of the peace in the *familia* or any army, and desertion from the field of battle – either on land or sea – as punishable crimes.[154]

The role of subordinate commanders in the maintenance of discipline was important. Legally, all soldiers were in the surety of their lords.[155] Clearly, as with the distribution of supplies, the army had to be broken into small units for the regular enforcement of rules and maintenance of order. Orderic characterizes an Angevin army which did not maintain such divisions as a hord of *indisciplinati*; the magnates, 'who in a properly

---

[149] Douglas, *William the Conqueror*, p. 358.
[150] WP, p. 150.
[151] WP, p. 232.
[152] Florence, 2:22–3.
[153] See above, p. 63.
[154] LHP, c. 10, 1; c. 13, 12; c. 80, 1.
[155] LHP, c. 8, 2a.

ordered army should have led separate units', were 'ignorant of the strictness of discipline of Roman warfare'.[156]

Discipline and order were closely related to loyalty, and it would seem that some of the same devices used by the Anglo-Norman kings to maintain the loyalty of their troops – oaths, regular pay, the hope of future rewards, personal friendship – also contributed to good order in the *familia* and its extensions. Furthermore, there is evidence, as Prestwich has pointed out, of a 'recognized professional pride and standing' among mercenary soldiers,[157] which undoubtedly made order easier to keep and prevented desertions. Good discipline made all an army's tasks easier and safer to perform: the disastrous lack of camp discipline in Duke Robert's army at Vignats in 1102 has been noted.[158]

Evidence for enforcement of discipline by the Norman kings on campaign is not all that plentiful, but this may be taken as confirmation of the general impression given by the sources that the internal discipline of royal forces was consistently good. Repeated episodes of disciplining would indicate a chronic problem rather than effective measures. It is significant that the examples we do have come from early in each of the three reigns of the period: at London in 1066, Rochester in 1088, and Carentan in 1105. Once established, it seems, discipline in royal forces was secure. This contributed greatly to the maintenance of Anglo-Norman armies on campaign. The critical role of discipline in battle will be discussed further in the next chapter.

---

[156] OV, 6:472, and n. 1. Too much should not be read into the reference to 'proper Roman discipline': Orderic was probably referring to Vegetius, whose theme, as I noted above, is discipline. Vegetius' work was well known in monastic circles but, I have argued, of less relevance among the practitioners of warfare in the twelfth century. But the division of armies into units for the purpose of keeping order may be taken at face value.

[157] Prestwich, 'War and Finance', p. 28; OV, 6:22; 28–9; 350.

[158] See above, p. 119.

Chapter Five

WARFARE II:
SIEGES AND BATTLES

SIEGE WARFARE

Besieging castles made up the vast majority of Anglo-Norman tactical action. This point does not receive the emphasis it should. Pitched battles were few and far between; even minor encounters were rare, and often occurred in the vicinity of a siege, at which point siege and battle tactics tended to become intertwined. The relative frequency of sieges as against battles reflects a real difference in intent, as outlined in the discussion of the role of field forces: sieges, as a means of taking enemy castles and cities, were actively sought after, whereas battles were avoided until they became absolutely necessary, for they furthered the primary goals of field forces only indirectly and were risky. Anglo-Norman field armies of any size were raised with sieges in mind, which accounts for the prominence of infantry forces in them. Even the elements of royal forces which were mounted for marching would normally have had to dismount to take part in assaults on a fortress, pointing out the distinction between use of the horse as a means of transport and use of the horse as a 'weapon', as it were, a distinction which will be important to bear in mind when battle tactics are examined.

Anglo-Norman siege tactics are relatively well known, for siege tactics at this time had not changed significantly since classical times, and would remain basically unchanged for several more centuries.[1] I shall discuss the techniques of attack first, then the measures open to defenders to resist assaults.

The first step in approaching a stronghold short of a full scale siege was to blockade it with troops placed in one or more counter-castles, or siege works on a scale comparable with the castle itself. The purpose of the

---

[1] Brown, *English Castles*, pp. 175–81, contains a useful discussion of common siege tactics. Cf. Vegetius, Book IV, for Roman siege techniques.

counter-castle and its garrison was to block access to and egress from the target castle. This served the double purpose of restricting the activities of the target castle's garrison, neutralizing it as a force in war, and preventing foraging by the garrison or the introduction of fresh supplies into the target castle, so as eventually to starve it into surrender. William I used four counter-castles to invest Rémalard, held by supporters of his rebellious son Robert, in 1079.[2] One advantage of using counter-castles was that it allowed prosecution of the blockade with a minimum of men, leaving the bulk of the king's army free to move against other targets. Thus in 1095 Rufus moved against Robert of Mowbray's castle at Bamburgh. But when he saw that it would be virtually impregnable to assault, he built a counter-castle which he named 'Malveisin', or Bad Neighbor.[3] During construction of the castle the king kept his field army mobilized,[4] and then marched against the Welsh, who had risen in revolt the year before. Similarly, Henry blockaded Robert of Bellême's castle at Arundel with counter-castles while he prepared his army to move against the rebel's strongholds at Bridgnorth and Shrewsbury.[5] Often, however, a counter-castle served as a base for closer investment and assault of the target castle by the king's entire army. Rufus built fortified siege towers at Rochester in 1088 to block egress from the castle, while at the same time closely investing the stronghold with a large field force,[6] so that one suspects the siege towers were erected to prevent the rebels escaping from the pressure of the attackers. Henry also used counter-castles in conjunction with his entire army against Brionne, held by Waleran of Meulan's steward against the king in April of 1124. Raising a great army, the king quickly constructed two siege-castles, which shortly brought the enemy to terms.[7] The assaults launched from the king's counter-castles resulted in the burning of the town before the garrison gave up.

If the besiegers of a castle did move to invest it more closely, three methods were commonly used to break down the defenses. First, machines of various types were used to weaken the actual walls of the stronghold, as well as to harry the defenders. Second, direct assault by storming the walls was effective if the walls had first been damaged, or it they were weakly defended. Finally, the defenses and the defenders could be burnt out.

The use of machines in siege work was a common technique. They were used in two different ways, generally. Bombardment machines were

2 OV, 2:360.
3 HH, p. 218.
4 OV, 4:282.

5 Florence, 2:49–50.
6 OV, 4:126.
7 OV, 6:354.

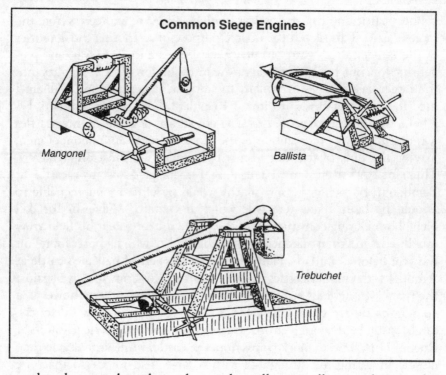

Common Siege Engines

Mangonel

Ballista

Trebuchet

used to batter a breach in the castle walls, as well as to damage the buildings inside a fortified area and harass and kill the defenders – in modern terms, to 'soften up' the target. Close assault methods of wall demolition such as rams and mining were used solely to open a path for storming parties.

Bombardment machines operated on one of three principles of applying force. The sources for Anglo-Norman warfare between 1066 and 1135 rarely offer enough detail about the machines in use at a siege for the historian to decide which was at work, nor is the terminology used in the sources of earlier and later periods always consistent in distinguishing the three. But the main types of bombardment machine were the mangonel, the trebuchet, and the ballista. The first gained its force from torsion, i.e. the torque of tightly twisted strands of rope or other material (the Romans preferred human hair). The second used a counterweight, suddenly released, to hurl its projectiles; of later invention than the mangonel (probably, in fact, after 1135), it was more accurate and powerful. Both were used mainly to hurl stones against walls and towers. The third type of machine, the ballista, used tension, i.e. the principle of a bow. It was, in fact, a large crossbow used to hurl spears and javelins with great accuracy at human targets. (More accurately, the crossbow was a handheld version of the ballista, by far the older device.) Finally, bombardment of a castle and its defenders was at times made more effective by the use of siege towers. Machines – ballistae particularly – placed on such platforms could fire down into a stronghold, greatly increasing their deadliness.

The use of such siege machinery by Anglo-Norman forces is fairly regularly illustrated throughout the sources. Robert of Bellême directed the use of 'a variety of siege engines', including a 'huge machine which is called a *berefredum*' – a siege tower – against Courcy in 1091, though to no avail, and of siege towers and catapults which 'threw huge stones onto the town and inhabitants' of Breval in 1092.[8] Henry directed the use of siege machines against Bridgnorth in 1102,[9] and against Waleran of Meulan's castle at Pont-Audemer in 1123, where he built a wooden tower twenty-four feet taller than the castle walls. Arrows and stones showered into the castle from this tower, inducing the garrison to surrender.[10] Royal forces found themselves on the receiving end of such attacks, as well. In 1118 Fulk of Anjou attacked La Motte-Gautier-de-Clinchamp in Maine, held by a detachment of Henry's *familia*. Repeated assaults and heavy bombardment of the castle with stones forced the 140 man garrison to terms even though they were as yet unharmed.[11] Henry was angry at this bloodless surrender, but the garrison protested that they had been shut in under a ceaseless bombardment and had seen no sign of the relief forces they had repeatedly asked for.

Close assault on walls to create a breach was always a slow process requiring skilled workmen and arrangements to protect the men and their machines from overhead defensive fire.[12] Such means of wall demolition came into use against stone walls, which were less vulnerable to bombardment and fire than wooden fortifications. The techniques included the use of battering rams, which were especially good against gates; manual attacks with picks and crow-bars; and mining. This last was the most effective when the terrain permitted its use, for it was virtually impossible to defend against. But in fact such methods were little used in this period. They gained in use later in the twelfth century partly in response to improvements in the design and building of fortifications, partly with the increasing sophistication of siege techniques generally. But this is beyond the scope of this study. One example of the use of mining between 1066 and 1135 comes from William I's siege of

---

8 OV, 4:232, 288.
9 Florence, 2:49–50.
10 Symeon, *HR*, p. 274; OV, 6:342.

11 OV, 6:194–6.
12 Brown, *English Castles*, pp. 180, 182.

Exeter in 1068, where his determined assaults included attempts to undermine the walls.[13]

Direct assault by escalade was frequently attempted throughout this period as a means of taking castles. There were two basic ways of getting over walls: with scaling ladders, and by using siege towers moved up to the walls. In either case, assaulting castles was the job of foot-soldiers: 'You could not take a castle by a cavalry charge.'[14] Thus it was Rufus' English troops who stormed Tonbridge in 1088.[15] Not only were horses useless in charging the walls of a fortress, using them in the vicinity of a hostile castle exposed them to the danger of the enemy's missiles. Rufus' army lost more than seven hundred horses in attacks on Chaumont in 1098, when the defenders fired at the exposed animals rather than their mailed riders.[16]

The walls of castles were often surrounded by a dry ditch – wet moats were rare in this period – to make escalade more difficult. Attackers had to fill the ditch where they wished to approach the walls. The five hundred Normans defending two castles in York in 1069 burnt the city lest the houses near the castles be used for filling the castle's ditches,[17] illustrating the importance of this feature of a castle's defenses. Besides filling the ditches, if any, attackers could increase their chance of success by covering the assault with heavy missile fire at defenders on the walls, and by attacking more than one place at once. The latter proved especially effective against small garrisons, but required a fairly large attacking force.

Assault by escalade was thus a fairly difficult technique to use. Success often depended on luck in finding an undefended section of wall, or better still, coming upon a fortress with its gates open and then rapidly forcing an entry. If the defenders of a fortress sallied out in attack, their return to the fortress presented an ideal opportunity for assault, the seizing of which gave mounted troops their one real attacking role in siege warfare. Henry's siege of Bellême in May 1113 concluded thanks to just such a piece of luck. A number of the *milites* of the garrison sallied against the besiegers, but turned and fled towards the east gate when the king's forces counterattacked. 'They were struck and thrown down by their pursuers in that entrance, and the gates could not be closed for the mass of enemy lances and were forced wide open.' The royal army rode in and took a large part of the walled town.[18]

---

13 OV, 2:212.
14 Brown, *English Castles*, p. 174.
15 Symeon, *HR*, p. 216.

16 OV, 5:216–18.
17 Symeon, *HR*, p. 187.
18 OV, 6:182.

In fact, this attack through a forced gate did not quite end the siege, for when the defenders of the tower continued to resist, 'fiery projectiles were launched, and the noble fortress was burnt'. The use of fire as a weapon against besieged strongholds was very common. It is rare, in fact, to read of a siege, particularly of a fortified town, where fire did not enter into the hostilities, at least in some quarter of the siege. Henry burned Brionne, Montfort-sur-Risle and Pont-Audemer as he supressed Waleran's rebellion of 1123–24, and Evreux when the king took the town in 1119, to cite only a few examples.[19] Fire made wooden houses in towns and wooden towers of motte-and-bailey castles equally vulnerable. The Bayeux Tapestry illustrates the use of fire against such a structure by William, at Dol in 1065.[20] But even stone structures had flammable parts. Duke Robert attacked Brionne in the early summer of 1090, in hot weather. After cutting the castle off from relief forces or supplies, he had arrows with heated metal tips fired onto the dry shingle roof of the castle. It caught fire, and forced the defenders to surrender.[21] About the only time, in fact, when fire failed to threaten was during wet weather. In late 1118, for example, Henry began an assault on Hugh of Gournay's castle of La Ferté-en-Bray, but a tremendous storm erupted forcing the king to retreat.[22]

The measures available to defenders to resist the tactics of besiegers were limited, and in the absence of relief forces could usually only prolong a siege. If the besieger could not afford a long siege or could not properly supply his besieging forces, this sufficed to maintain the stronghold. But the defenders of a castle could only drive off a besieging force by emerging for a full scale battle, as Robert Curthose's army did at Gerberoy in 1079, defeating his father's force in battle there. Most defensive garrisons lacked the size and strength to exercise this option with any chance of success: the garrisons of the two castles at York sallied against the entire Scandinavian army in the city in September 1069 and were overwhelmed by the superior numbers of the invaders.[23]

Short of full scale battle, the only options available to defenders of besieged castles were brief sorties at opportune moments, intended as hit-and-run-back-into-the-castle raids; and firing missiles of all sorts at the attackers. If attackers reached the walls, hand-to-hand fighting became the last resort to repulse the attack.

Of these tactics, missile fire was by far the most effective and safest:

[19] OV, 6:334–6, 354, 228.
[20] BT, pl. XXIII.
[21] OV, 4:208.

[22] OV, 6:200.
[23] OV, 2:228.

'Probably the most valuable members of the castle's garrison for its defense were the crossbowmen.'[24] The effect of missiles on the horses of Rufus' army at Chaumont was mentioned above; one of Henry's biggest losses in the campaign of 1106 was the death of Roger of Gloucester, struck on the head by a crossbow bolt at the siege of Falaise.[25] In addition to crossbows, the defenders could employ their own machines against the besieging army and against its siege machines.

Sorties were risky, as the defenders of Bellême discovered, because the gate of the castle had to be opened to let the sallying force out and back in. They were usually used only in extreme circumstances against a specific target, such as a siege tower that posed a dire threat to the garrison's safety within the walls. The defenders of Courcy sallied forth and burnt Robert of Bellême's siege tower in January 1091,[26] for example.

Hand-to-hand defense on the walls was, as mentioned, a last resort measure. Every effort would be made to keep assault parties off the wall tops in the first place: one reason covering missile fire played such a vital role in the success of an assault was that without it the defenders could simply push the scaling ladders over, sending the assaulters plunging to injury and death. The spirit of desperate defense is seen at Exmes in January of 1090. Besieged by Robert of Bellême, Gilbert of Laigle and a garrison 'few in number but brave' held out by launching missiles and stones against the enemy and throwing them back from the walls into the ditch; they wounded some and killed others of the assaulting troops.[27] But if enough attackers got onto the walls, the small size of most defensive garrisons virtually ensured the success of the assault.

Not every siege ended in a final assault or the destruction of the stronghold by fire, nor did many garrisons actually starve to death. Many garrisons surrendered on terms that reflect the importance of field armies to the defense of cities and castles. If the defenders saw no hope of relief after a suitable period of resistance – a period at times specified in agreement with the besiegers – they handed over the stronghold in exchange for their own freedom. Thus in December of 1118 Fulk of Anjou besieged Alençon. After he defeated a relief force under Theobald and Stephen of Blois, the defenders made peace; surrendering the tower, they marched out unharmed.[28] The situation of these defenders was made more urgent because Fulk had managed to cut the underground pipes

---

[24] Brown, *English Castles*, p. 188.
[25] Malmesbury, *GRA*, p. 475.
[26] OV, 4:234.
[27] OV, 4:200.
[28] OV, 6:208.

which supplied water to the castle: secure water supplies were a vital necessity to the defense of a stronghold.

It is often said that the defense had the advantage over the offense in siege warfare during the middle ages. The above discussion might seem to indicate otherwise, at least for the period 1066–1135. The besiegers had a great variety of techniques available to them for taking castles and cities, the defenders' possible responses were few. The passive, intrinsic strength of the fortification, especially a stone-built one, played as important a role as action by defenders in repulsing assaults. On the whole, more sieges ended in surrender than not. And we have seen that in the absence of relief forces, the defense almost always failed. But the relative strengths of attack and defense should not be measured simply by a ratio of surrenders to successful defenses. A besieging army was immobilized for the duration of a siege, which meant it could perform no other task during that time. In a short siege, this would matter very little. But a long siege might tie up the attacking army long enough to affect the course of a campaign significantly; the expectation of a long siege could discourage an attacker from even attempting to take a stronghold. Thus the time it took to force surrender should be weighed in the balance of attack and defense.

The shortest siege of the three reigns was Rufus' of Tonbridge in 1088: his English troops stormed the castle on the second day of the investment.[29] This was the best that could be expected, as a besieging army was unlikely to be prepared for an assault on the day of its arrival at a hostile castle. Henry's siege of Bellême in 1113 only took three days, but this success was unexpected and lucky.[30] At the other extreme, the siege of Norwich carried out by royal forces in 1075 and Henry's *familia's* siege of Arundel in 1102 both lasted three months.[31] In these two cases, the besiegers sat unthreatened by enemy field forces and had no other tasks impending, and so could spend as much time as necessary in subduing the rebel castles, without resorting to destructive tactics such as firing the stronghold or to costly assaults, either of which might have shortened the siege.

All four of these sieges were exceptional in terms of duration, however: there are no others whose recorded times are nearly so low as three days nor as high as three months. William I's eighteen day siege of Exeter, which ended not in surrender but by negotiated settlement, is closer to normal.[32] But the usual duration of sieges in this period seems to have

29 Florence, 2:23.   31 OV, 2:317; 6:22.
30 OV, 6:182.   32 OV, 2:212.

been between four and six weeks.[33] Even four weeks could be a long time in a campaign, so this would seem to indicate that yes, the advantage lay with the defense, at least initially. But this does not ring true, either, for it ignores the success of the majority of sieges. What seems to be the point is that the balance of attack and defense did not weigh heavily in either direction, with castles neither easily taken nor impregnable. This made the outcome of a siege depend very much on the larger strategic situation. That is, it was the actions of field armies against each other rather than the actions of evenly balanced offensive and defensive siege tactics that determined the success or failure of sieges. The point should be emphasized: the surest way to defend friendly castles and cities was to drive away besiegers with a friendly field army; the surest way to capture enemy castles and cities was to clear the field of enemy field armies first.

An assessment of the Anglo-Norman kings as besiegers of castles may therefore be divided into two parts. As siege tacticians they were unexceptional, for their sieges generally took about as long as those conducted by their enemies. It was Henry II who excelled as a siege tactician, shifting the balance decisively in favor of the attack.[34] But William I, Rufus, and Henry I generally succeeded as castle takers because they generally succeeded in controlling the strategic situation, so they did not have to be exceptional siege tacticians.

BATTLES: GENERAL CHARACTERISTICS

The number of major sieges conducted by the Anglo-Norman kings and their lieutenants precludes any treatment of these actions individually. Major battles, on the other hand, numbered relatively few, so they may be examined individually, at least for their major points of interest. The list of 'major' battles is not necessarily clear, however. Hastings and Tinchebrai were, of course, the major engagements of the age, with exceptionally large armies involved. In each case the king of England fought the duke of Normandy with possession of one or the other realm at stake. What were the others?

The usual list of the major battles of 1066–1135 is completed by

---

[33] Florence, 2:50 (Bridgnorth, 1102: *infra XXX dies*); OV, 6:334–6 (Montfort-sur-Risle, 1123: 1 month; Pont Audemer, 1123, 6 weeks – cf. Symeon, *HR*, p. 274: 7 weeks); HH, p. 215 (Pevensey, 1088: 6 weeks). William I had already been at Gerberoy for 3 weeks when he was defeated by the garrison: OV, 3:110.

[34] W.L. Warren, *Henry II* (London, 1973), pp. 231–2.

Brémule and Bourgthérolde. The former did see the meeting in battle of the kings of England and France; but neither was a large battle. Bourgthérolde was in fact an unusually small battle. But both are interesting tactically and offer valuable detail to the military historian, because both received some notice in the sources.

It would be ideal to have as much information about the engagements which seem to have been closer to major conflicts in terms of the size of the forces involved. The two engagements which stand out in this respect are Dol in 1076 and Gerberoy in 1079. The repulse of a Norman relief army by Fulk of Anjou at Alençon in 1118 should also be included. Possibly military historians have paid little attention to these 'battles' for a combination of reasons: inadequate source material; and the fact that each was so closely tied to an ongoing siege that they do not have the character of true pitched battles. Detailed discussion of these engagements may not be possible, but that they were major engagements should not be ignored.[35]

But in order to discuss individual battles, some general features of Anglo-Norman battle tactics should be examined, for certain unchanging factors affected the conduct of battle by the Anglo-Norman kings and their subordinates. These factors were leadership and command discipline; armor and weaponry; and the interaction of the three tactical arms: infantry, cavalry and archers. The last of these topics is especially in need of explanation, for much controversy attends it, particularly in arguments about the battle of Hastings. The crux of the problem concerns the alleged dominance of the mounted knight in medieval warfare, based supposedly on the introduction of the stirrup into European warfare at some point between the fourth and eighth centuries. To understand this controversy, and thus to understand Hastings and the other battles of the period, the mechanics of cavalry, infantry and missile combat must be examined.

Leadership

Leadership and command discipline concerns the control exercised by the leaders of an army over its actions in battle. The greater this degree

---

[35] The list should probably be extended even further. Jim Bradbury, 'Battles in England and Normandy, 1066–1154', Battle 6 (1983), 1 n. 4 lists the engagements which were at least as large as Bourgthérolde and probably qualify as battles. Those through 1135 not already noted include Fagaduna (1075), Chaumont (1098), Exmes (1102), and in Wales in 1088, 1095 and 1097.

of control, the more sophisticated are the actions the army can execute: the army may be divided into smaller tactical units, and the mobility and flexibility of each unit may be increased, when command control is good. The command control of Anglo-Norman royal armies was adequate, but it did not approach that of classical Macedonian or Roman armies, or of the professional standing armies of the seventeenth century and later.

Professional soldiers made up Anglo-Norman armies for the most part, as we have seen. The *familia*, at the heart of Anglo-Norman armies, was a professional force, and even the territorial troops of the fyrd and feudal host, though not professional in terms of pay, campaigned regularly and grew up as warriors. But the Anglo-Norman army was not a professional standing army in one important way. It did not train regularly as an army, that is in large groups. It thus had no opportunity to practice what is known today as close order drill: marching in formation, changing formation, massed weapons tactics and so forth.[36] Experience in battle counted as the only training Anglo-Norman armies received in such actions. Drill formed, for armies that practiced it – and outside of Byzantium drill was largely unknown in Europe between the breakup of the Western Empire and the fifteenth or sixteenth century – the basis of tactical maneuver, discipline and unit cohesion, especially for infantry, and the workings of the field chain of command.[37] When drill was lacking as the basis of these capabilities, it could be replaced to some extent by other factors, but the capabilities, especially tactical maneuver, suffered.

In short, Anglo-Norman armies could more easily disintegrate into

---

[36] Brown, 'The Battle of Hastings', p. 16, notes that 'Norman knights were *as professional as the age could make them*, born and bred to war and trained from early youth ... in the art and science of horsemanship and arms' [italics mine]. This is certainly true, but the limits of the age's professionalism are critical. And for the non-knightly elements of medieval armies, these limits were even greater and exercised decisive influence over tactical possibilities. To argue, as Brown does in 'The Status of the Norman Knight', p. 27, that knights 'were of necessity more expensive and more professional than infantry and foot-soldiers of whatever rank' is to miss this point. The expense of medieval knights was high, and was borne by a social system that then had no resources left for creating professional infantry. But the implication that medieval knights were more professional than any infantry could be is, if not wrong, at least confused in terminology. Roman legionaires were more professional than medieval knights because warfare was their profession, the job for which they were trained and paid; for the knights, warfare was their social role.

[37] Vegetius, *passim*, especially Book I, on the recruitment and training of masses of infantry – the part of Vegetius, as I have already noted, that clearly was not used by medieval generals, for they did not have the administrative resources to raise and train such forces.

armed mobs than classical or more modern armies.[38] This means they were in more danger of succumbing to 'crowd reactions': spontaneous mass movements not ordered and beyond the control of the leaders of the army, of which panicked flight was the ultimate disaster.

Interestingly, lack of drill also made individual actions in combat more likely. Group training and unit drill acted to direct a soldier's actions towards the preservation and success of the group. But if the group were not emphasized, glory and reputation became available through individual combat. The urge to individual combat could be just as destructive of army discipline as crowd mentality: the defenders of Bellême in 1113 were undone when some of the garrison's knights 'rode out of the castle to engage in single combat'.[39] But because soldiers perceived individual action as a way to glory, as it undoubtedly could be, it was even harder to control than the tendency to crowd reactions. Both crowd reactions and individual combat reduced the control of leaders over their men, which in turn reduced the leaders' control over the course of battle. That these two dangers hovered close to the surface in Anglo-Norman armies accounts for some of the wariness with which battle was approached. Even a skillful leader could not guarantee the outcome of the *ambiguum certamen*[40], the uncertain contest of arms.

Yet the armies of the Anglo-Norman kings were often, it seems, better controlled than those of their enemies. Several factors combined to replace peacetime training and drill and so contribute to the discipline and cohesion of royal armies in the heat of battle. Of these, the *familia*, with its regulations for and enforcement of discipline and its permanent structure both in war and peace, was the most important. It gave Anglo-Norman armies a professional core of leaders and soldiers serving together over a significant length of time. They had time to campaign and fight together, to become accustomed to each other's and the system's methods of operation, and to establish trust and friendship among themselves and with the king their master. The group identity this engendered, the loyalty of *familia* soldiers to their leaders, which

---

[38] I do not subscribe to Oman's position that medieval warfare was devoid of skill. The generals were as competent as those of any age, the warriors as brave. What I mean here is that medieval armies were more fragile, more likely to lose the cohesion that made them responsive to their commanders' wills. As John Keegan puts it, 'inside every army is a crowd struggling to get out' (*The Face of Battle*, p. 175); medieval armies' crowds were closer to the surface because the mass training that contains potential crowd reactions was lacking.

[39] OV, 6:182.

[40] OV, 2:308.

encouraged bravery and allowed tactical division of the army into separate units, and the coordination of these separate units in battle are all clear from Orderic's account of Bourgthérolde.[41] There is no better example of the critical role of the *familia* in holding Anglo-Norman royal armies together in battle.

The permanence of the *familia* allowed Anglo-Norman armies to make the most of their limited experience in battle. In effect, one battle served as a training ground for the next when the core of the army in each battle remained the same. And it made new recruits more effective, for they benefitted from the experience of the veterans beside whom they served.

The *familia* also provided, among other things, a permanent structure for leadership. The importance of leadership to Anglo-Norman battle tactics extended above and beyond the *familia*, as well. The leadership of the king or his lieutenant at the head of an army could be decisive in the course of a battle. The subordinate leaders of the fyrd and the feudal host had perhaps less importance, but still had their role.

Finally, the small size of Anglo-Norman armies made command control easier. Individual leaders could have a greater effect in a small army, and the chain of command never got long enough to cause significant organizational problems. A leader transmitted commands orally to his subordinates; voice commands, hand signals, and trumpets transmitted orders to masses of troops.[42] Command at the smallest levels of tactical division, the *familiae* of the subordinate commanders, centered around banners.[43] At this level the cavalry of Anglo-Norman armies, raised and trained in small groups, was fully professional in its capabilities, and could execute maneuvers such as feigned flights.[44]

The command control of Anglo-Norman royal armies was thus not up to the standard of the Roman legions, for instance, limiting the complexity of tactical maneuvers they could execute. But it was not so low that tactical division of the army was impossible, and some tactical

---

[41] OV, 6:350; see below, p. 173, for further discussion of this battle.

[42] WP, pp. 184, 188.

[43] Bennett, 'Wace and Warfare', p. 51.

[44] This point has been long debated. Richard Glover, 'English Warfare in 1066', *EHR* 67 (1952), 1–18, dismissed such tactical capabilities; John Carter, 'The Feigned Flight at Hastings Reconsidered', *The Anglo-Norman Anonymous* 6, no. 1 (1988) has taken up this banner more recently. But the concensus of scholarly opinion is on the side of the feigned flight. See Brown, 'Battle of Hastings', p. 16; Gillingham, 'William the Bastard at War', p. 154. That feigned flights were a natural maneuver even for small groups of non-professional horsemen is illustrated by the Turks' regular use of the tactics in crusading warfare: Smail, *Crusading Warfare*, pp. 78–9.

maneuvers – flanking attacks, for example – were certainly well within their capabilities.[45] And royal command control seems to have been superior to that of other armies of the time.

One of the most important results of limited command control for the conduct of battles was that it increased the uncertainty of the outcome. The riskiness of battle stood out as perhaps its most prominent characteristic for those who had to engage in combat – it was not a prospect to be faced lightly for the common soldier or the general.[46] The best laid plans and the most apparently sure advantages could disintegrate by the luck of the draw. It was for this reason, as well as because it furthered the aims of strategy only indirectly, that battle was a last resort, a strategy either of overwhelming confidence or of desperation.

Arms and Armor

The second factor affecting the conduct of battle was the type of armor and weaponry in use. First, weapons had a short range. Swords, axes, and spears reached only a few feet. Spears could be thrown, as could stones, hand-axes and clubs, but had an effective range as missile weapons of perhaps twenty-five yards. Even the true missile weapons, the short bow and the crossbow, had limited ranges. The former was effective to somewhat under 100 yards, the latter to perhaps 150 yards at most. Second, armor protected relatively effectively against contemporary weapons. King Henry himself twice escaped injury thanks to the strength of his armor: his *aerea cassis*, or bronze helmet, deflected a stone from his head in a fierce fight outside Laigle in November 1118, and his *capitium loricae*, the collar or headpiece of his hauberk, saved him from a sword stroke to the head at Brémule.[47]

The short range of weapons and the effectiveness of armor contributed to the relatively low casualties in Anglo-Norman warfare.[48] As a result of this, enemy armies usually succumbed to defeat not through casualties,

---

45 I refer here to division of the army into two or three 'battles', or major tactical divisions. See the discussion of Tinchebrai below for a flank attack by a hidden reserve.

46 Vegetius stresses the uncertainty of battle (p. 93), a sentiment echoed by Orderic when he refers to the uncertain verdict of battle: OV, 2:308. Gillingham stresses that battle was a high risk strategy ('William the Bastard at War', p. 146) and that medieval generals believed the outcome of battle to be in the hands of God (p. 147); see also the discussion of battle as divinely judged in Georges Duby, *The Legend of Bouvines*, trans. C. Tihanyi (Berkeley, 1990), pp. 109–112.

47 OV, 6:204, 238. See Peirce, 'Arms, Armor and Warfare in the Eleventh Century', for a good general introduction.

48 Class and cultural factors were also important, as discussed above, p. 21.

but through having their will to fight destroyed. This could be accomplished in two ways: by gaining a decisive psychological or physical victory over the enemy commander, for if he fled or was killed, his army would almost certainly disintegrate; or by outmanoeuvering, disordering, or surprising the enemy in such a way as to threaten to inflict more casualties than would normally be possible.[49] If disordering the enemy army did not panic the enemy commander, it would almost certainly reduce the enemy army to a panicked crowd and so remove it from the opposing commander's control. In other words, the low casualties resulting from the armor and weapons in use in Anglo-Norman warfare increased the importance of leadership and command control in the outcome of battles. A leader who could hold his army together when panic threatened to set in had a good chance of emerging as the master of the field.[50]

The role of experience and professionalism in command control and the importance of weaponry and armor in the conduct of battle together explain in large part the elite position of the knight in Anglo-Norman warfare. As A.L. Poole has noted, 'It was not so much his horse as his professional training and his better equipment which gave the knight his superiority in fighting.'[51]

'The Age of Cavalry'

Command control and weaponry were influences on the course of Anglo-Norman battles which, though at times somewhat overlooked, have caused no real controversy among historians. The interactions of cavalry and infantry with each other, on the other hand, expressed as a question of the dominance of one or the other, has been one of the central topics of medieval military history for many years. A brief outline of the theories involved is necessary, for although they concern a far longer time period than 1066–1135, they have had a direct, and in my opinion misleading, influence on interpretations of the battle of Hastings in particular and of the place of cavalry in Anglo-Norman combat in general.

That men who usually rode horses dominated warfare in the middle ages is not in question. 'Knights', men who counted horses among their valued possessions and used them in various ways in warfare, dominated

---

[49] Keegan, *Face of Battle*, pp. 104–5.
[50] William's rallying of his army at Hastings is the best example of this: WP, p. 190.
[51] Poole, *Obligations of Society*, p. 37.

the social and political landscape. Inevitably they would also dominate the conduct of warfare: they were the professional elite. But R.A. Brown speaks of the 'mailed knights which then dominated warfare',[52] and by this he means knights as cavalry and not, as A.L. Poole meant, as a professional elite. The distinction is a tactical one: Brown means men who fought on horseback in battle. This brings us to the heart of the problem: why was the middle ages an age of cavalry? There is a standard explanation, which I believe reveals a serious misunderstanding of the mechanics of medieval combat. A critical examination of that explanation and a reexamination of those mechanics will provide a basis for a new theory for the dominance of cavalry in medieval battles, a dominance more limited than is usually recognized.

I

That the knight is the dominant popular image of the middle ages is suggestive, for the best known military figures from other eras – the Greek hoplite, the Roman legionaire, the Napoleonic Imperial Guardsman, the Civil War rifleman – all fought on foot.

For the military historian, the Middle Ages as an Age of Cavalry received its most influential expression from Sir Charles Oman in his monumental *Art of War in the Middle Ages*. For Oman, the Age of Cavalry began, with Victorian precision if not accuracy, in 378 at the battle of Adrianople, 'the first great victory won by that heavy cavalry which had now shown its ability to supplant the heavy infantry of Rome as the ruling power of war.' The Goth 'had become the arbiter of war, the lineal ancestor of all the knights of the Middle Ages, the inaugurator of that ascendency of the horsemen which was to endure for a thousand years.'[53]

It has long been recognized that Oman's picture of an Age of Cavalry needs modification. In the first place, it must be made clear that Oman and those who have followed him have had battle tactics and battle tactics alone in mind when writing of cavalry dominance. This in itself is a major limit, for infantry never disappeared from warfare. They played an essential role in siege warfare, garrison duty, and engineering, activities all far more common than battles in medieval war, as this study has shown.[54] In addition, infantry could be useful in certain roles on the

52 Brown, *English Castles*, p. 173.
53 Oman, *Art of War*, p. 14.
54 See also John Gillingham, 'Richard 1 and the Science of War', pp. 78–91, for an

battlefield, and at times could even defeat cavalry.[55] So we are talking not of absolute dominance, but of a relative increase in the importance of cavalry in deciding battles. This focus on the battlefield requires a careful definition of cavalry. I use, as I have noted, a tactical, functional definition of cavalry and infantry : cavalry are soldiers fighting on horseback; infantry are soldiers fighting on foot. This maintains the important but much neglected distinction between horses as strategic transport and horses as battlefield 'weapons', and in fact follows the common medieval usage.[56] Thus, soldiers who rode to battle but fought on foot fought as infantry, not as 'dismounted cavalry', an anachronistic term which can only confuse our picture of medieval warfare.

In the second place, the temporal and geographical limits of the dominance of cavalry are subject to question. Lynn White dated the initial superiority of cavalry to the mid-eighth century in France, for instance.[57] But within broad limits which need not concern us here, there seems little question that the Middle Ages was, militarily, an Age of Cavalry. Why was this so?

The usual explanation for the dominance of cavalry in the middle Ages is simple and technological: the introduction of the stirrup into European warfare. The basic idea is that the stirrup made the horse a much more stable fighting platform, unified horse and rider into one massive attacking force directed through the couched lance of the rider, and so made cavalry so much more efficient that infantry no longer stood a chance against it.[58]

Lynn White, drawing on nineteenth century German histories of the stirrup, stated the case most completely in the first chapter of his *Medieval Technology and Social Change*, a chapter called 'Stirrup, Mounted Shock Combat, Feudalism, and Chivalry'.[59] This work has become the fountainhead for the spread of the Stirrup Theory. Though much

excellent discussion of the place of infantry and battles in medieval warfare. He builds on the fundamental work of Smail, *Crusading Warfare*.

[55] Beeler and Hollister have both pointed out the importance of infantry in England before and after the conquest, though Beeler still holds to the greater importance of cavalry in England after 1066: Beeler, *Warfare in England*, p. 1; Hollister, *Mil. Org. Norman Eng.*, pp. 127–9. See below for further discussion of infantry and cavalry roles on the battlefield and for discussion of individual battles where infantry beat cavalry, e.g. at Brémule and Bourgethérolde.

[56] E.g. OV 6:350, and see p. 10 above.

[57] L. White, *Medieval Technology and Social Change* (Oxford, 1962), ch. 1.

[58] E.g. Verbruggen, *Art of Warfare*, pp. 23–4; Beeler, *Warfare in England*, p. 57.

[59] White, *Medieval Technology*, Ch. 1. Oman, interestingly, did not really explain the rise of cavalry except by vague references to 'changes in military science' and the reliance of Rome on 'untrustworthy and greedy Teutonic Foederati': Oman, *Art of War*, 18, 19.

criticized in detail, particularly on the dating of the introduction of the stirrup and the conversion of Frankish armies to mounted combat,[60] White's account in broad outline seems to have passed into the realm of accepted textbook canon. It is in the major studies of medieval warfare which have succeeded Oman: J.F. Verbruggen places the stirrup at the heart of knightly dominance; Philippe Contamine notes some of the problems associated with dating the stirrup but accepts its eventual impact.[61] It has been used to explain aspects of Anglo-Norman warfare; in particular, it has been cited to explain the result of Hastings and thus the Norman conquest.[62] McKay, Hill and Buckler's History of World Societies is but one example of the theory's spread to introductory textbooks, while the first chapter of Michael Howard's War in European History, titled 'The Wars of the Knights', demonstrates the acceptance of the theory in a scholarly synthesis of European military history.[63] Martin van Creveld, in his recent survey Technology and War from 2000 BC to the Present sums up the case: 'Modern authors, however much they may differ in detail, are united in their opinion that, sometime between 500 and 1000 AD, the stirrup and the high saddle . . . spread to Europe. Add the horseshoe, the origin of which is simply unknown, and the ascent of cavalry over ancient infantry becomes at least understandable.'[64]

It is my contention that while the stirrup may indeed have appeared in Europe sometime between 500 and 1000, it explains nothing about the ascent of cavalry over infantry.

There is a purely logical problem with the Stirrup Theory: it leaves no room for infantry's return to dominance in the fifteenth century. The extension of the technological argument, that new weapons for the infantry – the longbow and, more importantly, gunpowder – turned the tide again, must ignore the fact that the Swiss pikemen, with weapons and tactics essentially identical with those of a Macedonian phalanx,

---

[60] E.g. Bernard Bachrach, 'Charles Martel, Shock Combat, the Stirrup and Feudalism', Studies in Medieval and Renaissance History 7 (1970), 47–75.

[61] Verbruggen, Art of Warfare, p. 5; Contamine, War in the Middle Ages, pp. 179–84.

[62] On the supposed impact of the stirrup, especially at Hastings, see R. Allen Brown, The Normans and the Norman Conquest (London, 1969), pp. 95–9, 166; F.M. Stenton, Anglo-Saxon England, 3rd edn (Oxford, 1971), pp. 585–8; EHD 2:1042–1189 (editors' introduction). For a different view of Hastings, arguing that the stirrup had little or no effect on its outcome, see S. Morillo, 'Hastings: An Unusual Battle', The Haskins Society Journal 2 (1990), 95–104. See below, p. 163 for a specific discussion of Hastings.

[63] John P. McKay, Bennett D. Hill and John Buckler, A History of World Societies, 2nd edn (Boston, 1988), 1:335; Michael Howard, War in European History (Oxford, 1976), Ch. 1.

[64] Martin van Creveld, Technology and War from 2000 BC to the Present (New York, 1989), p. 18.

could beat any stirrup-wearing cavalry in Europe.[65] Indeed, it was not until the invention of the bayonet that missile troops, whether they carried bows or guns, could stand against cavalry without the support of pikemen. The bayonet, of course, made every musketeer his own pikeman.

II

The more fundamental problem with the technological argument in general and the rise of cavalry because of the stirrup in particular, is that it is based on a misunderstanding of the mechanics of infantry and cavalry combat. I shall discuss infantry and cavalry tactics with specific reference to Anglo-Norman armies, but the principles apply throughout the wider period in question.[66]

The basic difference between infantry and cavalry on the battlefield was the superior mobility of the horseman. Mobility made cavalry the natural arm of attack and pursuit. Low mobility made infantry the natural arm of defense, though infantry, if it were experienced and well led, was capable of attack.

The classic cavalry attack, the charge in line, called for cohesion if it were to be effective. The French at Brémule launched the first attack, 'but charging *inordinate* they were overcome'.[67] The ability of Anglo-Norman cavalry to execute a charge *ordinate* – in line and maintaining good order – is suggested by this statement. The limited command control and training of Anglo-Norman armies undoubtedly limited the

---

[65] The significance of the Swiss pikemen is shown by the fact that Oman devotes all of Book XI (*Art of War* 2:233–280) to them. The lethality of early gunpowder handguns is often overestimated, and in fact before the invention of rifling in the 1830s remained no more lethal than bows and less so than the Roman gladius: Richard Gabriel, *The Culture of War. Invention and Early Development* (New York, 1990), p. 126. The advantage of guns was that they were easy to use (far easier than the much more effective longbow); large masses of conscript infantry could therefore be trained in their use. But this presupposes the ability to conscript and train large masses of infantry, a point I will return to later. Geoffrey Parker, *The Military Revolution. Military Innovation and the Rise of the West, 1500–1800* (Cambridge, 1988), pp. 6–45, traces the rise of infantry not so much to handguns as to cannon and related changes in fortifications, which made more infantry necessary for larger sieges. This argument has more merit, but does not deal directly with battlefield dominance (which theoretically could have remained unaffected by such developments – siege warfare was after all the domain of infantry in the middle ages), and again presupposes the ability to raise large masses of infantry.

[66] Many of the basic concepts of the following section are fully discussed in Keegan, *Face of Battle*, which provides an excellent introduction to medieval and modern combat at the level of the individual soldier.

[67] OV, 6:238.

cavalry's ability to wheel during a charge or regroup after one, but even these difficult maneuvers were not beyond the capabilities of small groups of horsemen.[68]

The stages of a cavalry attack were two: the charge itself; and its aftermath, which involved either regrouping for a second charge or breakup into many single combats. The mechanics of each stage varied according to whether the target was cavalry or infantry in formation.

Against opposing cavalry, a charge could result in the two lines meeting head on, in the style of a mass joust or tournament. At the moment of impact in such a collision, some riders were thrown from their horses by enemy lances; many lances undoubtedly shattered under the stress of blows. But the 'crashing together' of two lines of cavalry can be overdramatized. Depending on the density and depth of the formations, many of the horsemen were likely to pass through each other's lines. If the lines were too deep or tightly packed to allow this result, the charging lines had to slow before impact, and the soldiers then came together into a series of single combats.[69]

It was in cavalry against cavalry combat that the introduction of the stirrup made some difference in combat techniques. The stirrup allowed (but did not require) the lance to be carried couched, or underarm, with the weight of man and horse behind it. Stirruped cavalry would have had an advantage over cavalry without stirrups; but all cavalry in the eleventh and twelfth centuries had stirrups, so this is not a critical point for Anglo-Norman warfare.[70]

The introduction of the stirrup had even less effect in encounters of cavalry against infantry. Against a solid infantry formation, a cavalry

---

[68] R. Glover, citing the portrayal of the Norman charges at Hastings in the Bayeux Tapestry, which appears to show scattered groups of horsemen, has claimed that Norman cavalry did not charge in line: R. Glover, 'English Warfare in 1066', p. 13. But I doubt whether the Tapestry can be used to interpret mass formations. Its small format and lack of depth perspective would have made portraying a line of horsemen – or infantry, for that matter – very difficult. See also note 44 above on feigned flights. M. Bennett, 'La Règle du Temple as a Military Manual, or How to Deliver a Cavalry Charge', in Studies . . . to R. Allen Brown, pp. 7–19, explores the Rule of the Temple as a military manual; it too stresses the need for cohesion (pp. 16–17) and implies the ability of small groups to reform about their banner (p. 18). The Rule, as Bennett shows, is a valuable source for a number of aspects of cavalry warfare, especially in the Levant, including numbers of horses, camping, and tactics. Significantly, as this clearly was a military manual that saw use by military men, it contains no reference to Vegetius: p. 8 and n. 9.

[69] Keegan, Face of Battle, pp. 148–50.

[70] And even in the general history of warfare, the effect of the stirrup on cavalry technique may be exaggerated. Alexander's Companion Cavalry, who did not have stirrups, may have been the best cavalry unit ever, for as Robin Lane Fox has noted, 'What writing

charge was a psychological weapon. It had to depend on frightening at least some of the foot-soldiers into breaking ranks or fleeing, or the horses of the cavalry would 'refuse' in the face of an obstacle they could neither jump over nor go around – the solid wall of foot-soldiers. Individual horses and riders might accidentally crash into an unfortunate foot-soldier in rank, but on the whole the charge would draw up short of a mass collision.[71] The cavalry could then either retreat to charge again, or advance the last few yards to engage in single combat. The stirrup made no difference to the psychological value of the charge and little to individual combat between cavalry and infantry.

For infantry to stand up to a cavalry charge its formation had to be sufficiently deep and dense to force horses to refuse, and the men had to have the morale and courage to stand in the face of the terrifying sight of charging cavalry. The latter necessity accounts in part for the common practice by Anglo-Norman knights of dismounting: a front line of elite soldiers stiffened the morale of the less experienced masses behind them, making the whole formation more effective. This is the first way in which the Anglo-Norman practice of dismounting shows the influence of strong central authority: the Anglo-Norman kings could raise fairly large numbers of infantry of enough quality that casting the knights in with them was both possible and beneficial.

But this does not fully explain the dismounting of knights, for at Brémule and Bourgthérolde there was no infantry to stiffen. Nor does it explain how the knights were convinced to dismount, for there were conflicting group and individual motives at work in this process. It was to the advantage of any individual knight to fight mounted: it was more prestigious and glorious, there was a greater possibility of successful pursuit with the chance of prisoners and ransoms, and perhaps above all it was easier to run away safely if things went wrong. But it was to the advantage of the force as a whole that at least some of the knights dismount. Only a leader with enough authority to impose dismounting on his troops could overcome this individual tendency and reap the benefits of this tactic. Dismounting made the army as a whole more effective, and stiffened the resolve of the knights themselves, for it

has done to the memory, stirrups have done to riding; without them, men simply had to grip harder and ride better than they mostly do nowadays.' Robin Lane Fox, *Alexander the Great* (London, 1974), p. 75, and pp. 72–80 generally for an excellent discussion of the Macedonian army of Philip and Alexander; many of the points of tactics presented there bear directly on this argument. Fox probably overstates the case somewhat, but see also Archer Jones, *The Art of War in the Western World* (Oxford, 1987), p. 21.

[71] Keegan, *Face of Battle*, pp. 95–6, 156.

effectively removed flight as a safe alternative for them. As Amaury of Montfort told his fellow rebels before Bourgthérolde:[72]

> See, Odo Borleng has dismounted with his men, so you know he will fight tenaciously to win. When a warlike horseman becomes a foot-soldier with his men, he will not flee; rather, he will die or conquer.

Thus the authority and control of the Anglo-Norman kings over their military system, exercised through the institution of the *familia*, contributed directly to dismounting as a common Anglo-Norman tactic.

Given that dismounting regularly performed such important functions in Anglo-Norman battles, it does not seem to me that it has been over-stressed, as R.A. Brown has claimed.[73] In fact the change in Norman attitudes between 1066, when a knight dismounting was a matter for laughter and ridicule,[74] and Bourgthérolde, indicates a minor revolution in the Norman approach to battle. The importance of infantry tactics reflects the influence of the Anglo-Saxon tradition on Anglo-Norman combat and resulted from the effectiveness of the *familia* in replacing drill in disciplining Anglo-Norman forces.[75] The influence of effective infantry tactics on the Anglo-Norman knights may be guessed at as early as 1075, when royal forces under William of Warenne defeated Earl Ralph's rebel army at Fagaduna: Orderic writes of the royal troops that *obstantes*, they won the field.[76] Is it pushing the term *obstantes* too far to suggest that the *familia* knights and their fyrd support formed a shield wall at this engagement? The term certainly could not describe a cavalry charge. And it is worth noting that no dismounting took place in the Anglo-Norman defeats at Dol, Gerberoy and Alençon.

Because the horses of the cavalry of 1066–1135 were not, like their riders, covered in protective armor, cavalry charges were vulnerable to being broken up by archery. Even if the arrows did not kill very many horses or men, they would disorder the charge, for one injured horse, in falling, could trip or impede several others. And as Rufus' experience at Chaumont in 1098 shows, archery could take a heavy toll of knight's

---

[72] *Ecce Odo Borlengus cum suis descendit, scitote quia superare pertinaciter contendit. Bellicosus eques iam cum suis pedes factus non fugiet, sed morietur aut vincet.* OV, 6:350.

[73] Brown, *Origins of English Feudalism*, p. 35, n. 10.

[74] WP, p. 168.

[75] See below, pp. 183–84, for more on this point. For an alternate view, see Bradbury, 'Battles in England and Normandy', p. 11.

[76] OV, 2:316.

mounts.[77] Archery could, however, support cavalry attacks by 'softening up' a target, infantry or cavalry.

The terrain could also affect a cavalry charge. Broken ground or an obstacle such as a hedge or stream would disrupt a charge. Charging uphill was slower than on level ground and therefore less intimidating to the target troops, but charging downhill was impossible if the grade were too steep, for the horses would somersault under the weight of the rider.

The aftermath of a cavalry charge involved either the retreat of the cavalry, if possible to regroup and charge again, or single combat against the targets of the charge. Retreat and regrouping could be a difficult and dangerous maneuver. The retreat could easily degenerate into panicked flight, and disordered, retreating cavalry on blown horses were at the mercy of a mounted counter-attack. The concerted charge by the knights of Counts Theobald and Rotrou against the disordered and fleeing knights of the garrison of Bellême which resulted in the forcing of a gate and capture of the town in 1113 illustrates this.[78] The course of single combat, on the other hand, depended on the arms and condition of the defenders.

Against cavalry of similar training, weapons and tactics – and this describes all the mounted foes of Anglo-Norman royal armies – numbers were important in the outcome. The larger force clearly had an advantage. Otherwise, the outcome depended on morale, courage, and the factors mentioned above concerning retreating cavalry: formation (a scattered unit's members could not help each other very well) and fatigue of men and horses. The appearance of fresh forces in a cavalry melée was often enough to tip the balance: Henry's *familia*, arriving to aid Ralph of Gael against the French at Breteuil in 1119, drove away the tiring forces of King Louis with ease.[79]

Single combat between cavalry and infantry depended very much on the formation of the infantry, for the same factors which stopped a charge, density and depth, put infantry on close terms with cavalry in combat along the front of an infantry formation. Given some familiarity with the usual close range tactics of horsemen and given similar armor, professional infantry could more than hold its own against professional cavalry. Henry's instructions to his English infantry in 1101, when he taught them how to block and return the blows of his brother's mounted troops, are instructive on this point.[80] So too is the dismounting of

---

[77] OV, 5:218.
[78] OV, 6:182.
[79] OV, 6:246; cf. Keegan, *Face of Battle*, pp. 145–6, 150.
[80] Malmesbury, GRA, p. 472. See Barlow, *Feudal Kingdom*, p. 79, on Harold's familiarity with continental tactics at Hastings.

knights in the first rank of infantry: as experienced cavalrymen, the knights would have had a good idea how to counter a mounted attacker.

On the other hand, if cavalry caught infantry scattered in the open field, the superior mobility and attacking height of the horseman could be put to full use, and the foot-soldiers were easily butchered or rounded up as prisoners. A similar though less decisive advantage fell to cavalry which attacked infantry formations on the flank or rear before they had time to reface.

The stage of battle in which cavalry clearly performed better than infantry was the pursuit of a beaten foe, for although infantry could attack en masse, it could not hope to catch a fleeing enemy. Pursuit was also the stage of battle when the most casualties could be expected. But here we have a second explanation, in addition to good armor, for the low casualties of Anglo-Norman battles: the regular practice was to capture the beaten enemy, not to kill in pursuit. This was particularly true of battles on the continent between members of the knightly class, where the combatants all came from similar backgrounds, spoke the same language, and in many cases knew each other personally. Financial incentive to make prisoners of opponents also existed; indeed the prospect of ransoms was for some a major reason for fighting.[81] When royal forces fought other foes – Scandinavians and English rebels in front of York in 1069, for example – the pursuit ended up far bloodier.[82] Yet the closeness of Anglo-Norman cavalry to its continental foes, including the similarity of arms and armor, meant that in the pursuit stage of a battle, when clear battle lines no longer separated one side from another, there was much room for confusion and deception. After Brémule, for example, some of the French fugitives threw away their distinguishing shields and mixed with their pursuers.[83]

The role of infantry in Anglo-Norman battles was almost always defensive. When infantry attacked infantry, the resulting melée, like cavalry combat, depended on a variety of factors: density and cohesion of the opposing formations; morale; numbers; and armor and weaponry differences.[84] Infantry could not safely attack cavalry, because troops not trained in formation marching found it difficult to keep close order in an advance; if it lost close order, the infantry would open itself to counter-attack by the cavalry. But one cannot conclude that such attacks were

[81] OV, 5:216; see below p. 177.
[82] WJ, p. 140.
[83] OV, 6:242.
[84] Keegan, *Face of Battle*, pp. 99–100.

impossible. Harold Godwinson's infantry executed a swift and effective attack on Hardraada's army at Stamford Bridge, and one can only assume from Harold's actions in the Hastings campaign that he was confident in the ability of his troops to repeat the trick against the Normans. It was not by choice but because of William's generalship that the Anglo-Saxon king fought a defensive battle.[85]

Still, it did take very experienced, organized and well led troops to contemplate offensive action against enemy cavalry in the open field without the benefit of drill and peacetime practice. The Anglo-Saxon infantry were that good, probably the best in Europe by a good deal at the time; the Anglo-Norman infantry may have been that good, but had no need to attempt offensive action, as it always had cavalry support. Very few infantry forces in medieval Europe other than the Anglo-Saxon and Anglo-Norman even had the confidence to stand in defense, much less the cohesion to attack.

III

Here we have the key to the problem of the dominance of cavalry. Cavalry was not better from the fourth to the fourteenth centuries: infantry was worse. The confidence and cohesion infantry needed to be effective had to be instilled through training and discipline, which in large part required standing armies. Strong, rich central authority, the prerequisite for standing armies, was therefore the key to effective infantry forces.[86] The breakdown of the western empire left no central authority capable of maintaining and training infantry forces in peacetime. The decline of infantry standards is clear well before the final collapse of the Roman state.[87] With less training, infantry lost the ability

---

85 See below, p. 165.

86 Strong central authority was the prerequisite for development in most areas of warfare. For a provacative and convincing formulation of this argument, see Gabriel, *Culture of War*, pp. 124–5. Gabriel's entire book explores war and its institutions as phenomena driven by cultural and political constructs, not by technology, and is a necessary antidote to the overly technological outlook fostered by the industrial age. In European terms, at least, it is hard to argue with Gabriel's assertion that 'In almost all respects, the conduct of war after the fourth century did not return to the level of sophistication shown by the Romans until well into the nineteenth century' (p. 125). For a study of the role of government in the effect of gunpowder weapons on warfare, see S. Morillo, 'Guns and Government: A Comparative Study of Europe and Japan', *Journal of World History* (forthcoming).

87 Vegetius' constant emphasis on training and discipline arises out of his equally constant complaints that Roman infantry is no longer up to the standards of the ancients: Vegetius, *passim*.

to attack, which it surrendered to cavalry; with no training, it became incapable even of standing in defense.

Only in areas where drill and training were partially replaced by 'institutionalized experience', that is professionalism (money) and group continuity, did effective infantry forces appear between the fourth and fourteenth centuries. The *familia* of the Anglo-Norman kings, grafted onto the strong infantry tradition of Anglo-Saxon England, is a notable example of this, and in fact the infantry tradition survived in English forces to end Oman's 'Age of Cavalry' at Crecy. The independent and rich city-states of Italy and to a lesser extent of Flanders were virtually the only other governments capable of putting worthwhile infantry in the field in the Middle Ages. Warfare, at least on the battlefield, was therefore left to cavalry.

Why did cavalry emerge as the dominant arm in an age of weak central authority? Why didn't cavalry standards decline as well? The answer lies in the social structure of Europe. In the absence of central authority, the appropriation of economic surplus and the exercise of authority fell to the social elites. This had two consequences. First, as I noted earlier, one of the common ways elites displayed their status throughout the pre-industrial world was by owning and riding horses, which is simply one form of ostentatious display. So horsed elites are to be expected. Second, in the turbulent centuries of the early middle ages, it was also natural that the elite class should have a military function, as such horsed elites usually did. Given their monopoly of economic resources and organizational capacity (such as it was), the elite also monopolized whatever professionalism the age could afford. That this professionalism was in mounted combat was simply a product of the social structure. In effect, social dominance created a military elite in characteristic mounted form.[88]

Reinforcing the tendency for cavalry to dominate were several other

[88] This is the exact opposite of the formulation according to Brown, who states that 'the new military elite [based on the stirrup] became inevitably in the circumstances of the age a social elite also': 'Status of the Norman Knight', p. 27. While Brown refers to Bloch in this context, a careful reading of the latter in light of the above arguments reveals as much if not more of the social determinants in the decline of infantry as the technological factors in the rise of cavalry: Bloch, *Feudal Society*, 1:151–56. Brown says further of cavalry warfare, 'One need have no doubt that it was first adopted by rich nobles, as most good things in life descend from the top downwards' ('Status of the Norman Knight', pp. 27–8). While this general rule might surprise historians of the industrial revolution, or indeed of the technology that mattered in the middle ages, the heavy plow and the water- and windmill, it is revealing of Brown's attitude as a cavalryman himself, reflecting what Vegetius calls the 'natural antipathy' of the cavalry for the infantry: Vegetius, p. 55.

factors. Primarily, the lack of central resources meant that armies were small, and the effectiveness of infantry depends more on mass than does that of cavalry. The small groups in which cavalry can operate effectively were easily and naturally brought together and trained not by the institutions of central authority but by the social mechanism of the *familia*. Small armies also meant that it was practical to mount armies, *if only for reasons of strategic transport*. Once again, the Anglo-Saxon housecarls fit this European-wide pattern, as a socially elite force which rode to battle. And the small size of armies meant that strategic mobility was often at a premium, as the limited military resources of a ruler had to be moved around to meet needs that a larger military would have met with separate detachments. And as noted above, the lack of central authority weakened the restraint on each warrior seeking his own individual advantage, which was more likely to be found on horseback than on foot.

Finally, crediting the English archers at Crecy with ending cavalry's dominance is not quite accurate, for only the extreme range of the longbow transformed a still essentially immobile infantry into an offensive force. It is no coincidence that the first infantry forces to attack and defeat horsemen in the open field since the Roman legions, the pikemen of the Swiss cantons, were the first since the Romans to march in time to music.[89] Drill had returned to European warfare, and with it the dominance of infantry. The resurgence of central authority made that dominance permanent.[90]

As a final note to the whole question of dominance, the battles of this and other ages show that combined arms tactics almost always have an advantage over tactics which rely on one type of soldier alone. Supporting the attack mobility of cavalry with the defensive strength of infantry, and reinforcing each with missile fire, makes the most of each arm and minimizes the specific weaknesses of each.

---

[89] R. Ernest Dupuy and Trevor N. Dupuy, *The Encyclopedia of Military History from 3500 BC to the Present*, rev. 2nd edn (New York, 1986), p. 407.

[90] The rise of infantry resulting from resurgent central authority then stimulated further administrative advances: see Parker, *Military Revolution*, pp. 6–44. (But cf. Morillo, 'Guns and Government'.) It should be emphasized again that this entire discussion concerns battle tactics only, and is limited by geographic considerations (cavalry could not dominate in areas such as the Scottish highlands, where horses could not be raised easily and where terrain limited their use in battle anyway). For a further discussion of the relationship of political power and military force see Robert J. Bartlett, 'Technique Militaire et Pouvoir Politique, 900–1300', *Annales* 41 (1986), 1135–1159, who argues that the tactical combination of knights, castles and archers was the key to Latin expansion in the high middle ages. I am not entirely convinced by his argument; for the purposes of this discussion he does not adequately distinguish between knights as elite warriors and cavalry as mounted soldiers in battle (see especially pp. 1136, 1150).

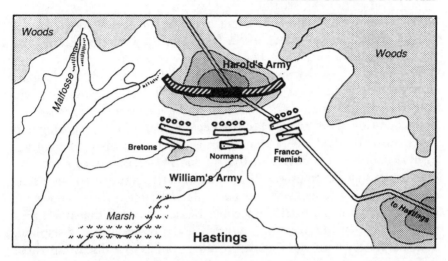

ANGLO-NORMAN BATTLES

With the general characteristics of Anglo-Norman battle tactics in mind – that is, the limits of command control, arms and armor, and the patterns of infantry and cavalry conflict – we may now briefly review the major battles of 1066–1135, highlighting their significant features.

Hastings (14 October 1066)[91]

The battle of Hastings has been discussed at great length by modern historians, and the general circumstances and course of the battle are

---

[91] The main primary sources for the battle are William of Poitiers and the Bayeux Tapestry. The *Carmen* also offers a full account. R.H.C. Davis, 'The Carmen de Hastingae Proelio', *EHR* 93 (1978), 241–61, casts doubt on the Carmen as an independent source for the battle, but see Davis, L.J. Engels et al., 'The *Carmen de Hastingae Proelio*: A Discussion', *Battle* 2 (1979), 1–20, for alternate views. It can at least offer useful information about common battle tactics. Brief narratives which provide a few extra details are found in *The Anglo-Saxon Chronicle*, William of Jumièges, and Florence of Worcester. William of Malmesbury, Orderic Vitalis and Henry of Huntingdon add even less and are more distant from the event. No one modern account of the battle is fully satisfactory, but most are useful to some extent. These accounts include Douglas, *William the Conqueror*, pp. 196–204; Brown, *Normans and the Norman Conquest*, pp. 158–74 and 'The Battle of Hastings'; Stenton, *Anglo-Saxon England*, pp. 585–8; J.F.C. Fuller, *A Military History of the Western World* (London, 1954), 1:360–385; C.H. Lemmon, 'The Campaign of 1066', in Whitelock et al., *The Norman Conquest*; A.H. Burne, *The Battlefields of England* (London, 1950); and, least

well known.[92] But there is nothing close to agreement about several critical stages of the battle, nor in fact about how to characterize the battle as a whole.

The feature of the battle that stands out and that sets the battle apart from any other medieval battle is its incredible length. Most medieval battles lasted less than an hour, and to find a medieval battle of several hours duration is difficult.[93] Hastings began about 9 in the morning and lasted into the darkness of that evening: over nine hours of fighting, even accounting for pauses in the battle. This certainly supports the conclusion that Hastings was a hard-fought battle between armies essentially equal in strength.[94] More particularly it reflects two important characteristics of the battle: a peculiar tactical standoff that developed mid-way through the day; and the high levels of leadership, discipline, and morale on both sides of the conflict. But before discussing these points in more detail, it is necessary to say what Hastings was not.

Hastings was not the inevitable victory of stirruped cavalry over helpless infantry,[95] infantry which was 'already obsolete in the greater part of Western Europe'[96] and which had failed 'to keep abreast with the latest developments in military science'.[97] Such a view subordinates the obvious realities of the battle – its extreme length alone argues against a predetermined result – to a theory of cavalry dominance which itself is untenable, as discussed above. Hastings was a battle between an army that included some of the best cavalry in Europe, and an army that included the best infantry in Europe.[98] The relative strengths and abilities

---

usefully, Oman, *Art of War*, pp. 149–66. Some of the problems of the battle are discussed in Morillo, 'Hastings: An Unusual Battle', pp. 95–104.

[92] Briefly, the major stages of the battle were as follows. An initial Norman attack commenced about 9 am involving archers and heavy infantry as well as cavalry (William of Poitiers, pp. 186–8; *BT*, pls 60–63). This was repulsed, and the Norman army began to retreat in growing disorder, with indications of an Anglo-Saxon pursuit (William of Poitiers, pp. 188–90; *BT*, pls 66–68; and see below p. 5). William rallied his army, halted the Anglo-Saxon advance, and led another unsuccessful attack (William of Poitiers, pp. 190–92). The rest of the day saw a series of Norman attacks and feigned flights which, though they failed to break the Anglo-Saxon line, depleted it to some extent, especially on the wings. Finally, with darkness falling and Harold dead, the Anglo-Saxon line gave way (William of Poitiers, pp. 196–204; *BT*, pls 70–73). See also the secondary accounts cited in the previous note.

[93] Vegetius claims that most battles last at most two to three hours: Vegetius, p. 86.

[94] Matthew, *Norman Conquest*, p. 84; Lemmon, 'The Campaign of 1066', p. 114.

[95] Brown, *The Normans and the Norman Conquest*, pp. 95–9, 166.

[96] Stenton, *Anglo-Saxon England*, p. 576.

[97] *EHD*, 2:20 (editors' introduction).

[98] William's army also included infantry, and not just archers but heavy infantry: WP, p. 184. They probably outnumbered the Duke's cavalry, and had to have played a greater role

of these troops as cavalry and as infantry played some part in certain stages of the battle, as I shall discuss in a moment, but Hastings cannot accurately be characterized as a victory of cavalry tactics over infantry tactics.

The dominant tactics of the day in fact were evenly matched. The English defensive formation of densely massed infantry[99] was just the sort that would turn back charging cavalry, especially since the Norman cavalry had to charge uphill to reach the English position. The hand-to-hand combat along the line matched Norman swords and lances against Anglo-Saxon battle axes 'which easily found their way through shields or other armor',[100] with no advantage either way. The other theme of the day's tactics was the ineffectiveness of missile fire on both sides, save for the high-angle fire of the final Norman attack.[101]

The key to the battle of Hastings seems to me to lie in the tactics and the leadership problems of the first Norman retreat, the general English counter-attack that was not general, and the Norman counter-attack on their scattered pursuers. To take the last point first, the ability of the cavalry forces under William to cut down their pursuers in the open field would seem to vindicate the superiority of the horsemen: unable safely to attack, the English were doomed to be attacked until defeated. But this misreads the episode. The Norman knights were able to cut down those Anglo-Saxon pursuers who scattered in the advance, but those pursuers who maintained their formation in the advance managed to defend themselves.[102] Had the entire Anglo-Saxon army advanced in close order, *densatim progredientes*,[103] as it had in taking up its battle position, no opening for the cavalry would have existed. The Duke's army,

---

in the battle than our sources, reflecting the knightly bias of their audience, let on. It is inconceivable that in the long hours of a hard, close battle William's spearmen would have been standing around using their spears to clip their fingernails. But the cavalry got all the glory. This is also the place to remember David Bates' warning about overestimating the Normans' prowess in war: Bates, *Normandy before 1066*, pp. 238, 245.

99 *pedites densius conglobati*; WP, p. 186. The *Carmen* also makes much of the density of the Anglo-Saxon mass: *Carmen*, lines 368, 415, 417–22.

100 WP, p. 188. See also Lemmon, 'The Campaign of 1066', p. 92.

101 Even this may have owed its effect as much to the single death of king Harold as to any general destructive or disruptive effect. The story of Harold's death by an arrow in the eye is much disputed and based largely on interpretations of the Bayeux Tapestry, which may show the event (BT, pls 71, 72). On the Tapestry and what it means, see David Bernstein, *The Mystery of the Bayeux Tapestry* (Chicago, 1986), and the convincing article by Shirley Ann Brown, 'The Bayeux Tapestry: Why Eustace, Odo and William?', *Battle* 12 (1989), 7–28, with the bibliographies cited in each.

102 *Pars ibi magna perit – pars et densata resistit. Carmen*, lines 429–35.

103 *Carmen*, line 367.

165

demoralized, disordered and thinking him dead,[104] seemed poised to be swept from the field by a general counter-attack. Why was it not?

Douglas concludes that Harold failed to order an advance and so missed the opportunity, and furthermore could not maintain discipline and hold back those of his troops who did advance.[105] But the matter is not clear. Failure to attack does not seem consistent with Harold's record as a general up to that point, including his probable intentions regarding William's invasion.[106] In addition, there are indications that a general advance was ordered: William saw 'a great part of the enemy army leave their positions, and pursue his troops.'[107] The question then becomes, if Harold did order a general advance, what happened to it?

Perhaps the answer lies in the deaths of Earls Gyrth and Leofwine, Harold's brothers and main subordinates. No conclusive moment has been found in the battle for their deaths, for the sources are not specific on this point. If Harold had ordered them to lead the counter-attack, which is not unlikely, and they were killed in front of the Anglo-Saxon army just as the advance was getting under way, the whole effort may have collapsed from this sudden loss of leadership. The placement of their deaths in the Bayeux Tapestry is not inconsistent with this

104 WP, p. 190.
105 Douglas, *William the Conqueror*, p. 200.
106 William of Poitiers describes Harold as 'eager for battle': WP, p. 154. For Harold's offensive intentions, see also Fuller, *Military History*, pp. 373, 375; Douglas, *William the Conqueror*, p. 197; Brown, *Normans and the Norman Conquest*, p. 159; Lemmon, 'Campaign of Hastings', pp. 95, 107. But cf. Morton and Muntz, *Carmen*, pp. 73–83, who argue that Harold's strategy was to trap William on the Hastings peninsula by establishing a strong defensive position on Battle Hill (and see maps in *Carmen*, pp. 110–11). But this does not necessarily imply a defensive approach to the battle itself; in fact, Morton and Muntz (following William of Poitiers and the *Carmen*) say that 'the king was preparing to blockade him [Duke William] by sea and surprise him in great strength on land', (p. 76) and suggest that the story of the fleet (for which there is no sure evidence) was 'calculated to bring the duke to battle forthwith.' (pp. 77–8, n. 5) In fact a real strategy of blockade and delay seems problematical: Harold is as likely as William to have run into supply problems from sitting still in the immediate vicinity, and unless there really were an Anglo-Saxon fleet able to contain and defeat William's fleet, William would not in fact be trapped. It should be noted that if William did land first at Pevensey (William of Poitiers, p. 164 and n. 3), then the move to Hastings would have involved use of the fleet as well as marching (see map in *Carmen*, p. 110).
107 WP, p. 190. Cf. OV, 2:174, who follows WP word for word on this point. Interestingly, the *Carmen* has the Anglo-Saxons pressing their attack against a feigned flight, turning it into a real rout: ll. 439–44. The problem, of course, is telling an abortive general advance from an undisciplined pursuit.

interpretation;[108] and the fact that their deaths were noticed by the sources may indicate that they died prominently – in front of their army, that is.[109] If, moreover, they were near the center of the Anglo-Saxon line to lead the attack, which is also not unlikely, this would account for the disordered advances taking place on the wings of the Anglo-Saxon army, which might not have seen their leaders' fate and thus been halted.[110]

In any case, the English attack faltered and William gained time to rally his army. The crisis of the battle, when one side or the other should have won the day, had passed with neither side winning. This is where Hastings becomes peculiar. An army which is rallied from panic rarely panics again. This accounts for the unusual length of the battle: the Normans recovered from their rout; the Anglo-Saxons recovered from the failure of their counter-attack. The Anglo-Saxons won no further opportunities to counter-attack, even if they had had the leaders to lead one; while the Normans faced the prospect of having to attack re-peatedly a still formidable target.[111] What followed seemed strange to those who saw it: 'there followed an unknown sort of battle,' says William of Poitiers, 'in which one side launched attacks and numerous manoeuvres, the other stood like rocks fixed to the ground.'[112] The rocklike immobility of the Anglo-Saxons gave the Normans the security to carry out the famous feigned flights, the existence of which I see no

---

108 *BT*, pls 62–8. The Normans charge (pl. 62), and are repulsed by the shield wall (pl. 63). Then Leofwine and Gyrth are killed (pls 64–5), apparently out in the open, away from the dense mass of the shield wall depicted in the preceding scene. Why would they be separated at this stage except to lead an attack? Following their deaths, we see French and English killing each other (pl. 66) and what appear to be less well-armed English troops isolated on a hillock (pl. 67). Finally, William bares his head and rallies his army for further attacks (pl. 68). The *Carmen*, line 478, may also support this view, as Gyrth is named as a victim of William himself (which we need not accept at face value) as the Duke led the counterattack on the Anglo-Saxon pursuit.

109 In addition to the Tapestry, Gyrth and Leofwine are mentioned as killed along with Harold in ASC (D, E) 1066, and Florence 1:227, but not (unsurprisingly) by William of Jumieges. William of Poitiers notes their deaths having taken place (p. 200), but does not name them or place their deaths in the sequence of events.

110 William of Poitiers, p. 206, states that their bodies were found near Harold's. Paradox-ically, the loss of leadership may have inspired the Anglo-Saxon army to fight even harder in defense, as the Anglo-Saxon tradition, at least in literature, emphasized rallying around a fallen lord. See, for example, the reactions of the followers of Ealdorman Byrhtnoth in *The Battle of Maldon: Anglo-Saxon Poetry*, trans. R.K. Gordon, rev. edn (London, 1970), pp. 332–3.

111 WP, p. 192.

112 WP, p. 194.

reason to doubt.[113] Yet the issue still hung in the balance; the Anglo-Saxons were by no means doomed.[114] The death of Harold in what must have been the final attack of the day, whatever its outcome, proved the decisive factor in the end, and remarkably even this led not to a rapid rout but a slow, hard-fought collapse.[115] Harold's death, like that of his brothers, shows the decisive role of leadership in a battle which on the Norman side, and in the final outcome on both sides, was dominated by Duke William.[116]

Dol and Gerberoy (November 1076 and January 1079)

As noted above, the source for these two conflicts offer insufficient detail even to be sure what happened. King William's army at each siege seems to have been fairly large; but his forces had undoubtedly been worn down by several weeks of siege work in each case before the major fighting occurred. It is not even clear, however, what form the fighting took, especially at Dol. There, William's forces seem to have been taken by surprise and to have retreated precipitously in the face of suddenly overwhelming opposition. They lost heavily in men and material.[117] Dol was a defeat, but calling it a battle may be inaccurate. We may be more sure that some sort of pitched battle occurred at Gerberoy, in which William himself was unhorsed and wounded, and only saved by the actions of an Englishman in his army.[118] But the unexpected success of the defender's sally may suggest that they took the besiegers by surprise, had to fight only a portion of William's forces, and that William's wounding had a demoralizing effect on his army. About infantry and cavalry tactics we can conclude virtually nothing.[119]

---

113 WP, p. 194; Douglas, *William the Conqueror*, p. 201, n. 2; see above, p. 148, n. 44.

114 The strategic situation meant that the Anglo-Saxons could afford a draw, while the Normans could not. Had the Anglo-Saxons held together for an hour more, or through one more Norman attack, they might have won the war without winning the battle. William's army was not going to get any bigger; Harold probably fought with only a part of his military forces gathered: ASC (E) 1066; Florence 1:227. William, in a hostile country, without a firm base of operations, and probably having to contend with the Anglo-Saxon fleet (William of Poitiers, p. 180), was also more likely to run into supply problems than was Harold. Finally, Harold was the sitting king, and a boxing analogy is here apt: the challenger has to win, the champion only has to not lose.

115 WP, pp. 202–4, and see note 110 above.

116 Douglas, *William the Conqueror*, p. 204.

117 ASC (E) 1076; OV, 2:352.

118 ASC (E) 1079.

119 Orderic speaks of many horses killed: OV, 3:110.

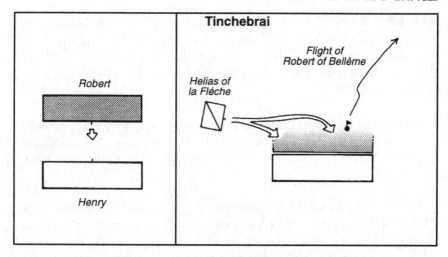

Tinchebrai

Robert

Henry

Helias of
la Fléche

Flight of
Robert of Bellême

Tinchebrai (28 September 1106)

The general course of the battle of Tinchebrai is fairly well known.[120] It was not a long battle – about an hour, according to one source.[121] In another respect also the battle was far more 'normal' than Hastings: prisoners seem to have significantly outnumbered casualties.[122] The feature of the battle which has attracted most comment, not surprisingly, is the role of foot-soldiers, including dismounted knights on both sides. As C.W. David noted, 'Whatever the theorists may hold, foot-soldiers did play an unusually large part in the battle of Tinchebrai.'[123] The only part of this assessment that might be questioned, given the dismounting of royal forces at Brémule and Bourgthérolde, is how 'unusual' the prominence of infantry was, at least for Anglo-Norman royal armies. The conduct of the battle in this respect is instructive, and shows how little the Anglo-Saxon tactics at Hastings were determined by 'obsolete thinking'.

Henry of Huntingdon informs us that 'the king, the duke, and their lines were on foot, in order to fight more resolutely.'[124] Stand or die: the dismounted knight could not flee, and so was a better, more determined fighter, in addition to making less elite infantry behind him better by

---

120 OV, 6:88–90, and the priest of Fécamp's letter: *EHR* 25 (1910), 296, are the primary sources for the battle. HH, p. 235 and the king's own letter to Anselm: Eadmer, p. 184, also add details.
121 *EHR* 25, 296.
122 Eadmer, p. 184.
123 C.W. David, *Robert Curthose* (Harvard, 1920), p. 247.
124 . . . *rex namque, et dux, et acies ceterae pedites erant, ut constantius pugnarent.* HH, p. 235.

example. Dismounted units of Henry's *familia* received the initial attack – a mounted charge it would seem – from Duke Robert's army; though disordered, they held.[125] The two main bodies of foot-soldiers, led by the king and duke respectively, must then have joined the fight, and a mass melée ensued:[126]

> When the two armies came together . . . they were so densely packed, and stood with their weapons so closely locked, that they could do nothing to each other, and all attempted in turn to break the solid lines.

A clever bit of prearranged generalship then turned the tide for Henry. Helias of Maine, who with his troops had been posted some distance away and remained mounted, led a charge on the exposed flank and rear of the duke's engaged column of foot-soldiers. In marked contrast to the repulse of the duke's frontal charge, Helias' troops slew a number of infantry in short order and completely broke the cohesion of Robert's army.[127]

Even more decisively, the flank attack convinced Robert of Bellême, second in command of the duke's army, to flee the field; his flight led to the collapse of the Duke's entire army.[128] Once again the critical role of leadership in determining the course of battle is demonstrated.

Finally, the different fates of Duke Robert and Robert of Bellême emphasize the greater stability of infantry over cavalry, but show its potentially negative side for the loser in a battle of foot-soldiers: the mounted baron fled, saving himself but losing the battle; the dismounted duke fought bravely but was captured.

Alençon (December 1118)

Like Dol and Gerberoy, Alençon is an engagement about which the Norman sources are not expansive or clear, but there is an account with more detail from the Angevin side.[129] What we know of the fighting is interesting. Fulk had gathered an army consisting of *milites*, *sagittarios* and *pedites* and drew it up in battle line to meet Henry's relief forces.[130]

---

125 OV, 6:88; HH, p. 235.
126 OV, 6:88.
127 HH, p. 235; OV, 6:88–90.
128 *EHR* 25, 296.
129 OV, 6:206–8; *Gesta Consulum Andegavorum* in *Chroniques des Comtes d'Anjou*, pp. 155–61.
130 OV, 6:206, 208; *Chroniques*, p. 156.

Henry's army split into at least two division. Theobald and Stephen of Blois led the first, which may have contained more of the young and eager members of the *familia*.[131] The king led the second division, probably with more of the footsoldiers.[132] 'Greedy for glory', the first division advanced ahead of Henry's main force, it appears; Fulk's line repulsed their mounted attacks with no small loss in killed and captured Norman knights. The Angevins relied heavily on archery and used the solid mass of heavy infantry as a base from which to launch mounted counterattacks.[133] Fulk himself is presented as leading the defense, saying 'Behold your leader' and urging his troops of all types on by word and example.[134]

Alençon is interesting because it teaches many of the same lessons as the other battles of the period, but with the Normans on the losing side. Leadership again plays a crucial role, with Fulk in control of his whole force and leading the fight, while Henry lost touch with a major part of his forces. The advantages of combined arms tactics, especially the vulnerability of an unsupported and ill-organized cavalry charge against a mixed force of archers and heavy infantry supported by cavalry, is particularly clear. The results of the battle also show what victory could bring when battle was successfully risked: Fulk not only went on to capture the town, left without hope of relief, but set the stage for a favorable peace settlement with Henry.[135]

Brémule (20 August 1119)

The details of the battle of Brémule have never been clear because the primary sources – Orderic, Henry of Huntingdon, Suger and The Hyde Chronicle[136] – are completely at odds with each other concerning Henry's order of battle. Of these accounts, that of the Hyde Chronicle seems best able to make sense of the others' conflicting accounts.

It seems that Henry had about 500 knights with him, including some *familia* troops; 400 or so of these dismounted. The mounted troops were

---

131 *Chroniques*, p. 156.
132 *Chroniques*, p. 156; Henry's army is said there to have been composed of '*Francigene, Angli, Normanni, Flandrenses, Britones cum adjutoriis suis*'.
133 OV, 6:208; *Chroniques*, pp. 157–9. We may perhaps see in this battle the first signs of one of Stephen of Blois' consistent characteristics as a general: rashness in committing to battle. His impetuosity was to serve him ill several times in the civil war with Matilda.
134 *Chroniques*, p. 159.
135 *Chroniques*, pp. 160–1.
136 OV, 6:236–42; HH, 241–2; Suger, *Vita Ludovici grossi regis*, ed. H. Waquet (Paris, 1929), pp. xxvi, 196–8; *Liber Monasterii de Hyda*, ed. E. Edwards (RS 1886), pp. 317–18.

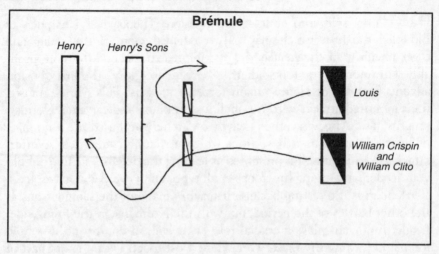

stationed forward of the foot-soldiers, in two groups, either side by side or one behind the other, and were led by William of Warenne, Henry of Eu and Walter Giffard. Behind the mounted line – thrown forward, it appears, to induce a French attack – Henry put the dismounted knights drawn up in a dense formation.[137] Since the sources agree that Henry and his sons led different columns, and since the circumstances of their parts in the battle suggest that all had dismounted – Orderic states explicitly that Henry was on foot, Henry of Huntingdon that Richard and Robert were on foot[138] – there may well have been two lines of infantry, the first under the royal sons, the second under the king, as the Hyde Chronicle claims.[139]

Whatever the exact disposition of Henry's forces, the sources agree on the general course of the battle. Charging in roughly two groups, the first led by William Crispin and William Clito, the second by King Louis, the French rode headlong and completely without order at the Norman army. The first group appears to have ridden straight through the initial line (or lines) of Henry's cavalry, scattering them a bit without causing much damage. According to the Hyde Chronicle, they then split into two groups, rode completely around the first dense line of infantry, pursued by the Norman cavalry they had just ridden through, and attacked Henry's line, where William Crispin delivered a glancing blow to the king's head. Surrounded by the various portions of Henry's army, nearly

137 *Hyda*, p. 317.
138 OV, 6:338; HH, p. 241.
139 *Hyda*, p. 317.

all the first group were captured. The second group of French knights, under Louis, probably followed the first and attacked the front of Henry's first line of infantry after Henry's cavalry had fallen back in pursuit of the first attackers. Some of the second attack were also captured; some, including Louis, fled, pursued by Normans who had remounted.

The general character of this battle is in fact admirably summed up by Oman:[140]

> The conflict of authorities on minor points does not prevent us from having a very clear idea of the military significance of Brémule. Disorderly charges of cavalry, unaided by either infantry or archers, avail nothing against a solid mass of well-armed knights on foot.

Or as the Hyde Chronicle has it, 'He who charges rashly often falls.'[141] The disorder of the French army reflected Louis' lack of command control and more generally the small degree of control he exercised over his military system, though in the event it also reflected the king's rashness and lack of self-control, for he made no attempt to draw up his troops in an ordered way.

Bourgthérolde (26 March 1124)[142]

The minor battle of Bourgthérolde is of interest because it demonstrates the remarkable capabilities of the royal *familia* in independent campaigning. The tactical lessons of the conflict reinforce what the other battles show: the importance of firm leadership, cohesion and group loyalty, and the impotence of the traditional cavalry charge in the face of a firm line of well-armed infantry. In fact the battle plan of Odo Borleng is a minor masterpiece of medieval combined arms generalship, and bears a remarkable similarity to the dispositions of Edward III's army at Crecy: a central line of dismounted knights, supported by archers thrown forward on the flanks, with a mounted reserve ready to exploit the infantry's success.[143] The archers of the *familia* at Bourgthérolde were even mounted for campaigning[144] as Edward's were.

---

140 Oman, *Art of War*, 1:338.
141 *Qui praeceps graditur saepe cadit. Hyda*, p. 317.
142 OV, 6:348–53 is the only source for this battle.
143 OV, 6:348.
144 WJ, p. 294.

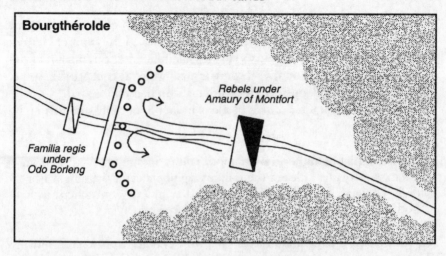

The unifying themes of Anglo-Norman battle tactics may be stressed again: the critical role of leadership in determining the outcome of battles; and the use of infantry, cavalry and, at times, archers in combination. It should be remembered that William's army at Hastings was mixed, and that the archers and cavalry worked together in the end. Even the duke's heavy infantry may have played a greater role, especially late in the battle, than the pro-knightly bias of the sources reveals. The continuing use of infantry, including the dismounting of knights, reflects the importance of combined-arms tactics in Anglo-Norman royal warfare.

NAVAL COMBAT

Sieges and battles were the two forms of tactical action engaged in by the Anglo-Norman royal army. As has been noted, the number of battles between 1066 and 1135 is small compared to the number of sieges. Yet land battles appear frequent compared to the number of battles conducted by the Anglo-Norman royal navy. Indeed the very existence of a combat navy may be questioned after 1101. Only the fact that warships as a special class probably did not exist, and so any transport vessel filled with soldiers was a potential warship, prevents us from asserting that no combat navy existed for most of Henry's reign.

The one real naval battle of the entire period occurred in 1088 in connection with Rufus' siege of Pevensey. Duke Robert sent ships from Normandy with supplies and reinforcements for the defenders, but 'the

English who guarded the sea fell on them and sank a great many of them.'[145] This shows that the Anglo-Norman combat navy was still English – probably the remains of the Anglo-Saxon navy which had been a major cause of concern to the Norman nobles before the invasion in 1066, but which had met with such ill-fortune in that campaign.[146] It may be indicative of the declining fortunes of these Anglo-Saxon survivors that Symeon of Durham refers to them as Rufus' *piratae*.[147] Yet they did manage to sink Robert's fleet decisively, which led directly to the surrender of the castle.[148]

Unfortunately, we have almost no information on the types of ships and tactics used in this battle.[149] Naval tactics before the advent of gunpowder consisted of a combination of three techniques: grappling and boarding; ramming; and hurling missiles from siege engines carried on board. The effectiveness of the last was immeasurably increased if the missiles were fire-causing. Which of these methods might the Anglo-Norman navy have used at Pevensey?

There is no evidence that the limited naval resources of the Norman kings included ships specially fitted out with engines of war. Ordinary archers could of course have made up part of a ship's contingent of marines, but their effect would have been limited to anti-personnel fire. Lacking some specially flammable substance such as Greek fire, incendiary missiles must have been somewhat ineffective if used at all by the Anglo-Norman navy.

It is easy to imagine the use of grappling and boarding by *butescarls* experienced in fighting on shipboard, and this must have been one of the common tactics of Anglo-Saxon naval warfare. There are two problems with supposing the use of this tactic on any great scale at Pevensey, however. First, soldiers destined for the castle filled Robert's ships, and even if they lacked experience as marines they must have presented formidable opposition to a scraped up force of *piratae*. Second, Henry of Huntingdon and Symeon of Durham both refer to large scale sinking of Robert's fleet. Boarding is not a tactic which sinks the enemy's ships.

This leaves ramming, or more generally using friendly ships as weapons

---

[145] HH, p. 215.
[146] WP, p. 156; Florence, 1:225.
[147] Symeon, HR, p. 216.
[148] HH, p. 215.
[149] A general introduction to the sorts of ships and tactics used in northern European waters in this period is available in Lewis and Runyon, *European Naval and Maritime History, 300–1500* (Bloomington, 1985), pp. 111–43. See also Neumann, 'Hydrographic and Ship-hydrodynamic Aspects of the Norman Invasion, A.D. 1066'.

to damage enemy ships. We know that Mediterranean-style galleys with bronze beaks designed specifically for ramming did not see use in the rougher seas of the Atlantic, the Channel and the North Sea: they lacked the seaworthiness to operate outside of the calm waters of the Mediterranean. Designs derived from the Viking longboat dominated in northern waters, as the Bayeux Tapestry shows. These could easily accommodate the oar-power necessary for ship-to-ship combat, but do not seem particularly suited to ramming. Yet this is the tactic we must assume worked for Rufus' navy at Pevensey, unless incendiary or other missiles had more effect than I have allowed and the spectacular burning of Robert's fleet that would have resulted from such missiles went unnoticed by the sources.

The fact that ramming tactics require experienced oarsmen to carry them out may support this interpretation. Rufus' Anglo-Saxon *butescarls* probably were experienced oarsmen, and would have been at a great advantage against Norman sailors unaccustomed to the tactics of oared combat. It should be remembered that in 1066 the Normans worried whether they could find enough experienced oarsmen for the invasion fleet within the space of a year.[150]

Whatever the means used – and in truth whatever we say of the naval tactics of this period is speculation – Rufus' fleet gained a decisive but unrepeated victory at Pevensey. We see the royal navy in tactical action on only two other occasions. In 1072 William I 'led a naval force and a land force to Scotland, and blockaded that country from the sea with ships.'[151] There was no enemy fleet to fight, and it is not clear what the ships blockaded. Probably they served to demonstrate the English power at sea in conjunction with the king's show of force on land, in addition to acting as supply carriers for the army. The second occasion on which the royal navy appears had the same potential for battle as existed in 1088: Robert's threatened invasion of England in 1101. Henry's preparations included naval defense: 'he ordered his *butescarls* to guard the sea, and watch lest any force from Normandy reach the shores of England.'[152] In the event, however, the fleet defected to Robert on the eve of his sailing and the invaders crossed without a fight. Perhaps not surprisingly, this is the last we hear of *butescarls* and combat navies.

The question is why do we not hear more of royal fleets when we might expect to: during the Scandinavian invasions of 1069 and 1075,

150 WP, p. 156.
151 ASC (D) 1073 (1072).
152 Florence, 2:48.

and the threat of invasion in 1085. Undoubtedly William felt much more confident in the strength of his army and his castles to repulse an invasion than in the ability of his small Anglo-Saxon war fleet to stop an invasion before it landed. Indeed the discrepancy we may assume between the size and experience of the Scandinavian and Anglo-Norman fleets must have made even the prospect of damaging the invaders' fleet at anchorage seem fairly remote. Thus, not surprisingly, William's defense efforts were concentrated on land defense, for building up a large combat navy might not have been effective, would have been a long-term project rather than an immediate response to a specific invasion, and went against the traditions and strategies of Norman military experience.

PRISONERS

As noted above,[153] prisoners often outnumbered casualties in Anglo-Norman battles. Furthermore, sieges or assaults on strongholds often took the garrison along with the building, though some garrisons marched free as part of the settlement of a siege. What happened to prisoners in Anglo-Norman warfare? The answer to this question varied depending on the captor, the prisoner, and the circumstances of the capture.

If the prisoner were of sufficient social standing, in other words rich enough, he could be ransomed. The prospect of ransoms could be an incentive for some to go to war, as Orderic notes of French forces fighting Rufus' *familia* in 1097, skirmishes in which both sides took some prisoners.[154] But it seems that the traffic in ransoms occurred mainly at levels below the king – that is among equals fighting as individuals rather than in the king's service.

Guibert of Nogent claims, in fact, that Duke William sold no captives: 'It was the custom of this count never to hold prisoners for ransoms, but to condemn them to captivity for life.'[155] Henry of France did in fact obtain the release of some of his vassals captured at Mortemer in 1054[156] – including Guibert's father – but the decision to release royal prisoners depended ultimately on political rather than financial considerations.

---

153 See above, p. 149.
154 OV, 5:216.
155 *Self and Society in Medieval France. The Memoirs of Abbot Guibert of Nogent*, ed. and trans. John F. Benton (New York, 1970), p. 69. Guibert exaggerates, but William probably encouraged such contributions to a fearsome reputation.
156 WP, p. 77.

Henry I, having captured his brother Robert at Tinchebrai, held him in captivity the rest of his life to eliminate possible competition for the throne. Similarly, Henry threw Robert of Bellême, captured not in war but arrested on an embassy from the King of France, into prison permanently, ending his career of rebellion.[157] Ransom in these cases was out of the question.

Prisoners of a lower social standing were clearly not very good for lucrative ransoms. The treatment of such captives – including enfeoffed soldiers serving feudal duty, mercenaries of various types, and even townspeople captured in a siege – varied greatly and is thus difficult to generalize about. But a few conclusions may be drawn.

The most important consideration in the captor's decision about such prisoners may have been the perceived intent, or honorability, of the captives' part in hostilities up to their capture. Thus William I's lieutenants mutilated and exiled the plundering Flemish mercenaries they captured at Fagaduna in 1075, and confiscated their possessions.[158] But Henry I allowed the mercenaries who defended Bridgnorth for Robert of Bellême to go free with their arms and horses, because they had 'stayed faithful to their lord as they ought'.[159] Of course class, ethnicity and style of fighting probably enhanced the 'honor' of these mercenaries, as opposed to that of the Flemings: some mercenaries undoubtedly had higher status and thus more respect than others.

Other factors influencing the treatment of captives included the relative security of the victor (this factor also distinguishes the Flemings in 1075 from the rebels of 1102), and the captives' potential usefulness. Mercenaries who might be re-employed by their captor would clearly receive better treatment than those who could not. A closely related consideration was the degree of resistance the prisoners had offered. Particularly where castle garrisons were concerned, long resistance could mean harsh treatment in defeat, as an example to other strongholds.

Finally, treatment of prisoners could vary with the captor. The Breton nobles and other mercenaries captured at Norwich, just months after Fagaduna, were granted their lives and spared mutilation, and swore to leave the kingdom within forty days (thirty for the mercenaries) and never return without the king's permission. As Clover and Gibson point out, 'The council of London had just agreed that ecclesiastics should not

---

157 Barlow, *Feudal Kingdom*, p. 195.
158 OV, 2:316.
159 OV, 6:28.

be party to judgements of death or mutilation; the Norwich garrison may have benefited by this ruling when Lanfranc and/or Geoffrey of Coutances came to sentence them.'[160] As in non-military questions of justice, the church's methods tended to be more moderate than those of the temporal power.

[160] *Letters of Lanfranc*, no. 35 and n. 1.

Chapter Six

CONCLUSIONS

The disputed succession which followed the death of Henry I posed a grave danger to one of the foundations of royal military power: the bonds of friendship which tied the barons and soldiers of the realm to the king. Of course in itself succession dispute was nothing new to Anglo-Norman history. Duke Robert and his son William Clito had claims to the throne in the reigns of Rufus and Henry; Robert pressed his claims militarily in 1088 and 1101. Only on the death of the Clito in 1128 could Henry finally feel the problem settled. But Rufus and Henry had been able to meet this threat to their power and solidify their hold on the military system. Within three years Stephen's inability to overcome this danger left the realm divided by civil war. This struck at the other basis of royal military strength, money.

When the kingdom split into warring factions, the machinery of government split as well, and disruption ensued. The capacity of the military system to make war weakened directly, since it operated as a branch of government. The most obvious case of this is that the division of the kingdom disrupted the shrieval organization of taxation and territorial army service. The king no longer had use of the full resources of the realm. Some of what the king lost, his opponents gained; some simply disappeared. William of Malmesbury's picture of Stephen's resulting impecunity[1] is probably exaggerated – there is no evidence that the coinage was debased, for instance – but the task of maintaining the military system with reduced resources undoubtedly put a strain on the king's finances.

Reduced resources and weak leadership seriously hampered the effectiveness of royal warfare. Stephen could not bring the war in England to a conclusion in under ten years; in the meantime, Normandy had been lost to the Angevins. But the weakness of royal warfare between 1135 and 1154 resulted from the deficiencies of Stephen as a leader, not from

---

[1] Malmesbury, HN, p. 42.

any fundamental deficiency of the Anglo-Norman military system. Nor did the troubles of the civil war do irreparable damage to that system.

The basic continuity and underlying strength of the Anglo-Norman military system during Stephen's reign is demonstrated by the quick recovery of royal military power under Henry II. In this recovery, the military system parallels the history of the government as a whole. And as with the royal systems of justice and finance, the new king did not simply recover the military efficiency of his grandfather's time. He developed his resources to an even greater degree. Henry's achievements as a castle builder are well documented, and had a farreaching effect: 'these years saw nothing less than a drastic alteration of the balance of power, expressed in terms of castles, as between king and baronage, in favor of the former.'[2] Furthermore, they reflect the basic strength of the financial and military institutions left to Henry by Stephen, and are the clearest demonstration of the vital ties between money and military power:[3]

> Angevin castle-building in England during this period represents the latent military power of a strong centralized government, no less necessary to its success than its other assets of economic superiority and administrative efficiency.

Henry's development of his resources also had a critical effect on the conduct of warfare in the field. His increased financial resources enabled Henry to maintain a substantial force of Brabançon infantry, trained, it seems, in siege tactics like those that took Malmesbury in 1153: sudden, bloodthirsty assaults from all sides at once, with the men on scaling ladders covered by continual missile fire, designed to overwhelm the usually small garrisons.[4] This force made Henry a feared castle taker as well as builder.[5] Combined with his vast building programs, Henry's siege tactics fundamentally altered the patterns of warfare.

Yet Henry built his achievements from essentially the same system, with the *familia* at its heart, that his predecessors had used. Henry simply made the system work even better with the addition of more money. And in the increased emphasis on the infantry arm of his army, we see the extension of principles already clearly demonstrated earlier: money strengthens central authority, strong central authority tends to favor good infantry. The cavalry forces of Anglo-Norman armies, like the

---

[2] Brown, 'A List of Castles, 1154–1116', *EHR* 74 (1959), 249.
[3] Brown, 'Royal Castle-Building', p. 361.
[4] *Gesta Stephani*, ed. and trans. K.R. Potter (Oxford, 1976), p. 230.
[5] Warren, *Henry II*, pp. 231 ff.

cavalry of warfare in general, were less affected by changes in central strength. Changes in the ability of governments to pay their troops and maintain forces thus affected infantry more than cavalry use.

It would take separate studies to do justice to the military systems and warfare of Stephen and Henry II's reigns. But continuity of the military system and of the English infantry tradition through the Civil War into the warfare of Henry's reign points to two of the central conclusions that may be drawn from this study of Anglo-Norman royal warfare from 1066 to 1135: from the military system, the centrality of the *familia*; and from warfare, the continued use of effective infantry tactics that the *familia* allowed. The central role of leadership in Anglo-Norman warfare is the only other topic calling for further discussion, including an evaluation of the 'generalship' of each of the three kings who reigned from 1066 to 1135.

THE MILITARY SYSTEM

The clearest point to emerge concerning the Anglo-Norman military system in the period 1066–1135 is the centrality of the *familia regis*. Its organization was at the heart of the entire system. Its regulations concerning terms of service were the basis for the large scale employment of mercenaries, who were, over the whole period, the most important source of manpower available to the Anglo-Norman kings. It provided a permanent framework within which the temporary soldiers of the territorial armies, the fyrd and the feudal host, could be employed effectively. It allowed the kings to retain military specialists – engineers, merchants, artillerists, and so on – without whom the field army could not have operated, but who could not have been provided for in any other way. Finally, the 'institutionalized experience' that the *familia* embodied – professional (paid) service in stable groups over a significant period of time, tied to the king by firm bonds of profit and friendship – was the basis for many of the tactical capabilities and practices of Anglo-Norman royal armies in the field. In particular, the discipline and cohesion of *familia* troops allowed them to be used as infantry or cavalry as the situation called for.

The significance of the centrality of the *familia* to the wider institutional history of medieval England lies in the connection of the military household with the structure of the Anglo-Norman government as a whole. As has been pointed out, the military system of 1066–1135 was a branch of government. One cannot separate the history of the military system from the institutional history of the realm. This has a bearing on the contentious problem of Anglo-Saxon to Anglo-Norman continuity.[6]

In this context, the military similarity of the housecarls and the *familia* is significant, especially in that the professionalism and permanence of both had a direct effect on battle tactics. In other words, the similarity of the two military systems allowed continuity of the infantry tradition of Anglo-Saxon England. The continued use of the fyrd as a major source of support for the professional elite of the army, whether housecarls or *familia*, was another point of continuity between Anglo-Saxon and Norman military practice, and reinforced the tendency towards infantry tactics. It should not be overlooked, however, that the *familia* did improve on the tactical capabilities of Anglo-Saxon armies: *familia* knights could fight on horseback as well as on foot; the housecarls, though they used horses for strategic transport, fought exclusively on foot. It is true that Norman knights were not trained to fight on shipboard, but given the vastly greater number of engagements fought on land than at sea by Anglo-Saxon or Norman forces, it would seem that the gain in tactical flexibility was clearly on the Norman side.

The close ties of the *familia* to the government as a whole are also significant in terms of the continuity of the Anglo-Norman military system into later periods of English history. As Prestwich has pointed out, 'Anglo-Norman military forces were not then so different in structure from those of Edward I as historians have often supposed.'[7] Undoubtedly the intimate connection of the military system with the government accounted for the system's continuity, in addition to the fact that the *familia's* sophistication and flexibility enabled it to adapt to changing conditions of warfare fairly easily. The permanence of the *familia* at the heart of the military system also allowed territorial forces to remain a useful part of English royal armies. The reform of militia duty undertaken in the Assize of Arms of 1181 owes its organization to the principles of the Anglo-Saxon fyrd; but the usefulness of the force it produced resulted from the professional body of troops the militia supported. On the other side, the evidence for continuity of the military system is by implication evidence for the continuity of the wider governmental institutions of which they were a part.

The most important result of the continuity of the *familia* structure of English military organization, however, was the continuity of battle tactics that resulted from it, for the permanence, professionalism and central

---

6 Prestwich, 'Continuity', p. 39; pp. 22–28 above.
7 Prestwich, 'Continuity', p. 51.

control that gave the *familia* the ability to fight effectively on foot or horseback in the twelfth century had the same effect in the fourteenth. In fact a description of the tactics of Edward I's *familia* could apply to the tactics of virtually any small English army between 1042 and 1450:[8]

> Although the English normally fought on foot at this epoch, they moved from place to place on horses and frequently utilized their steeds in the pursuit of fleeing foes; . . .

The only reason the qualifier 'small' is needed is that large English armies usually included substantial bodies of foot-soldiers, such as the fyrd or Henry II's Brabançons, who did not have horses for transport or pursuit. As I mentioned concerning the Assize of Arms, the role of the *familia*, in terms of organization and discipline, in making such forces into effective parts of the army was critical.

The significance of the continuity of the English infantry tradition lies in the adoption of the longbow in the thirteenth century, a development that had a huge impact on European warfare during the Hundred Years' War. It is reasonable to say that the institutional and tactical continuity of the *familia* (and, in support, of militia duty) allowed English armies to adopt the longbow and make effective use of it. The similarity of the tactics at Bourgthérolde and Crecy should be remembered in this context. It may also be pointed out that 'technology', in the form of weapons changes, has rarely altered warfare by itself, for the armies that adopt new weapons must have the organization to incorporate them and must have tactical capabilities compatible with their use.[9] The point is made by Michael Howard in connection with the changes in weapons and warfare in Europe between the time of Gustavus Adolphus and that of Frederick the Great:[10]

> Indeed it is doubtful whether the improvements in weapons would have taken place at all, much less have been fully exploited, if full-time

---

8 A.E. Prince, 'The Army and Navy', in *The English Government at Work 1327–1336*, ed. J.F. Willard and W.A. Morris, 1:337.

9 This general rule is true at least before the invention of a practical rifled musket in the 1830s, which did have major tactical implications. This change accompanied the broader technological changes resulting from the Industrial Revolution, which inevitably revolutionized warfare. But even in the age of technology, the successful tactical application of new weapons systems depends on the framework of military and political institutions using them. See Morillo, 'Guns and Government', for more on this point.

10 Howard, *War in European History*, p. 62. Gabriel, *Culture of War*, develops this theme for both the institutions and practices of warfare in Europe and the Near East from

professionals had not been available to put them to good effect and – perhaps more important – full-time officials had not been in a position to take decisions about their development, arrange for their manufacture and supply, and pay for them.

The connections of the *familia* with the government as a whole are even more significant in the context of this last point. Indeed if organization were not so vital to the adoption of new weapons, one would have expected the French armies of the Hundred Years' War to have adopted the longbow themselves; they clearly did not have the organization to do so. This point also casts further doubt on the role of the introduction of the stirrup in the transition from classical to medieval forms of warfare.

The second point concerning the Anglo-Norman military system to emerge from a study of the period 1066–1135, after the centrality of the *familia*, is the small role of feudal forces and the feudal system of military obligations, strictly defined, in the actual warfare of the time. As I have noted, the money raised by the collection of scutage was perhaps the feudal system's most significant contribution to Anglo-Norman armed forces in this period. Given the prominence of the feudal system in the secondary literature, this conclusion calls for some comment.

In the first place, the level of military use of the system says nothing about its importance in the legal and social structure of medieval England: the Anglo-Norman realm was a feudal society. But in broad terms, Anglo-Saxon society functioned very similarly to Norman society. Perhaps the whole problem of the introduction of feudalism into England should be recast in other terms and in the light of the lack of military use of the feudal system. The problem of continuity between fyrd and feudal host would seem to be affected by the feudal system's small role. Historians who see a transition from the five-hide army to the feudal host in terms of 'ancient obligation, discharged in a new way, through the feudal hierarchy'[11] – that is, that the fyrd became the host – would have to explain the transformation of a militarily useful system into a militarily under-used system. But once again, most of the territory covered by the term 'feudalism' is beyond the scope of this study. It may simply be noted, in terms of wider definitions of feudalism, that the central role of the knights of the *familia* in Anglo-Norman warfare should warn medieval

pre-historic times through the fourth century; his conclusions are completely applicable to the middle ages.

11 Matthew, *Norman Conquest*, p. 127; clearly, I have not accepted this point of view.

historians that militarily, mailed horsemen plus castles does not equal feudalism, no matter how closely they are intertwined.

Returning to the feudal system as a military institution, its small role in the warfare of England and Normandy in the period 1066–1135 does raise some questions about its military significance in other countries. Feudal society has been called a society organized for war. But the Anglo-Norman military system was organized for war partly in non-feudal ways. Where was feudalism militarily significant? When, and most importantly why, did it have significance as the basis for a state's military organization? The answers to these questions are also beyond the scope of this study, but one of the major points I hope this study has emphasized is that answering such questions involves not just a study of military institutions, but of the warfare they waged and of the non-military context of both. Studying military systems and warfare in isolation from each other and their context leads to distortions, and at best can present only an incomplete picture of each.

WARFARE

The feature of the warfare waged by Anglo-Norman armies which emerges in a variety of ways is the central role of leadership in the conduct of war. Whether in preparing the field of war by diplomacy, choosing the target of a campaign, holding an army together on the march, or conducting sieges and battles, the actions and decisions of the king and his subordinates had a tremendous influence on the ability of Anglo-Norman royal armies to execute their tasks successfully.

Given this dominant influence of the leadership of the king on Anglo-Norman warfare, an evaluation of the 'generalship' of William the Conqueror, Rufus and Henry is virtually an evaluation of the effectiveness of their warfare itself. Such an evaluation would therefore seem to be worthwhile. But first, the term generalship has often been used in military history for an analysis of a general's strategy and tactics in terms of abstract standards of military theory. Such an analysis assumes levels of command control high enough that armies were always responsive instruments of the commander's will, and assumes the dominance of warfare as a tool of policy. As we have seen, neither of these assumptions is justified in Anglo-Norman warfare, particularly the latter. An analysis of the generalship of the Norman kings must therefore be a somewhat broader topic, encompassing several additional factors beyond strictly military strategy and tactics. The king's skill as a diplomat was an essential part of his role as a strategist, for example. The most important additional factor may be called personal influence; that is, the king's ability to control his subordinates and his troops before, during and after warfare. This ability resulted from a combination of leadership by example, reputation and record of success, and personality or charisma. Clearly it is not a precise factor, but just as clearly it had a decisive influence on the king's ability to execute his strategy and tactics.

William I

In the generalship of the Conqueror, his personal influence over his troops was the keystone of his achievements. Before 1066, he had managed to harness the energies of the Norman baronage to his purposes; without this, he could never even have planned the conquest of England. In the course of the 1066 campaign, he held his army together through supply shortages, one of the hardest fought battles of the middle ages, disease, and the pacification of a hostile population. He managed to exert more influence over the course of the battle of Hastings than his opponent, no mean leader himself. In the ten years following the conquest, he tirelessly defended his realm. His energy probably accounts for part of his personal influence in war; if we detect some decline in his effectiveness after about 1076 – and Dol was the first major setback of his career – advancing age and increasing corpulence may both have affected his role on the battlefield, if not on campaign. William's tremendous personal influence allowed him to plan and execute strategy far more boldly than any of his contemporaries. His strategic planning had to be good, because he faced greater challenges than most of his contemporaries, whether he set them himself, as in 1066, or had them thrust upon him, as was mostly the case after 1066. He showed a keen appreciation of where the greatest threats to his security lay: he never really ended up in the wrong place at the wrong time. And his strategy was at times brilliant and daring. His winter march across the Pennines in January of 1070, during which he himself led the foot-soldiers, and his late 1072 land and sea invasion of Scotland, which pushed his army far beyond the normal limits of its supply bases, were bold strokes that could easily have ended in disaster for a leader with less control of his men. He knew the value of time in strategy: he could move quickly when necessary, as his 1073 invasion of Maine demonstrates; but he also knew when lack of haste intimidated, as his deliberate approach to London in 1066 shows. And he knew how to play his opponents: his strategy in 1066 was designed to encourage Harold's natural impetuosity, and he succeeded in persuading the Anglo-Saxon king to abandon the advantage of time as a result. In all, William I must be ranked among the best leaders and strategists of medieval military history.

William's battle tactics were not so exceptional. Apparently he only coordinated the actions of his archers, infantry and cavalry very late in the battle of Hastings. He lost at Dol and Gerberoy, and – to go back a bit – was not on the battlefield at the Norman victory at Mortemer in 1054 nor did he lead the army at Val-es-Dunes.[12] But his tactics did not need to be exceptional, at least early in his reign, because his personal influence was so decisive in battle. His siege tactics were adequate, even good for his time; and the calculated balance of savagery and leniency which characterized many of his operations against cities rose at times to the level of a strategic weapon of some value.[13]

The overall effectiveness of William's warfare, in offense and defense, was thus exceptional, as the achievements of his reign testify. Because of his success, his sons were in an easier position. They faced challenges, it is true, but not quite of the magnitude that the Conqueror had met.

William II

Though not as dominating as his father, Rufus always had full control of his leaders and soldiers. His dominance over a situation tended to increase over time, indicating that the consistency of his personal approach made up for any initial lack of natural authority.

As a strategist Rufus had two sides: one when dealing with internal, defensive wars; and quite another when conducting external, offensive campaigns. In the former case, Rufus could nearly match his father, though he never faced the combination of threats his father had. His direct and determined approach focused on the key to the strategic situation. The campaign of 1088, the first and biggest crisis of his reign, illustrates this. Leaving rebel castles on the periphery of the kingdom to be dealt with by subordinates, he concentrated his efforts against the heart of the rebellion: the castles of Rochester, Tonbridge and Pevensey. And the order in which he attacked these is significant. Tonbridge, which linked the other two castles together, fell first, fragmenting the rebellion. He next beseiged Pevensey, the port for communications with

---

[12] Douglas, *William the Conqueror*, p. 68; Gillingham, 'William the Bastard at War', p. 143.
[13] Gillingham, 'William the Bastard at War', p. 151, also mentions the value of William's brutality.

Normandy, from land and sea. After these two had fallen, taking Rochester proved almost a formality.

By contrast with the decisiveness and lasting success of Rufus' internal defensive warfare, his offensive campaigns showed uniform caution and conservatism to the point of ineffectiveness. His gains in Normandy between 1090 and 1094, for instance, depended much more on money and Duke Robert's incompetence as a ruler than on Rufus' military actions. He only gained the duchy by non-military means. Once in possession, however, he swiftly and effectively pacified the duchy.

Rufus' Maine campaigns of 1098 and 1099 also demonstrate the contrast. His conquest of the county in 1098 owed much to the luck of Robert of Bellême capturing Count Helias and to Fulk of Anjou's defeat by the garrison of Ballon; and even given these advantages, he took months to actually take control of the county, finally gaining Le Mans by treaty rather than military action. The contrast with his father's conquest of Maine in 1073 is dramatic. On offense, Rufus had none of his father's daring or concentration of effort – or success. But when the county, now his, rose in rebellion in 1099, his swift reaction struck at the heart of the rebellion in Le Mans and overwhelmed it.

Rufus' caution is reflected in the complete lack of battle tactics from his reign. This is not necessarily a point against his generalship, however. It simply admits of no judgment. Like his father, Rufus was an adequate besieger of castles. He was not, overall, a great general, but he effectively defended the lands in his possession.

Henry I

Henry's personal influence seems to have been as natural and powerful as his father's. The same power of coercive persuasion that Henry used to establish the succession settlement in 1128 made the king an effective military commander in the field.

The strength of Henry's strategy lay in its connection with his diplomatic skill as king. As a diplomat Henry was perhaps the most skillful of the Norman kings. He was thus able to build up coalitions that either did his fighting for him or made his fighting easier. His conquest of Normandy in 1105 and 1106 was the crowning achievement of this approach: he isolated Robert by a ring of alliances, weakened him by raids and induced rebellions, and finished him off in two campaigns.[14] But Henry's strategy

---

[14] The contrast with the Conqueror's diplomatic history is interesting. The great success of William's reign was the favorable diplomatic situation of 1063 to 1067 which made the

was not great, and even in the conquest of Normandy displayed some of the same caution that characterized Rufus' offensive strategy. Henry, content not to push the pace of a war militarily, relied instead on patient diplomacy to break up enemy attacks. Such a policy was undoubtedly the cheapest and safest course available, but it does reflect the fact that Henry, like Rufus, never faced the level of threat that his father had. Henry's strategy was therefore effective but not great.

On the other hand, Henry was the best tactician of the Norman kings. He knew the strengths and weaknesses of his troops in attack and defense and developed the infantry tactics which proved so effective throughout the reign. His influence in this respect is apparent when Anglo-Norman armies started dismounting even in the absence of the king, as at Bourgthérolde and, after his death, at Northallerton. The mounted line thrown forward of his main force at Brémule to induce a French attack shows that he knew how to exploit the characteristics of enemy troops to his own advantage. Finally, his use of a flanking force at Tinchebrai under Helias of Maine constitutes one of the better pieces of tactical generalship during the eleventh and twelfth centuries. As a besieger of castles Henry was at least as effective as his father and brother had been; he took a personal interest in the tactics of siege warfare and is several times found directing the use of siege machinery. Henry's strength as a tactician lent valuable support to his strategic operations, as the results of Tinchebrai demonstrate. So on the whole, Henry was a good general – certainly an effective one – if not, overall, quite in the same class as his father.

Leadership was important in Anglo-Norman warfare because the influence of leaders touched all aspects of warfare. To present a complete picture of warfare has been one of the aims of this study: medieval warfare, like the warfare of any period, consisted of much more than battle tactics. Yet battle tactics have dominated studies of the medieval 'art of war'. What does a more complete view of warfare have to say about battle tactics? Put another way, where does Anglo-Norman royal warfare fit into the medieval art of war as it has commonly been understood?

For one thing, looking at all aspects of warfare shows how misplaced the emphasis on battle really is. The role of field armies called for battles

conquest possible. But this alignment of forces was due as much if not more to luck as to William's skill. Henry's diplomatic constructions lasted longer and were more of his own making.

only as a last resort, and a successful campaign could easily be conducted without a battle being fought. Simply in terms of tactical action, sieges were far more common and, in terms of the goals of warfare, more important than battles.

For another, a broad view of warfare sheds new light on the dominance of cavalry in medieval warfare, showing that it needs to be redefined and explained very differently from the way it has been, as I have already noted in connection with battle tactics.[15] To restate the major points in this context, first, the dominance of cavalry is strictly confined to battle tactics. For one thing, siege tactics had to be conducted by foot-soldiers, which accounts in part for the fairly constant presence of infantry forces in all medieval armies, whatever the superiority of cavalry on the battle-field. For another, the strategic use of horses as a means of transport should not be used to determine whether a soldier was an infantryman or a cavalryman, as the tactics of the Anglo-Saxon housecarls show. Failure to maintain a distinction between campaigning and battle tactics leads to nonsensical statements such as, 'The fight at Wherwell and the Rout of Winchester in 1141 seem to have been cavalry actions, although both sides dismounted at Wherwell.'[16] The elite soldiers of medieval armies were mounted on campaign for mobility, and because they were elite soldiers and so received the best equipment, which included horses.

Second, the dominance of cavalry on the battlefield was never as complete or as widespread as has at times been claimed. To the extent that cavalry did dominate, it did so not due to the introduction of the stirrup, but because of the lower quality of infantry in medieval warfare. Poor infantry resulted from the inability of medieval governments to maintain and train armies on a large scale and permanent basis, for training – close order drill in particular – was vital to the efficiency of infantry in battle. Anglo-Norman royal warfare, in this context, demon-strates that a small-scale, permanent and professional military system could partly replace large-scale peacetime drill as the basis for infantry efficiency. Such a system, under strong leadership, could produce armies proficient in infantry tactics. Some reevaluation of medieval military history in the light of these conclusions would seem to be called for.

[15] See above, p. 160.
[16] Beeler, 'The Composition of Anglo-Norman Armies', *Speculum* 40 (1965), 414.

Bibliography

Primary Sources

The Anglo-Saxon Chronicle. A revised translation by D. Whitelock with D.C. Douglas and S.I. Tucker. London, 1961.

The Battle of Maldon: Anglo-Saxon Poetry. Trans. R.K. Gordon. Rev. edn., London, 1970.

The Bayeux Tapestry. A Comprehensive Survey. Ed. Sir F. Stenton. 2nd edn. London, 1965.

Calendar of Documents Preserved in France, Illustrative of the History of Great Britain and Ireland. Vol. 1, AD 918–1206. Ed. J.H. Round. London, 1889.

The Carmen de Hastingae Proelio of Guy Bishop of Amiens. Ed. C. Morton and H. Muntz. Oxford, 1972.

Chronica de Hida. Ed. E. Edwards in *Liber Monasterii de Hyda.* RS, 1886.

Chroniques des Comtes d'Anjou et des Seigneurs d'Amboise. Ed. Louis Halphen and Rene Poupardin. Paris, 1913.

Constitutio Domus Regis in EHD, 2.

De Expugnatione Lyxbonensi. Ed. and trans. C.W. David. New York, 1976.

Diplomatic Documents Preserved in the PRO. Vol. 1, 1102–1272. Ed. P. Chaplais. London, 1964.

Eadmer. *Historia Novorum in Anglia.* Ed. M. Rule. RS, 1884.

English Historical Documents. Vol. 2, 1042–1189. Ed. D.C. Douglas and C.W. Greenaway. London, 1953.

Flavius Vegetius Renatus. *Epitoma Rei Militaris.* Ed. C. Lang. Stuttgart, 1967. Translation of Books I–III available in T.R. Phillips. *Roots of Strategy.* Harrisburg, 1940.

Florence of Worcester. *Chronicon ex Chronicis.* 2v. Ed. B. Thorpe. London, 1848–9.

Gesta Stephani. Ed. and trans. K.R. Potter. Oxford, 1976.

Guibert of Nogent. *Self and Society in Medieval France. The Memoirs of Abbot Guibert of Nogent.* Trans. J.F. Benton. New York, 1970.

Henry of Huntingdon. *Historia Anglorum.* Ed. T. Arnold. RS, 1879.

John of Hexham, in *Symeonis Monachi Opera Omnia,* 2:284–333. Ed. T. Arnold. RS, 1885.

Lanfranc. *The Letters of Lanfranc Archbishop of Canterbury.* Ed. and trans. H. Clover and M. Gibson. Oxford, 1979.

Leges Henrici Primi. Ed. and trans. L.J. Downer. Oxford, 1972.

Liber Monasterii de Hyda. Ed. E. Edwards. RS, 1886.

Orderic Vitalis. *Ecclesiastical History*. 6v. Ed. and trans. M. Chibnall. Oxford, 1969–78.

The Pipe Roll of 31 Henry I. Michaelmas 1130. Facsimile from the 1833 edition, ed. J. Hunter. 1929.

Priest of Fécamp, letter of. *EHR* 25 (1910), 295–6.

Regesta Regum Anglo-Normannorum, 1066–1154. Vol. 1, 1066–1100, ed. H.W.C. Davis. Oxford, 1913. Vol. 2, 1100–1135, eds. C. Johnson and H.A. Cronne. Oxford, 1956. Vol. 3, 1135–1154, eds. H.A. Cronne and R.H.C. Davis. Oxford, 1968.

Select Charters and Other Illustrations of English Constitutional History. Ed. W. Stubbs. 9th edn., revised H.W.C. Davis. Oxford, 1921.

Suger. *Vie de Louis le Gros*. Ed. H. Waquet (Classiques de l'Histoire de France). Paris, 1929.

Symeon of Durham. *Historia Regum*. Ed. T. Arnold. RS, 1885.

William of Jumièges. *Gesta Normannorum Ducum*. Ed. J. Marx. Rouen, 1914.

William of Malmesbury. *Gesta Regum Anglorum*. 2v. Ed. W. Stubbs. RS, 1887, 1889.

William of Malmesbury. *Historia Novella*. Ed. K.R. Potter. London, 1955.

William of Poitiers. *Histoire de Gillaume le Conquerant*. Ed. R. Foreville. Paris, 1952.

Secondary Sources

Abels, Richard. 'Bookland and Fyrd Service in Late Saxon England.' *Battle* 7 (1984), 1–25.

———. *Lordship and Military Obligation in Anglo-Saxon England*. Berkeley, 1988.

Bachrach, B.S. 'Some Observations on the Military Administration of the Norman Conquest.' *Battle* 8 (1985), 1–26.

———. 'The Practical Use of Vegetius' *De Re Militari* During the Middle Ages.' *The Historian* 47 (1985), 239–255.

———. 'Some Observations on William the Conqueror's Horse Transports.' *Technology and Culture* 25 (1985), 506–517.

———. 'Charles Martel, Shock Combat, the Stirrup, and Feudalism.' *Studies in Medieval and Renaissance History* 7 (1970), 47–75.

Barker, Juliet R.V. *The Tournament in England, 1100–1400*. Woodbridge, 1986.

Barlow, F. *The Feudal Kingdom of England 1042–1216*. 3d. edn. London, 1972. 4th edn. London, 1987.

———. *William Rufus*. London, 1983.

———. *Edward the Confessor*. Berkeley, 1970.

———. *William I and the Norman Conquest*. London, 1965.

Barraclough, G., ed. *Social Life in Early England*. London, 1960.

Bartlett, Robert J. 'Technique Militaire et Pouvoir Politique, 900–1300.' *Annales* 41 (1986), 1135–1159.

Bates, David. *William the Conqueror*. London, 1989.

———. *A Bibliography of Domesday Book*. Woodbridge, 1986.

———. *Normandy before 1066*. London, 1982.

Beeler, J. 'The Composition of Anglo-Norman Armies.' *Speculum* 40 (1965), 398–414.

———. *Warfare in England 1066–1189*. Cornell, 1966.

Bennett, Matthew. 'Wace and Warfare.' *Battle* 11 (1988), 37–57.

———. 'Poetry as History? The *Roman de Rou* of Wace as a Source for the Norman Conquest.' *Battle* 5 (1982), 21–39.

———. 'La Règle du Temple as a Military Manual, or How to Deliver a Cavalry Charge' in Harper-Bill et al., *Studies in Medieval History presented to R. Allen Brown*.

Bernstein, David. *The Mystery of the Bayeux Tapestry*. Chicago, 1986.

Bloch, Marc. *Feudal Society*. 2v. Trans L.A. Manyon. London, 1961.

Boussard, J. 'Les Mercenaires au XIIe Siècle. Henri II Plantagenet et les Origines de l'Armée de Mètier.' *Bibliothèque de l'Ecole des Chartes* 106 (1945–6), 189–224.

Bradbury, Jim. 'Battles in England and Normandy, 1066–1154.' *Battle* 6 (1983), 1–12.

Brooks, F.W. 'The Battle of Stamford Bridge.' *East Yorkshire Local History Series* no. 6, 1963.

Brooks, N.P. and Walker, H.E. 'The Authority and Interpretation of the Bayeux Tapestry.' *Battle* 1 (1978), 1–34.

Brown, Elizabeth A.R. 'The Tyranny of a Construct: Feudalism and Historians of Medieval Europe.' *AHR* 79 (1974), 1063–1088.

Brown, R.A. *English Castles*. London, 1976.

———. 'A List of Castles, 1154–1216.' *EHR* 74 (1959), 249–80.

———. *The Normans and the Norman Conquest*. London, 1969.

———. *Origins of English Feudalism*. New York, 1975.

———. 'Royal Castle-Building in England, 1154–1216.' *EHR* 70 (1955), 353–398.

———. 'The Battle of Hastings.' *Battle* 3 (1980), 1–21.

———. 'The Status of the Norman Knight' in *War and Government in the Middle Ages*, ed. Gillingham and Holt.

———, Colvin, H.M. and Taylor, A.J., eds. *The History of the King's Works*. Vols. 1, 2. London, 1963.

Brown, Shirley Ann. 'The Bayeux Tapestry: Why Eustace, Odo and William?' *Battle* 12 (1989).

Burne, A.H. *The Battlefields of England*. London, 1950.

Chibnall, M. 'Mercenaries and the Familia Regis under Henry I.' *History* 62 (1977), 15–23.

———. 'Feudal Society in Orderic Vitalis.' *Battle* 1 (1978), 35–48.

————. 'Military Service in Normandy before 1066.' *Battle* 5 (1982), 65–77.

————. 'Orderic Vitalis on Castles', in Harper-Bill et al., *Studies in Medieval History presented to R. Allen Brown.*

————. *Anglo-Norman England.* Oxford, 1986.

————. 'Women in Orderic Vitalis.' *The Haskins Society Journal* 2 (1990), 105–121.

Contamine, P. *War in the Middle Ages.* Trans. M. Jones. Basil Blackwell, 1984.

Cowdrey, H.E.J. 'Towards an Interpretation of the Bayeux Tapestry.' *Battle* 10 (1987), 49–65.

Cronne, H.A. *The Reign of Stephen 1135–1154.* London, 1970.

Crouch, D. *The Beaumont Twins.* Cambridge, 1986.

David, C.W. *Robert Curthose.* Harvard, 1920.

Davis, R.H.C. 'The Carmen de Hastingae Proelio.' *EHR* 93 (1978), 241–61.

————. *King Stephen.* 3d edn. London, 1977.

————. *The Normans and their Myth.* London, 1976.

————. 'The Warhorses of the Normans.' *Battle* 10 (1987), 67–82.

————. L.J. Engels, et al. 'The Carmen de Hastingae Proelio: A Discussion.' *Battle* 2 (1979), 1–20.

Douglas, D.C. *William the Conqueror.* London, 1964.

Duby, Georges. *The Legend of Bouvines.* Trans. Catherine Tihanyi. Berkeley, 1990.

————. *The Early Growth of the European Economy. Warriors and Peasants from the Seventh to the Twelfth Century.* Trans. Howard B. Clarke. Ithaca, 1974.

Dupuy, R. Ernest and Trevor N. Dupuy. *The Encyclopedia of Military History from 3500 B.C. to the present.* 2d rev. edn. New York, 1986.

Engels, Donald. *Alexander the Great and the Logistics of the Macedonian Army.* Berkeley, 1978.

Fleming, Donald F. 'Landholding and *Milites* in Domesday Book: A Revision.' *Battle* 13 (1990), 83–98.

Freeman, E.A. *History of the Norman Conquest of England.* Oxford, 1867–79.

Fuller, J.F.C. *A Military History of the Western World.* 3v, London, 1954.

Gabriel, Richard. *The Culture of War. Invention and Early Development.* New York, 1990.

Gillingham, John. 'William the Bastard at War,' in Harper-Bill et al., *Studies in Medieval History presented to R. Allen Brown.*

————. 'Richard I and the Science of War,' in Gillingham and Holt, *War and Government in the Middle Ages.*

————. 'The Introduction of Knight Service into England.' *Battle* 4 (1981), 53–64.

Gillingham, John, and J.C. Holt, eds. *War and Government in the Middle Ages. Essays in Honour of J.O. Prestwich.* Woodbridge, 1984.

Gillmor, C.M. 'Naval Logistics of the Cross-Channel Operation, 1066.' *Battle* 7 (1984), 105–131.

Glover, R. 'English Warfare in 1066.' *EHR* 67 (1952), 1–18.

Godfrey, John. 'The Defeated Anglo-Saxons Take Service with the Eastern Emperor.' *Battle* 1 (1977), 63–74.

Green, Judith A. 'Lords of the Norman Vexin' in *War and Government in the Middle Ages*, ed. Gillingham and Holt.

Hardy, Robert. *Longbow. A Social and Military History*. Cambridge, 1976.

Harper-Bill, Christopher. 'The Piety of the Anglo-Norman Knightly Class.' *Battle* 2 (1979), 63–77.

Harper-Bill, Christopher, Christopher J. Holdsworth and Janet L. Nelson, eds. *Studies in Medieval History presented to R. Allen Brown*. Boydell, 1989.

Harvey, S. 'The Knight and the Knight's Fee in England.' *P&P* 49 (1970), 3–43.

Hollings, M. 'The Survival of the Five-Hide Unit in the Western Midlands.' *EHR* 63 (1948), 453–87.

Hollister, C.W. *Anglo-Saxon Military Institutions on the Eve of the Norman Conquest*. Oxford, 1962.

———. *The Military Organization of Norman England*. Oxford, 1965.

———. 'The Significance of Scutage Rates in Eleventh- and Twelfth-Century England.' *EHR* 75 (1960), 577–88.

———. 'The Campaign of 1102 against Robert of Bellême', in Harper-Bill et al., *Studies in Medieval History presented to R. Allen Brown*.

———. 'Henry I and the Anglo-Norman Magnates.' *Battle* 2 (1977), 93–107.

———. 'War and Diplomacy in the Anglo-Norman World: The Reign of Henry I.' *Battle* 6 (1983), 72–88.

Holt, J.C. 'The Introduction of Knight Service in England.' *Battle* 6 (1983), 89–106.

Hooper, N. 'Some Observations on the Navy in Late Anglo-Saxon England', in Harper-Bill et al., *Studies in Medieval History presented to R. Allen Brown*.

———. 'The Housecarls in England in the Eleventh Century.' *Battle* 7 (1984), 161–176.

Howard, M. *War in European History*. Oxford, 1976.

John, Eric. *Land Tenure in Early England*. Leicester, 1961.

Jones, Archer. *The Art of Warfare in the Western World*. Oxford, 1987.

Kapelle, William E. *The Norman Conquest of the North. The Region and Its Transformation, 1000–1135*. Chapel Hill, 1979.

———. 'Domesday Book: F.W. Maitland and his Successors.' *Speculum* 64 (1989), 620–40.

Keegan, J. *The Face of Battle*. London, 1976.

Keen, Maurice. *Chivalry*. New Haven, 1984.

Latouche, R. *Histoire du Comté du Maine Pendant le Xe et le XIe Siècle*. Paris, 1910.

Lane Fox, Robin. *Alexander the Great*. London, 1974.

Le Patourel, J. *The Norman Empire*. Oxford, 1976.

————. *Feudal Empires, Norman and Plantagenet.* London, 1984.

Lewis, Archibald and Timothy Runyon. *European Naval and Maritime History, 300–1500.* Bloomington, 1985.

Lot, F. *L'Art Militaire et les Armées au Moyen Age en Europe et dans le Proche Orient.* 2v. Paris, 1942.

Loud, G.A. 'The *Gens Normannorum*–Myth or Reality?' *Battle* 4 (1981), 104–116.

Luttwak, E.N. *The Grand Strategy of the Roman Empire.* Baltimore, 1976.

Lyon, B.D. 'The Feudal Antecedent of the Indenture System.' *Speculum* 29 (1954), 503–11.

————. *From Fief to Indenture.* Harvard, 1957.

————. 'The Money Fief Under the English Kings, 1066–1485.' *EHR* 66 (1951), 161–93.

Mann, J. 'Arms and Armour', in Poole, *Medieval England.*

Matthew, D.J.A. *The Norman Conquest.* London, 1966.

Morillo, Stephen. 'Hastings: An Unusual Battle.' *The Haskins Society Journal* 2 (1990), 95–104.

————. 'Guns and Government: A Comparative Study of Europe and Japan.' *Journal of World History* (forthcoming).

Morris, J.E. 'Mounted Infantry in Medieval Warfare.' *TRHS* 8 (1914), 77–103.

Mortimer, Richard. 'Land and Service: The Tenants of the Honour of Clare.' *Battle* 8 (1985), 177–197.

Murray, K.M.E. 'Shipping', in Poole, *Medieval England.*

Musset, L. 'Une Institution peu Connue de la Normandie Ducale: les Prés et le Foin du Seigneur Roi.' *Annales de Normandie,* 1979, 375–6.

Nelson, Janet L. 'Ninth Century Knighthood: The Evidence of Nithard', in Harper-Bill et al., *Studies in Medieval History presented to R. Allen Brown.*

Neumann, J. 'Hydrographic and Ship-hydrodynamic Aspects of the Norman Invasion, A.D. 1066.' *Battle* 11 (1988), 221–242.

Oman, C. *A History of the Art of War in the Middle Ages.* 2v. London, 1924.

Parker, Geoffrey. *The Military Revolution. Military Innovation and the Rise of the West, 1500–1800.* Cambridge, 1988.

Peirce, Ian. 'Arms, Armor, and Warfare in the Eleventh Century.' *Battle* 10 (1987), 237–257.

Poole, A.L., ed. *Medieval England.* Oxford, 1958.

————. *Obligations of Society in the Twelfth and Thirteenth Centuries.* Oxford, 1946.

Powers, James F. *A Society Organized for War. The Iberian Municipal Militias in the Central Middle Ages, 1000–1284.* Berkeley, 1988.

Powicke, F.M. *The Loss of Normandy (1189–1204).* Manchester, 1913.

Powicke, M.R. *Military Obligation in Medieval England.* Oxford, 1962.

————. Review of Hollister, *A–S Mil. Inst. Speculum* 39 (1964), 159–61.

Prestwich, J.O. 'Anglo-Norman Feudalism and the Problem of Continuity.' *P&P* 26 (1963), 39–57.

———. 'The Military Household of the Norman Kings.' *EHR* 96 (1981), 1–35.

———. 'War and Finance in the Anglo-Norman State.' *TRHS* 5th series, vol. 4 (1954), 19–43.

Prince, A.E. 'The Army and Navy,' in J.F. Willard and W.A. Morris, eds. *The English Government at Work 1327–1336* 1:332–393.

Round, J.H. 'The Introduction of Knight Service into England.' *EHR* 6 and 7 (1891–92).

Russell, Frederick H. *The Just War in the Middle Ages*. Cambridge, 1975.

Searle, Eleanor. 'The Abbey of the Conquerors: Defensive Enfeoffment and Economic Development in Anglo-Norman England.' *Battle* 2 (1979), 154–164.

———. 'Emma the Conqueror.' in Harper-Bill et al., *Studies in Medieval History presented to R. Allen Brown*.

———. *Predatory Kinship and the Creation of Norman Power, 840–1066*. Berkeley, 1988.

Smail, R.C. 'Art of War', in Poole, *Medieval England*.

———. *Crusading Warfare 1097–1193*. Cambridge, 1956.

Stenton, F.M. *Anglo-Saxon England*. 3d edn. Oxford, 1971.

———. *The First Century of English Feudalism 1066–1166*. 2d edn. Oxford, 1961.

———. 'The Development of the Castle in England and Wales' in Barraclough, *Social Life*.

———. 'Norman London', in Barraclough, *Social Life*.

———. 'The Road System of Medieval England.' *EcHR* 7 (1936), 1–21.

Strickland, Matthew. 'Securing the North: Invasion and Strategy of Defence in Twelfth-Century Anglo-Scottish Warfare.' *Battle* 12 (1989), 177–198.

Suppe, Frederick. 'Castle Guard and the Castlery of Clun.' *The Haskins Society Journal* 1 (1989), 123–34.

Taylor, A.J. 'Military Architecture', in Poole, *Medieval England*.

Thompson, Kathleen. 'Robert of Bellême Reconsidered.' *Battle* 13 (1990), 263–286.

Van Creveld, Martin. *Supplying War. Logistics from Wallenstein to Patton*. Cambridge, 1977.

———. *Technology and War*. New York, 1989.

Van Houts, Elizabeth M.C. 'The Ship List of William the Conqueror.' *Battle* 10 (1987), 159–183.

Verbruggen, J.F. *The Art of Warfare in Western Europe during the Middle Ages, from the Eighth Century to 1340*. Trans. S. Willard and S. Southern. Oxford, 1977.

Ward, Jennifer C. 'Royal Service and Reward: The Clare Family and the Crown, 1066–1154.' *Battle* 11 (1988), 261–278.

Warren, W.L. *Henry II*. London, 1973.
White, G.H. 'The Household of the Norman Kings.' *TRHS* 30 (1948), 127–55.
White, L. *Medieval Technology and Social Change*. Oxford, 1962.
Whitelock, D., et al. *The Norman Conquest*. London, 1966.

Index